Asylum after Empire

KILOMBO: INTERNATIONAL RELATIONS AND COLONIAL QUESTIONS

This is the first series to mark out a dedicated space for advanced critical enquiry into colonial questions across International Relations (IR). The ethos of this book series is reflected by the bricolage constituency of Kilombos – settlements of African slaves, rebels and indigenous peoples in South America who became self-determining political communities that retrieved and renovated the social practices of its diverse constituencies while being confronted by colonial forces. The series embraces a multitude of methods and approaches, theoretical and empirical scholarship, alongside historical and contemporary concerns. Publishing innovative and top-quality peer-reviewed scholarship, Kilombo enquires into the shifting principles of colonial rule that inform global governance and investigates the contestation of these principles by diverse peoples across the globe. It critically re-interprets popular concepts, narratives and approaches in the field of IR by reference to the 'colonial question' and, in doing so, the book series opens up new vistas from which to address the key political questions of our time.

Series Editors:
Mustapha K. Pasha, Aberystwyth University
Meera Sabaratnam, SOAS University of London
Robbie Shilliam, Queen Mary University of London

Titles in the Series
Meanings of Bandung: Postcolonial Orders and Decolonial Visions, Quỳnh N. Phạm and Robbie Shilliam
Politics of the African Anticolonial Archive, Shiera S. el-Malik and Isaac A. Kamola
Asylum after Empire: Colonial Legacies in the Politics of Asylum Seeking, Lucy Mayblin
Decolonising Intervention International Statebuilding in Mozambique, Meera Sabaratnam (forthcoming)
Unthinking the Colonial Myth of Complexity: Ethnocentrism, Hierarchy and the Global in International Relations, Gennaro Ascione (forthcoming)

Asylum after Empire

Colonial Legacies in the Politics of Asylum Seeking

Lucy Mayblin

ROWMAN &
LITTLEFIELD
——INTERNATIONAL
London • New York

Published by Rowman & Littlefield International Ltd
Unit A, Whitacre Mews, 26-34 Stannary Street, London SE11 4AB
www.rowmaninternational.com

Rowman & Littlefield International Ltd.is an affiliate of Rowman & Littlefield
4501 Forbes Boulevard, Suite 200, Lanham, Maryland 20706, USA
With additional offices in Boulder, New York, Toronto (Canada), and Plymouth (UK)
www.rowman.com

Copyright © 2017 by Lucy Mayblin

All rights reserved. No part of this book may be reproduced in any form or by any electronic or mechanical means, including information storage and retrieval systems, without written permission from the publisher, except by a reviewer who may quote passages in a review.

British Library Cataloguing in Publication Data

A catalogue record for this book is available from the British Library
ISBN: HB: 978-1-78348-615-1

Library of Congress Cataloging-in-Publication Data Available

ISBN: 978-1-78348-615-1 (cloth : alk. paper)
ISBN: 978-1-78348-617-5 (electronic)

∞™ The paper used in this publication meets the minimum requirements of American National Standard for Information Sciences—Permanence of Paper for Printed Library Materials, ANSI/NISO Z39.48-1992.

Printed in the United States of America

Contents

Acknowledgements		vii
1	Introduction	1
2	The Asylum 'Problem'	13
3	Decolonising the 'Problem': An Alternative Standpoint for Analysing the Exclusionary Politics of Asylum	29
4	Slavery and the Right to Be Human	51
5	Colonialism, the League of Nations and Race Equality	83
6	The United Nations and the Right to Be Human	113
7	Dehumanisation: Asylum Seeker Support in the Twenty-First Century	147
8	Asylum after Empire	175
References		181
Index		197
About the Author		201

Acknowledgements

I started this project in 2009. Seven years, one PhD, two babies, two house moves, three job changes, and two postdocs later, I am amazed to find that I have finally finished (to the extent that any academic project ever really ends). There are, of course, many people to thank. The first is Gurminder K. Bhambra, who has been a mentor, advocate, critic and friend over these seven years, and without whom the book certainly would not be in existence. I need also to acknowledge Robbie Shilliam, who supported and encouraged me in pursuing this thesis-to-book project; Joe Turner, whose incisive critical comments improved the introductory chapters tenfold; and Bob Carter, who championed my arrival in the Warwick Sociology Department, a place which has opened up many intellectual challenges and opportunities to me. I must also acknowledge the unwavering support of Roger Mayblin, Chris Booth-Mayblin and the amazing Michael Farrelly. The research in this book was supported by the UK's Economic and Social Research Council.

Chapter One

Introduction

In spring 2015 the UK-based *Guardian* newspaper featured a gallery of images taken by photographer Christian Sinibaldi which showed the conditions in the migrant camp in Calais – the so-called 'Jungle'. On a wall covered in political graffiti one contributor had written, 'Why always black man?' in both French and English. In the French text 'noir' is capitalised for emphasis – NOIR.[1] Just four words, which presented an analysis of the camp as embedded in a global historical web of racial power relations. This is not an unusual occurrence; asylum seekers, refugees and undocumented migrants often draw attention to the global colonial histories which give context to their present situation (Langa 2015; Robinson and Sergott 2002). The Sans Papiers movement in France, for example, which includes many forced migrants, explicitly draws attention to the colonial relations that connect not only their home countries with France but also their present situation with histories of French colonialism (see Cissé 1997: 2) – what Gurminder Bhambra calls 'connected histories' (2007). So if migrants make these connections so frequently, so automatically, why is it that these connections are not made frequently or automatically by academics?

The task of this book is to take the first steps towards theorising asylum policy within the context of such histories and to make sense of contemporary public policy developments on asylum within the context of histories of colonialism. The book is a historical sociology which brings together postcolonial and decolonial theories on the hierarchical ordering of human beings; it troubles the supposedly universal category of 'man' within the epistemological framework of 'modernity' and names the response of the British state (which acts as the case study) to contemporary asylum seekers as an example of the coloniality of power. It is an attempt to make sense of the dehumanisation of asylum seekers not as racism but as enmeshed within interconnected histories – of ideas of distinct, geographically located 'races', of human beings as hierarchy organised in relation to civilisation and of colonial power relations. In this sense, I am taking as my starting point the sophisticated analyses of forced migrants and sans-papiers and elaborating their conclusions with academic study.

ASYLUM IN BRITAIN

In the period since 1993 huge sums of public money have been spent on preventing people from seeking refuge from persecution in Britain. The country is typical of Western states in this sense. Policy measures have included preventing would-be asylum seekers from arriving and preventing those who do manage to arrive and therefore make a claim for asylum from working, travelling or living in a city of their choosing and detaining and deporting the many whose claims are unsuccessful back to unstable countries with poor human rights records (Zetter, Griffiths and Sigona 2005; Gibney 2006; Squire 2009). Since the early 2000s this policy approach has been taken and regularly intensified, despite numbers of applications generally decreasing (Schuster 2003a). In the year ending June 2015 the largest number of applications for asylum to the United Kingdom came from Eritrea (3,568), Pakistan (2,302), Syria (2,204) and Sudan (1,799) (Home Office 2015). These are all places known to be experiencing the kinds of situations where persecution is likely to occur, and yet at the same time as limiting the rights of asylum seekers, British politicians have often boasted that theirs is a country for which respect for equality and human rights and the provision of refuge is of the utmost importance. For example, in the government's 2005 white paper 'Controlling our borders: Making migration work for Britain', the authors wrote that the 1951 Convention 'is part of the legal and ethical framework that enshrines basic principles of human decency' – and must not be undermined – while in the next sentence proposing new legislation that would do just that (Home Office 2005: 17).

To put the proliferation of new legislation in context, between 1793 and 1870 there were three new pieces of asylum legislation, one of which extended the rights of asylum seekers and one whose provisions were never actually acted upon. Between 1871 and 1993 there was no new national legislation passed to deal with asylum seekers or refugees. These were not periods which did not see the arrival of large numbers of people fleeing persecution; Jews from Eastern Europe in the nineteenth century and those fleeing the aftermath of the Russian Revolution are two examples. In the twenty years since 1993, however, there have been *nine* rafts of new legislation covering asylum. The policy framework which has resulted is now widely termed 'the non-entrée regime' (Orchard 2014). So what has changed? Or, more precisely, how have social scientists conceptualised this change? For many scholars, the policies have changed because the asylum seekers have changed. This change is often said to be about numbers, methods of travel and reasons for flight. More specifically, there are more asylum seekers facilitated by the rise of mass international air travel, with many seeking an alternative route to legal economic migration as avenues for this have closed.

Political analyses of the current asylum regime in Britain often point to the unprecedented nature and context of contemporary asylum flows (Zolberg et al. 1989; Loescher 1993; Spencer 1995; Joly 1996; Appleyard 2001; Koser 2001; Gibney 2003; Hansen 2003; Spencer 2003; Bohmer and Shuman 2008) or to longstanding political formations, such as the nation state system (Boccardi 2002; Nyers 2003; Haddad 2008; Malkki 1995), as leading to this (inevitable) policy response. There is also a tendency to focus on recent deviations from the 1951 United Nations (UN) Convention obligations by wealthy nations as lying at the core of 'Western' asylum problems. Beneath many of these explanations presented for the current asylum regime, discussed further in chapter 2, is a set of unelaborated assumptions. The set includes the following: The assumption that readers understand that non-European asylum seekers arriving in Europe will be seen as undesirable, or even dangerous, to the integrity of communities and nation states. The assumption that this fact is so obvious that it does not require explanation. The assumption that responsibility for non-European asylum seekers, who are 'other', is obviously not generally seen to rest with host states. The assumption that, irrespective of the circumstances of their flight, some human bodies are simply more easily and acceptably degraded than others. A core aim of this book will be to unpack some of these assumptions and examine the connections between such assumptions, Britain's colonial past and current asylum policy.

Refugee studies, as an inter-disciplinary field of study which straddles the modern/traditional, developed/developing divide, is an obvious place to look for the application of broadly *postcolonial* analyses within the context of asylum. Bearing in mind that its object of study – the refugee – is the embodiment of the darker side of modernity and of the global fallout from colonialism, is a figure who migrates from the 'non-modern' to the 'modern' world and is treated all over the world as not quite human enough to deserve full access to human rights, one would have thought that refugee studies would have fully incorporated postcolonial analyses decades ago. This is not the case. The reason is in part because refugee studies is a field which has not tended to engage to any great extent with history (Marfleet 2007) or to any great extent with thorny social and political phenomena such as racism.

In contrast to mainstream refugee studies scholars, some in sociology and cultural studies have brought a critique of 'Western' asylum policy regimes together with analyses of the wider social contexts in which the media and general public are broadly hostile to asylum seekers and refugees in order to diagnose this societal response as racism (Cole 2009; Garner 2013; Hubbard 2005; Fekete 2009). Anti-asylum sentiment, as well as the actions of the state, is therefore conceptualised as one of many contemporary racisms alongside Islamophobia and hostility to white Eastern European immigrants. I will argue in the next chapter that while hostility to asylum seekers is certainly historically entangled with the formation of ideas of 'race' and the proliferation of racism as both a sociocultural and a political-institutional phenomenon, that does not mean that it can straightforwardly be conceptualised as racism, or that such a conceptualisation helps us to make sense of it. What is missing from this analysis is an engagement with those inter-connected histories – colonial histories – which have allowed for the assignment of differential worth to various human bodies.

Those working in sociology and cultural studies have of course long held an interest in the impact of colonialism on patterns of not just migration and settlement but also identity, inter-cultural encounters, racism, race relations and community cohesion (Gilroy 2003, 2004, 2002; Rex 1970; Wemyss 2009). There is a well-established literature which speaks to the links between colonialism and immigration, particularly in the British context. Economic migrants travelling from the colonies and former colonies to Britain have been the subject of a great deal of study, which inevitably brings issues of racism, 'race' and 'race relations' to the fore. From case studies of specific areas (Patterson 1965; Rex and Moore 1967; Rex and Thomlinson 1979) to histories of immigration and integration policy in response to colonial immigrants (Joshi and Carter 1984; Dean 1987; Rich 1990; Spencer 1997; Bleich 2005; Hansen 2000; Hampshire 2005), the cultural articulations of the racialised immigrant experience (Gilroy 2002), inequality in employment (Jowell and Prescott-Clarke 1970; Brooks and Singh 1978; Berthoud 1999), education (Bhatnagar 1981; Gillborn 1990) and housing (Peach and Byron 1993; Peach 1998; Phillips 1998) to 'race riots' (Keith 1993; Amin 2003), this cornucopia of scholarship consistently makes explicit links between colonialism, racism and the economic immigrant experience in post-war Britain. Is it not strange, then, that this same postcolonial analysis has not been extended to the politics of *asylum*? That it is not integral to a political and sociological analysis of asylum policy today?

Post–Cold War forced migrants, and the policies designed to deal with them, have tended to be the focus instead of empirically engaged social and public policy research (e.g. Bloch and Schuster 2002; Gibney 2004; Hassan 2000; Joly 1996; Koser 2001; Morris 2002; Phillimore and Goodson 2006; Schuster 2003a; Silove et al. 1997; van Wetten et al. 2001; Vink and Meijerink 2003; Zetter, Griffiths and Sigona 2005). This is an important body of work but nevertheless again leaves broader transnational, historical political concerns under-explored. Indeed, the historical geopolitical linkages made so commonly by forced migrants are decisively not the starting point for mainstream *political* analysis of contemporary Western asylum regimes.

As a first step towards rethinking the way we approach the turn to restrictive policies, I would like to highlight one key change in the contemporary period, rarely systematically and critically addressed in academic literature, though of course decisively identified by migrant activists. It is this: since the early 1990s, for the first time in British history, the majority of asylum seekers making applications for refuge come from outside Europe. They are, in fact, by and large people who originate from countries which until thirty to sixty years ago were under British colonial rule. Rather than depicting contemporary asylum seekers as fundamentally different to those of the past, this book suggests an alternative perspective. Underpinning this perspective is the idea that histories of asylum should not be considered as exclusively European. This may not seem to be a radical statement, and indeed others have attempted such an intervention previously. For example, Chimni's work on the 'myth of difference' argues that academics contribute to a pervasive myth that European refugees in the past and 'Third World' refugees in the present are fundamentally different. He has argued that the idea that Third World asylum seekers are in some sense 'new' asylum seekers is incorrect, and yet this idea has proved powerful in justifying restrictive asylum polices in both the academic and policy-making communities. Though nearly two decades old and widely cited, the driving thrust of this paper, a call to rethink the imperialist foundations upon which refugee studies sits, appears to have remained largely unheeded. Indeed, the vast majority of academic accounts of refugee and asylum history are European histories.

Yet even periods of massive displacement in Europe, such as the middle of the twentieth century, were not periods in which only Europeans were displaced. Before the 1980s refugees and asylum seekers existed in a wide range of locations outside of Europe in numbers comparable to, or even in excess of, those seen within Europe in the wake of the Second World War. This is an issue I take up in chapters 2 and 5. Acknowledging the existence of such refugees means that non-European asylum seekers cannot be understood as appearing as a global 'problem' only since the 1980s. Furthermore, these histories of displacement need to be incorporated *into* European understandings of the history of asylum, not as external and consequently irrelevant occurrences.

The book takes as its starting point the exclusionary history of 'man' upon which the right to asylum is founded. It shows the durability of ideas of differential humanity through time, even when equality and universal rights have been central to international discourse. This is done through a diachronic analysis – four snapshots of very different periods in history but through which run threads of ideational continuity. These snapshots are as follows: the debates surrounding the abolition of slavery in 1833, when black bodies became human in law; the legacies of scientific racism in debates around the introduction of 'race equality' rules at the League of Nations in 1919; the discussions surrounding the establishment of the human rights framework, including the right to asylum, in 1951; and debates around levels of asylum support in 2012–15. The thread running through these snapshots is then pulled right through to the present with an analysis of the contestations over the levels of financial support to be provided to destitute asylum seekers in contemporary Britain.

Developing such an argument requires a postcolonial and decolonial analysis. Indeed, it requires us first to accept that Britain is a post-colonial country and that the legacies of colonialism live on beyond the facts of historical events. Britain is used as a case study here but coloniality, a concept which is elaborated further in chapter 3, can be found in many other contexts. In other words, the worldviews that are discussed in this study of Britain in domestic and world politics can certainly be observed in other post-colonial contexts, which would include at least the European former colonial powers and the white settler colonies.

KEY TERMS

The Right to Asylum

Before moving on it is important to clarify some key terms. First, the refugee and the asylum seeker. The category 'refugee' has been subject to considerable scrutiny. There are many who reject the use of the purely legal definitions 'asylum seeker' and 'refugee' since these are bureaucratic, arbitrary, exclusionary and imply classifications of deservingness (Zetter 1991; Sigona 2003). However, because my interest here is in policy and the chapters that follow interrogate the exclusionary nature of legal definitions deployed in policy contexts, it is appropriate that the legal categories are used in this case. Asylum seekers and refugees are, then, legally distinct categories of person in both international and national law. An asylum seeker is someone who has made an application for asylum. Their application is in the process of being assessed, a process which can take up to ten years in the United Kingdom. The application is a legal document with which evidence must be submitted as proof of persecution. The purpose of the application is, therefore, to prove to the host state that an individual has been persecuted.

The definition of a refugee in international law is as follows:

> A person who owing to a well-founded fear of being persecuted for reasons of race, religion, nationality, membership of a particular social group or political opinion, is outside the country of his nationality and is unable or, owing to such fear, is unwilling to avail himself of the protection of that country; or who, not having a nationality and being outside the country of his former habitual residence as a result of such events, is unable or, owing to such fear, is unwilling to return to it. (UNHCR, 1951)

This definition is contained in Article 1 of the 1951 Geneva Convention on the Status of Refugees. Initially this legal framework for protecting persecuted forced migrants was only applicable to those displaced in Europe. The process through which this decision was made is the focus of chapter 6. From 1967 a new protocol expanded the convention to cover other international contexts. Applications are made on an individual basis for adults; children (under sixteen) are included in their parents' application (if accompanied). Asylum seekers are subject to special legal conditions, and in the United Kingdom this includes, amongst other things, restrictions on working (the majority are forbidden to take employment) and a duty to report to a reporting centre on a regular basis.

A failed asylum seeker is someone whose application for asylum has been refused; they have been judged not to have experienced persecution and, in theory, to be in no danger if they return to their home country. Appeals on a decision may be submitted, or a second application may be completed if new evidence of persecution is obtained. If an application has been rejected but an applicant's country of origin is found to be unsafe to return to, an applicant may be granted 'temporary leave to remain' which is subject to periodic review. This is not uncommon.

A refugee is an individual whose application for asylum has been successful. However, the UK government now rarely grants refugee status but instead favours the immigration status of 'indefinite leave to remain' or 'temporary leave to remain'. These categories are, again, subject to review. As previously stated, this book focuses on policies oriented towards asylum seekers, including border controls and the asylum determination process, not refugee policy, which, though linked, has a different character.

Colonialism, Imperialism and the West

The book will draw links between this legal regime and histories of colonialism, imperialism and the British Empire. When referring to colonialism, I will primarily be addressing British colonial activities since the fifteenth century.

At times this may be expanded to include the Western European colonial empires more widely, over the same time span, at which point I will make this reference clear. 'The Empire', then, refers to the territory of the British Empire, inclusive of the metropolitan hub. 'Colonialism' here will refer to 'a form of domination, the control of individuals or groups over the territory and/or behaviour of other individuals or groups' (Horvath 1972: 45). These are the activities through which Britain was able to maintain the Empire. Colonialism, like all concepts, has been subject to varying interpretation according to the shifting morality of the day. As Horvath (1972: 45) points out, 'it has either been a dirty business engaged in by evil people or a praiseworthy endeavour undertaken by fine gentlemen for the purpose of saving the wretched, the savage, the unfortunate'. Though I do not view histories of colonialism in a positive light, my concern is less with asserting this opinion and more with mapping the ways in which such moral judgements were enabled by a particular worldview, and how aspects of that frame endure in the present.

'Imperialism' is often used interchangeably with 'colonialism'. There are subtle differences between the two, primarily the fact that imperialism does not necessarily involve the occupation of territory. It can take a much more fluid form, incorporating the imposition of cultural, economic and political customs without involving the taking of formal political control over a territory by a foreign power (Page 2003). These differences are not foregrounded for the purposes of this book, as discussion of imperial activities is largely done in association with discussion of territorial and political domination. Where the distinction becomes relevant is in modes of thinking at the international level which might be characterised as imperialist, while the topic under discussion (such as 'race equality' in general in chapter 5) is not solely focused on the colonies.

Linked to these historical geographical configurations are the concepts of 'the West' and 'the non-West', or 'Western' and 'non-Western'. These terms will be employed at various points in the book, though I am mindful of the problems inherent in their use. Not only is 'the West' very difficult to pinpoint as a territorial entity, but the distinction between 'the West' and what is essentially encapsulated by 'the non-West' – the rest – can be taken to imply superiority on the part of the former. These are also somewhat lazy categories which allow for generalisation but ignore diversity amongst those categorised below their headings (Hall 1996). Nevertheless, here 'the West' will refer to those powerful states in Western Europe and the white settler colonies populated by European emigrants between the fifteenth century and the present, who have had the most influence on global politics and economics over recent centuries. In tandem with this largely colonial history of political and economic power, this group of states has held a hegemonic influence over epistemology, society and culture, what is often described as 'globalisation' but is better represented as 'Westernisation' through the influence of powerful Western institutions.

These concepts are therefore about commonality of experience as opposed to identifying difference. Commonality of experience in the 'non-West' is one of existing under the hegemony of the West, despite the diversity of experience on other measures being multitudinous. These are therefore categories which are both practically useful for generalising about areas of the world in forming a metanarrative and also ideological in their deployment. That is not to say that I do not appreciate that there is tremendous diversity of experience within 'Western' and 'non-Western' states respectively. I simply say that accounting for the specificities and nuances of that tremendous diversity of experience is beyond the parameters of this book.

'Race'

The concept of 'race' will also appear throughout the book. As this concept has a highly contested status in social-science analysis, it is worth addressing briefly here some of the issues raised by its employment, my own position on this subject and how the term will be deployed within the book. The word 'race' is often put in inverted commas in academic work in order to indicate that the author is aware of the problematic status of the term. This stems from the fact that the idea of separate human 'races' with biologically, and particularly intellectually, distinguishable characteristics has been widely discredited (Banton 2009). Nevertheless, as many of the old ideas about the inherent differences between 'races' endure, whether in the form of racism or identity politics, 'race' continues to hold meaning for many people in terms of how they experience the world and interact with others. Racially marked individuals are today more commonly identified on the basis of a subjective judgement of visible difference than a systematised science, though scientific research has not completely thrown off its interest in 'race' (Carter 2007). Thus, though 'race' is now rarely seen as a category with any analytical use in and of itself for social researchers, its enduring resonance in many societies around the world, and particularly the problems created by the apparent resilience of the idea, means that social scientists must engage with it. A shorthand way of acknowledging these issues is to write 'race' instead of race.

I am sensitive to these debates and reject the idea that the concept 'race' has any factual basis or meaning beyond that which human beings invent for it. However, like many researchers, I can see that 'race' means something to many people in the world and appears to have causal properties in the sense that it is sometimes deployed as a basis for action. Furthermore, ideas around 'race' and difference continue to shape local, national and international politics in the present (Gilroy 2003). For me, this is a clear illustration of the enduring resonance of ideas derivative of colonialist modes of thinking about the world. In this book I will therefore be placing 'race' in inverted commas when discussing its deployment in particular contexts. When referring to historical texts where the author did not approach the concept with such caution, I will leave the punctuation out. As there are few concepts in social science which are not subject to contestation, this decision clearly raises issues around which concepts to make tentative and which to leave as having some assumed validity. However, I feel that the particularly problematic nature of the concept 'race', and the fact that its existence and continued usage is almost entirely a product of histories of domination, violence, subjugation and struggle, makes this not simply an issue of scholarly nuance but a vitally important political statement.

STRUCTURE OF THE BOOK

The next chapter explores the rise of asylum as an issue of great political significance, public interest and media coverage in Britain over the past thirty years. Starting with an overview of British asylum policies since the Act of Union in 1707, it charts how the presence of asylum seekers, of this specific category of alien body on British territory, has come to be seen by policy makers as presenting a problem *in itself*. Following this, academic responses to the recent perception that asylum seekers are a problem are explored, and a 'standard narrative' on the topic identified. This narrative focuses on a select European history which inevitably leads to contemporary asylum seekers being conceptualised as 'new' and 'different', rather than historically consistent. I critique this standard narrative by focusing on the 'sociology of absences' – what is missing from the dominant account.

Chapter 3 offers an alternative standpoint from which to approach the politics of asylum. The standard narrative is discredited as a 'myth of difference' using scholarship from Third World Approaches to International Law (TWAIL), and the inadequacy of theories of 'racism' or 'racialisation' to account for the hostile policy regime is explained. Hostility to asylum seekers is then re-theorised using the work of scholars from postcolonial and decolonial studies including Michel-Rolph Trouillot, Walter Mignolo and Sylvia Wynter. Central to this re-theorisation is the critique of 'modernity' as a worldview, rather than a geographical and temporal phenomena, and an exploration of the entanglement of exclusionary and hierarchical ideas of 'man' and the 'human' with ideas of modernity. In order to trace histories of continuity over time a methodological framework is required. The chapter therefore closes with a description of the approach taken in this book – a historical institutional analysis. This offers a means of mapping continuity and change in detail, which is able to get at some of the organisational and institutional practices and processes that have allowed for continuity and also for continuity to go unrecognised in the face of social and political change.

Chapters 5, 6 and 7 trace three critical junctures which together provide the empirical evidence required for wider claims to be made about the connections between colonialism and contemporary asylum policy. Chapter 5 is concerned with the role that slavery played in influencing early conceptions of humanity and differential rights, and how this ideology was augmented by the campaign for abolition. It is fundamentally about one of the earliest legal expansions of the category of 'man' which would later be used as a basis for human rights. In the eighteenth and early nineteenth centuries the humanity of enslaved people was considered at best ambiguous within European discourses, and they were consequently largely excluded from the suite of rights being promoted by European philosophers and politicians of the day. Thus, an institutional analysis of the political campaigns and debates which led to the abolition of slavery in the British Empire in 1833 provides a means of exploring the debates around the humanity of black bodies and the possibility of extending rights to them in the past. This legislation represents the first critical juncture in a long series of connected histories which have contributed to the framing and understanding of the deserving and the undeserving, the familiar and the 'other' in Britain.

Chapter 6 is concerned with the rise of conceptions of racial hierarchy in the nineteenth century and the ways in which these taxonomies influenced international relations in the twentieth century. More specifically, it investigates the Japanese proposal in 1919 that race equality be included in the Covenant of the League of Nations. The proposal was rejected, twice. Leading the resistance was the British Empire delegation, strongly supported by the United States. The evidence presented in the chapter shows that their resistance can be understood clearly within the context of contemporaneous ideas of racial hierarchy derivative of the colonial experience. Such ideas facilitated the domination of colonial subjects, understanding their place in the world as being below that of the European 'race' in a world hierarchy of humanity. This chapter shows that these powerful ideas had an enduring impact in world politics into the twentieth century. The final section entails a discussion of racial hierarchy and the ongoing relevance of this event in the history of differential conceptions of humanity, not least at the UN, which have such an important place in the realpolitik of asylum policy today.

Chapter 7 is concerned with the institutionalisation of human rights, and by extension the right to asylum, in the mid-twentieth century. The focus here is on the 1951 UN Geneva Convention on the Status of Refugees, one part of the international legal framework for human rights which emerged in this period. The Geneva Convention is central to scholarship on refugee and asylum issues and has come to be associated with the very idea of a universalised rights-bearing human being. Yet the focus on European asylum seekers is only one part of the story. The period in question was also one of the dismantling of colonialism and a profound reshaping of the world order, which involved massive displacements outside of Europe. Drawing out the relevance of these histories to the founding of human rights in international law is the task of this case study. The themes addressed in chapters 5 and 6 are of course of vital relevance here. By selecting this founding moment of contemporary asylum rights as a critical juncture, I am able to exposit the entanglement of colonialism and decolonisation with the institutionalisation of asylum policy, and thus call for a reconsideration of the bases for critical analysis in which we engage.

The final chapter before the conclusion takes a contemporary policy area – the economic rights of asylum seekers and failed asylum seekers – and explores the ways in which long-standing (and modern) notions of human hierarchy continue to be quietly active in the contemporary asylum regime. As a whole, the book is an effort at reading the contemporary hostility of the British state to postcolonial asylum seekers as dehumanisation within the context of colonial histories and in dialogue with the work of theorists from postcolonial and decolonial studies. In the next chapter this effort begins with a discussion of the asylum 'problem' and the way that social scientists have tended to approach this sociopolitical 'problem'.

NOTE

1. Available at: http://www.theguardian.com/world/gallery/2015/apr/06/life-in-calais-migrant-slum-jules-ferry-in-pictures-christian-sinibaldi.

Chapter Two

The Asylum 'Problem'

The extent of policies and laws designed to deal with asylum seekers has proliferated in the West since the early 1990s, as have the resources required to manage them. In Britain, as in many other countries, this process is related to the rise of asylum as an issue of great political significance, public interest and media coverage. More specifically, the presence of asylum seekers, of this specific category of alien body on British territory, has come to be seen by policy makers as presenting a problem *in itself*. Starting with an overview of British asylum policies since the Act of Union in 1707, this chapter demonstrates this process in the British context. Britain here is used as an example country, though the story is very similar in many other Western contexts. Academic analyses of this phenomenon are then explored, and a 'standard narrative' on the topic identified. This narrative focuses on a select European history which inevitably leads to contemporary asylum seekers being conceptualised as 'new' and 'different', rather than historically consistent. I critique this standard narrative by focusing on the 'sociology of absences' – what is missing from the dominant account. This critique sets the stage for the next chapter, where an alternative analysis, drawing on a different theoretical grounding, is presented.

ASYLUM POLICY IN BRITAIN: A SHORT HISTORY

This section will provide an overview of the policy response of the British government to the phenomenon of refugees, and then asylum seekers after the distinct legal category was introduced. While some mention will be made of the various countries of origin of asylum seekers and refugees at particular points in time, the focus will be on the policy response. This story in itself maps the emergence of the perception among policy makers of asylum as a problem for British society. As this example focuses on *British* asylum policy, it is important to point out that the British state came into existence only in 1707 with the Act of Union. The ruling nation state England, however, preceded this by 800 years, and there was much political continuity after the transition. England, and then Britain, was involved in both producing forced migrants (e.g. through the slave trade up to 1807) and hosting them (e.g. the Huguenots fleeing France in the seventeenth century) long before there were any laws in place defining or addressing the rights of refugees, or indeed before all human beings were categorised as rights-bearing individuals.

The first legislation to deal with refugees came in 1793 with the Aliens Act. This act was introduced in response to French refugees arriving in Britain following the revolution. Concern was expressed by members of the government, aristocracy and monarchy, and the purpose of the legislation was to protect the British state against French subversives who might stir up revolutionary fervour in the domestic population. Ships' masters were obliged to give details of foreigners carried by them or else face a fine. Some people were to be prohibited from landing, and the act legalised the removal of those who were ordered to leave on the grounds that they might be subversives (Schulte Beerbühl 2003).

The 1848 Alien Removal Bill was again proposed on the grounds of national self-protection. That is, protecting Britain from refugee republican propagandists originating in continental Europe. In introducing the bill, Sir George Grey said:

> We think that the present are extraordinary times, and that they are such as to justify exceptional legislation, with a view to prevent the accomplishment of the designs of that class of foreigners to which I have already alluded, who have availed themselves of their residence in this country, or who have come to it for the purpose of intriguing against its institutions. (House of Commons, 1 May 1848)

In any event, no 'aliens' were removed and immigration legislation was not debated in Parliament again for ten years, and not at serious length for forty years. The failure of Parliament to pass legislation in this period reflects the fact that there was liberal resistance in the Houses of Parliament and Lords, and particularly the strength of the feeling that Britain must resist anti-Semitism (see House of Lords, 23 May 1898).

In 1870, the Extradition Act provided for the non-extradition of fugitives who had committed an offence of 'a political character'. Indeed, throughout the nineteenth century the principle of asylum was fiercely defended in Parliament. For example, Sir George Grey stated in 1848:

It has long been the boast of England – and a just cause of boast it is – that she has been the protectress of constitutional liberty throughout Europe, and has at all times afforded an asylum to those individuals who have been oppressed in, and exiled from, their own countries on account of the political opinions they entertained. (House of Commons, 1 May 1848)

The belief amongst prominent sections of the political classes that asylum was a fundamental value of the British nation and hence must be defended did much to temper any hostilities bubbling up among communities receiving refugees, as well as diminishing Parliament's willingness to legislate on the matter. Yet, note the specification of Europe. At this time, refugees coming to Britain were European in a broad sense (encompassing Russia), but they were nevertheless European. They were Europe's internal 'others', and the duty to protect them was implicitly accepted. Importantly, colonialism and associated practices were not considered persecution.

During the early twentieth century, despite a proliferation of legislation to control the entry of immigrants, particularly 'coloured' immigrants (see key acts: Aliens Act 1905 and the Aliens Restriction (Amendment) Act 1919), asylum was not subject to new legislation. The management of European refugee flows following the Russian Revolution and the First World War was fulfilled initially by the League of Nations' High Commissioner Fridtjof Nansen, who issued certificates of identity to the displaced. An intergovernmental committee on refugees, focused on the German situation, was set up in 1938 and the International Refugee Organization (IRO) was founded in 1946 to deal with those displaced in Europe by the Second World War. In this period Britain fulfilled those duties that were expected of it by the international community in Europe and North America through ad hoc policies put in place for managing particular refugee populations, but no domestic legislation was passed. These responses were certainly influenced by racially based prejudices. For example, in 1938 visas were introduced to 'distinguished persons assured of hospitality in Britain and non-refugees who are known not to have any Jewish or non-Aryan affiliations' (cited in Dummett and Nicol 1990: 157). Later that year some Jews were allowed entry on temporary visas, and by the time the war was over, bowing to international pressure, tens of thousands were permitted to enter.

In 1951 the British government signed the Geneva Convention on the Status of Refugees, though they went to great lengths to see that it wasn't globally applicable (see chapter 6). The convention defined refugeehood and proscribed in international law the rights to which asylum seekers were entitled and the duties of states in relation to them. This made the categories 'asylum seeker' and 'refugee' legally distinct: an asylum seeker, as noted in the introduction, is someone who has made an application for asylum in a host state, while a refugee is someone whose application is successful. The immediate context for the next forty years of asylum policy was the Cold War, with the majority of applications for asylum in Britain under the convention coming from Soviet refugees. Though no legislation was put in place, Britain followed the convention, refusing refugee status for some and granting it to others, occasionally in large groups. In 1970 the immigration rules were changed so that persecution was listed as a reason for granting leave to appeal against refusal of entry clearance. However, the following year the Immigration Act gave the Home Secretary and immigration authorities powers to detain 'new commonwealth' (mostly non-white) asylum seekers indefinitely without charge. This was a part of a wider agenda of restricting 'coloured' commonwealth immigration through the late 1960s and in to the 1970s (Spencer 1997; Hampshire 2005).

It was in the early 1990s that legal instruments seeking to limit the number of asylum applications, and the number of people granted refugee status, began to proliferate. As the 'main property of the refugee regime [in the West] is its restrictiveness', the phrase 'non-entrée regime' has become one of the most common ways of describing the policy approach taken (Orchard 2014: 206). In the United Kingdom, in the fourteen years to 2007, there were seven Acts of Parliament which collectively established a non-entrée regime and two further acts in 2014 and 2016 which further targeted the growing category of refused asylum seekers created in part by the restrictiveness of the regime. Thus, it was in the late 1980s that asylum seekers began to be categorised explicitly as a 'problem' around which government policy must be focused (Schuster 2003b; Squire 2009). It was also at this time that applications for asylum from non-Europeans began to increase as a proportion of all applications as a consequence of peace in Europe, conflict elsewhere and increased international mobility.

The 1993 Asylum and Immigration Appeals Act, brought in by the Conservative government, incorporated the provisions of the 1951 Convention into UK law. This was not so that rights could be more fully extended to asylum seekers, however. The act introduced fingerprinting requirements for asylum seekers and fast-track procedures for assessing asylum applications (including criteria for decreasing the chance of an application being successful) and reduced the duties of local authorities towards homeless asylum seekers. However, it also extended appeal rights to people who had not previously had them. Three years later the 1996 Asylum and Immigration Act removed welfare benefit entitlements from in-country asylum applicants. Though ruled unlawful by the courts when introduced as a change in regulations (as it would leave people destitute), this change nevertheless made it in to the final act. In addition, the act introduced safe country lists (if your country of origin was on this list, you were deemed not to have been persecuted), reduced appeal rights for asylum seekers who had travelled through safe third countries, introduced new immigration-related criminal offences and removed the right of asylum seekers to register for local authority housing.

The first piece of asylum-related legislation to be passed under the New Labour government was the 1998 Human Rights Act, which incorporated the European Convention on Human Rights (ECHR) into domestic law, making it enforceable in UK courts. This limited the ability of the government to remove asylum seekers from the United Kingdom if they were at risk of having their ECHR rights breached. Such concessions were not, however, a good indication of what was to come. The following year the 1999 Immigration and Asylum Act sought to limit the rights of asylum seekers. It removed all remaining mainstream welfare benefit entitlement from asylum applicants and created the National Asylum Support Service (NASS) to provide basic support and accommodation to asylum applicants on the basis of a no-choice national dispersal policy. Financial support was set below citizen welfare payments. Carriers' liability was extended and immigration officers were given new powers to enter premises and search, arrest and detain asylum seekers. While the 2000 Race Relations (Amendment) Act extended anti-discrimination legislation into the public sector, those making decisions on immigration and asylum cases were exempt. This meant that public sector officials could legally make blanket decisions on immigration status on the basis of country of origin, a clause described by one journalist as 'the bluntest piece of state-sponsored ethnic discrimination in 35 years' (Hugo Young in the *Guardian*, 24 April 2001, cited in Sales 2002: 457).

The 2002 Nationality, Immigration and Asylum Act made it illegal for asylum seekers to travel without identity documents (this aspect of the act actually contravened the 1951 Convention). It introduced a list of behaviours to be taken into account when assessing an asylum seeker's credibility in relation to their application for asylum and removed the automatic right to support from families with children if applications were unsuccessful. It also granted the government the right to make support conditional for failed asylum seekers who could not be returned to their own countries as it was too unsafe, on the performance of unspecified community activities. The appeals system was simplified, deportation to safe third countries introduced, and resisting deportation made a criminal offence. That year the prime minister announced that the number of asylum seekers entering the United Kingdom would be halved within a year, 'as though the causes of flight were less relevant than the will of governments in the receiving states' (Schuster 2003a: 237).

The same year government ministers called for policies to discipline countries not cooperating with measures aimed at the repatriation of refused asylum seekers. Such disciplinary measures might include the withdrawal of trade privileges and development aid, with the armed forces being called upon to implement these and other asylum-related measures. For example, the use of the Royal Navy in intercepting asylum seekers at sea who were headed for Europe at sea, partnered with the Royal Air Force who would remove them in mass airlifts (Flynn 2005). In 2003 the 'New Vision' initiative made a case for the processing of all asylum applications outside of the United Kingdom in 'transit processing centres' or 'regional protection areas' which would be located outside of Europe (Noll 2003). These proposals did not make it into law.

Nevertheless, there were several more punitive pieces of legislation to come. The 2004 Asylum and Immigration (Treatment of Claimants) Act prohibited the provision of cash to asylum seekers whose first application for asylum was rejected. It also extended the grounds on which the government could exclude people from the 1951 Convention. Two years later, the 2006 Immigration, Asylum and Nationality Act removed the right to be granted 'indefinite leave to remain' from people recognised as refugees under the 1951 Refugee Convention. Instead, they were now to be given 'limited leave to remain' for five years, at which time their home country situation would be reviewed. The act gave the Home Office the power to withdraw support from families at the end of the asylum process (making them destitute as a means of encouraging their departure) and extended border controls, including the use of biometric data. It also enforced more strict regulations on attending fingerprinting appointments, extended the list of convention exclusion reasons and made asylum seekers whose first application had been refused exempt from eviction and housing laws designed to protect tenants. However, it did open up the possibility for local authorities to provide destitute asylum seekers with housing.

The 2007 UK Borders Act extended the use of biometric border technologies, making it a requirement for asylum seekers to have a biometric ID card, an imposition which was strongly resisted and ultimately rejected for citizens but nevertheless brought to bear on asylum seekers. It allowed for the imposition of 'reporting' conditions (much like an individual on police bail) upon anyone with limited leave to enter or remain in the United Kingdom, including those with refugee status, humanitarian protection or discretionary leave to remain. Reporting was already a standard part of being an asylum seeker. The act gave immigration officers further powers of apprehension and detention and put the right to deport foreign criminals seeking asylum in law. It also confirmed the right to support for asylum seekers who had not exhausted appeal rights.

The New Labour government, led by the then prime minister Tony Blair, introduced more pieces of legislation on the topic of asylum than any other in history, while simultaneously seeking to distance itself from the 1951 Convention. In 2001 Home Secretary Jack Straw said that the convention was no longer working as the framers had intended, as the environment for host states had completely changed as a consequence of the increasing number of applicants (Flynn 2005). Measures such as detention have proliferated and are now a part of the 'normal' asylum regime (Bloch and Schuster 2005; Hall 2012). Indeed, every effort has been made to limit the number of people who are legally recognised as having been persecuted, irrespective of the country contexts from which they flee.

The Conservative/Liberal Democrat coalition government (2010–15) introduced a new Immigration Act in 2014 which further enhanced the power of airlines to prevent migrants without visas boarding flights to the United Kingdom (thus preventing would-be asylum seekers from reaching the United Kingdom); reduced the appeal rights of asylum seekers who have received a negative decision on their application; increased restrictions on accessing public services, working and renting accommodation for those whose application has been refused; and removed barriers to swift deportation. In this period the United Kingdom resettled just 143 Syrian refugees fleeing the crisis in their country (Germany by contrast resettled 30,000). The 2015 Conservative government opted out of a European Union (EU) plan to offer resettlement to a limited number of migrants from North Africa in response to the crisis in the Mediterranean; instead, it supported only the plans to limit search and rescue operations and to bomb boats used by people smugglers on the Libyan coast.

Under pressure from NGOs and some vocal publics within the United Kingdom, the then prime minister David Cameron eventually agreed to take on twenty thousand quota refugees from within the refugee camps in the Middle East and North Africa over a period of five years. Only a fraction of this quota has been filled at the time of writing. In contrast to Germany, the United Kingdom sought to distance itself from responsibility to help asylum seekers and refugees arriving in Europe as part of the Syrian crisis. At the same time the government passed the 2016 Immigration Act, which sought to further crack down on refused asylum seekers remaining in the United Kingdom through sanctions on private renting and illegal working and constraints on the rights of parents not to be separated from children. The 'Brexit' referendum on the United Kingdom's membership of the EU, which saw 52 percent of the UK public vote to leave the Union, involved explicitly hostile and racist images of the 2015–16 European 'refugee crisis' being used in order to argue for leaving.

This overview clearly charts the emergence of asylum as a 'problem', for which policy solutions must be sought. But what has not been addressed is why the British government began to see the presence of asylum seekers in the United Kingdom as a problem and pursued measures to limit the likelihood of claims being accepted, limited asylum seekers' rights under the Geneva

Convention and made their lives in the United Kingdom as uncomfortable as possible. While one might have an intuitive idea of why these migrants may be considered undesirable – perhaps because of their countries of origin, or perhaps because of their number – it is important to interrogate these beliefs if a truly critical analysis of asylum policy is to be made.

THE RISE OF THE ASYLUM 'PROBLEM': THE STANDARD NARRATIVE

In response to the policies outlined above, a large body of academic analysis has emerged which reports on the poverty and almost total social exclusion which asylum seekers in Britain experience today. This includes research on the common incidence of mental health problems (self-harm, post-traumatic stress disorder, suicide), as well as arbitrary imprisonment, harassment, hate crime, media witch-hunting and inadequate access to basic services and resources (Silove et al. 1997; Buchanan, Grillo-Simpson, and Threadgold 2003; Schuster 2003a; Phillimore and Goodson 2006; Gabrielatos and Baker 2008; Fekete 2009; Hall 2012). Much of the literature about asylum has appeared since the 1980s, with the cross-disciplinary 'refugee studies' growing in this period in response to developments in Europe, North America and Australasia (Chimni 1998).

This is undoubtedly an important body of critical work. However, there is a common thread running through this work: the accepted historical context to this policy regime, a story which is widely accepted and is generally seen to be uncontroversial. Allowing for variations in individual accounts, the narrative goes like this: the number of asylum seekers coming to the United Kingdom, to Europe and to other Western countries today is unprecedented (Zolberg, Suhrke, and Aguayo 1989; Loescher 1993; Spencer 1995; Joly 1996; Appleyard 2001; Koser 2001; Gibney 2003; Hansen 2003; Spencer 2003; Bohmer and Shuman 2008). Present-day asylum seekers are unprecedented not only in number but also in character – they are different from previous cohorts in various ways including the reasons for their flight and the range of countries they come from. This 'newness' is set within the context of two cohorts of refugees who are often depicted as prima facie refugees, the original and the genuine who unequivocally were the intended subjects of the international refugee regime. The first are those displaced within Europe as a result of the Second World War. Other refugees in other parts of the world at the time of drafting the Refugee Convention, let alone those before or after, are not a part of this story. The second group are Cold War refugees, again from within Europe, who fled communism in favour of the capitalist West (see Goodwin-Gill 2001; Keely 2001; Joly 2002; Crisp 2003; Hansen 2003; Friedman and Kelin 2008; Haddad 2008; Squire 2009).

Once it has been established that the Refugee Convention was devised in response to European refugees following the Second World War, and that Cold War refugees were small in number and were clearly politically persecuted, the sudden presence of large numbers of non-European asylum seekers at the gates of Europe, or within European territories, at the close of the twentieth century becomes a logical explanation for a tightened policy regime. These new refugees are *different*, and there are a lot of them. They also come from poor countries, meaning that they implicitly blur the boundaries between economic migrant and refugee, casting doubt on their claim to have been persecuted (Spencer 1995; Joly 1996; Koser 2001). Hansen (2003: 35), for example, writes that 'for much of the post-war period, asylum was a Cold War sideshow ... accepting rare large-scale outflows ... allowed the West to assert, without much financial cost, its moral superiority'. Then, in the 1980s, numbers began to increase; after 1989 'they exploded' (Hansen 2003). He suggests that despite all efforts on the part of European governments to the contrary, the numbers of applications remain 'at intolerably high levels. At the same time, only the most resourceful – generally the young and male – can make it to Europe's shores and they are by definition not always the most deserving' (Hansen 2003: 36). Haddad (2008: 31) echoes this: 'when numbers reached hitherto unimaginable heights, something had to change – one refugee is an individual in need who should be let in, a thousand refugees are a threat and a burden'.

Applications for asylum are said to have increased for a number of reasons, including the advent of cheap international air travel and global telecommunications (Appleyard 2001; Gibney 2003, 2006). Gibney (2003) dubs these 'jet-age' refugees and describes how the economic downturn in the 1980s and 1990s meant that fewer foreign workers were required. This meant the 'closing off [*sic*] the major avenue through which the denizens of the world's poorer countries could enter the West', thus increasing applications for asylum. What this opened up was 'the prospect of a truly "globalized" system of asylum-seeking, driven as much by economic disparities between North and South, as by refugee generating events, strictly defined' (Gibney 2003: 145).

This narrative has been taken up by politicians, who justify restrictive asylum policies on the basis that there are too many asylum seekers coming to the United Kingdom and that most of them are not genuine refugees. At the same time, it is acknowledged with a shrug of the shoulders that these policies are likely to prevent genuine refugees from being able to access their human right to claim asylum. In the next section I problematise this narrative, describing my critique as a sociology of absences.

THE STANDARD NARRATIVE: A SOCIOLOGY OF ABSENCES

Refugee studies has been repeatedly criticised for being ahistorical. Kushner (2006: 40), for example, writes of the inability of refugee studies scholars 'to see history and refugees as linked or relevant', while Marfleet (2007: 136) suggests that forced migration studies scholars appear actively 'averse' to history. In the absence of a serious engagement with history, the standard narrative has gone largely uncontested. It provides a brief introductory context to many books and articles but is rarely questioned (Marfleet 2007 and Chimni 1998 are exceptions). But the status of the narrative described above as a generally accepted historical context has implications for how we critically respond to asylum policy and for the challenges that it is possible to make.

My critique is not of what is present but of what is absent. The histories which I seek to explore are not necessarily refugee histories, but are rather histories which explain the hierarchical ordering of human beings according to place of origin, those which might make sense of the response of states such as Britain to asylum seekers today. Therefore, while there are many histories which might be incorporated into contemporary analyses and which might therefore complicate them (such as Long 2013), the omissions which I will focus on here are around histories of colonialism. Not all of the absences mentioned below will be addressed in the subsequent chapters of the book, which focus on the legacies of colonialism in relation to ideas of differential human worth and access to the rights of 'man' and 'human'. However, it is worth noting here a number of the silences within the standard narrative and their implications for how we study and theorise forced migration and the response of Western states to asylum seekers. Four are identified below and they all individually, as well as in combination, raise questions about how we approach the actions of Western states to asylum seekers in the present.

Silences around Non-European Refugees Before the 1990s

In terms of refugee history in a specific sense, it is striking that displacements outside of Europe, often as a result of colonial activities and struggles around decolonisation, as well as the reception of European refugees in former colonies, are not a part of the standard narrative. This is despite the vast exodus from China between 1949 and 1950, millions of refugees created by the Korean War (1950–53), and seven hundred thousand Palestinians becoming refugees during the Arab–Israeli conflict of 1948 – what would become one of the most long-lasting refugee crises in history (Sandler 1999; Morris 2003; Chi-Kwan 2007). Talbot and Singh (2009) estimate that fifteen million people were forcibly displaced during the partitioning of India to create the new state of Pakistan in one of the largest migrations of the twentieth century. These refugee crises were raised on a regular basis in the British Parliament throughout the 1950s (more than European refugee issues, in fact) and the country provided significant sums of bilateral aid to alleviating them (House of Commons, 19 March 1951). Large numbers of refugees were also displaced as a result of decolonisation, in disputes over borders and sovereignty which in some cases continue today. It might therefore be assumed that a discussion of the history of refugee policy, at least in Britain, would include some mention of such movements. But rarely is this the case. Typically neglectful of these broader issues, Barber and Ripley (1988: 53) suggest that in 1951 'the overwhelming majority of refugees were European'. Starting from this same assumption, a decade later Bloch (1999: 1) describes how the 1967 Protocol opened up recourse to the 1951 Convention to people from all over the world 'which reflected changes as refugees were no longer just a European phenomenon; instead refugee migration was occurring from conflicts all over the world'. What scholars usually mean is that asylum seekers and refugees seeking sanctuary *in wealthy Western states* were almost always European in 1951, but two vital pieces of information are missing from this representation. First, the Refugee Conventions prevented non-Europeans from being considered refugees until 1967. Second, and most importantly, just because most refugees in Europe were European in the middle of the twentieth century, it does not mean that most refugees *in the world* were European until the 1990s.

This slippage is vital, as it allows for a whole host of assumptions about contemporary (non-European) asylum seekers. One key issue is that contemporary asylum seekers are then widely described as different from previous cohorts in character and number, even though this is demonstrably not the case. The evidence suggests that asylum seekers today, though from poor countries, are migrating not because of poverty but as a result of the same kinds of forces that plagued Europeans in the 1930s and 1940s – the threat or experience of persecution. A focus on numbers, in fact, reveals that numbers spike when refugee-creating situations, such as wars, occur. Research on this topic has shown that poverty alone is not sufficient to compel someone to leave their home country and seek asylum in the West; war, violence and human rights abuses must also be present to explain flight (Neumayer 2005). This demonstrates that asylum is not the mechanism through which 'the denizens of the world's poorer countries could enter the West', as Gibney (2003: 145) has suggested, but rather a mechanism for seeking protection from a foreign state as in the past. And yet the myth of difference, which I discuss further in the next chapter, endures. Their difference is not in the legitimacy of their claim to persecution but in their national origins.

Silences around Colonial Exclusions from the Refugee Conventions

Not only were there millions of refugees outside of Europe at the time of drafting the Refugee Conventions, but non-European refugees were *purposefully* excluded from these conventions. This history is described in detail in chapter 6, and so it is perhaps sufficient here to explain that this exclusion occurred despite extensive and protracted resistance from the representatives of formerly colonised states at the United Nations negotiations. As Antony Anghie (2008) has argued so convincingly in relation to international law more broadly, colonialism was central to the constitution of international law. This includes a variety of areas that have a direct impact on refugee-producing situations and the rights of those fleeing them. Colonialism was not simply 'an unfortunate episode that has long since been overcome by the heroic initiatives of decolonization that resulted in the emergence of colonial societies as independent, sovereign states' (Anghie 2008: 3). Rather, it was in fact central to the formation of international law in that it provided in the first instance a legal framework for colonial relations. The standard narrative does not include this history; the popular framing of the birth of the right to asylum is entirely different, which again has implications for how we interpret the present moment.

Silences around the Legacies of Colonialism for Mobility and Immobility

Because colonialism is absent from the standard narrative, and displacements resulting from colonialism and decolonisation in the past are left out of many accounts of the history of asylum policy that precede analyses of the present, it then also becomes logical to leave unmentioned the legacies of colonialism for refugee-producing situations, for destination country choice and for ongoing practices of border control. Colonial practices involved restricting the mobility of colonised peoples and facilitating the mobility of the colonisers. As the world has become seemingly more mobile through processes and practices related to what has come to be labelled 'globalisation', it is easy to forget that these same mobilities and immobilities characterise the contemporary period. As the formerly colonised have become more mobile, legal and practical barriers have been developed to re-inscribe that very immobility which characterised colonial subjugation. As Wendy Brown (2010: 7–8) has observed:

> what we have come to call a globalized world harbours fundamental tensions between opening and barricading ... These tensions materialise as increasingly liberated borders, on the one hand, and the devotion of unprecedented funds, energies and technologies to border fortification, on the other.

This is, in part, about ideas of citizenship and belonging which can be traced back to the days of Empire, but which take on new forms today. Citizenship depends on controlling mobility in order to support the 'sedentarist ideology of the nation state', an ideology which constantly clashes with the reality of human mobility (Kotef 2015: 11). But once this image of stability and rootedness is established for particular groups of people, it then serves to facilitate their growing mobility at the same time as the mobility of others (who are not rooted by belonging to the privileged group) is constrained (Kotef 2015). While British citizens are made ever more mobile, their privileged status as travellers and 'expats' is contrasted against – or even made possible by – continued efforts to immobilise non-European, often racially marked, 'others' – immigrants and asylum seekers. Globalisation is said to have created 'mobility gaps' – new regimes of mobility and immobility (Shamir 2005) – and yet these gaps have a long history which we might pay more attention to.

The technologies – the methods of containment and restriction – that are used in contemporary border regimes around the world follow the very same patterns of mobility and immobility that began in the colonial period. Until recently, the rise of cheap international air travel meant that asylum seekers could flee contexts of violence and persecution and get to stable, wealthy countries relatively easily. That is, assuming they had the financial means, which the vast majority did not (86 percent of refugees live in 'developing' countries, often those neighbouring their country of origin). The introduction of carrier sanctions, an effort at containing refugees in regions of original displacement, means that people either are successfully immobilised or risk their lives on hazardous land and sea crossings in order to circumvent such controls. Thus, while carrier sanctions are new, the rationale behind them is not, and it is this fetishisation of the new in policy analysis that needs to be overcome if the standard narrative is to cease to have such popularity.

Silences around the Legacies of Colonialism in Ideas of Asylum Seekers as Undesirable and Excludable

What we therefore lose from the standard narrative is the acknowledgement of continuity that a postcolonial analysis necessarily demands. How can we make sense of the exclusionary impulse without discussing ideas of 'us' and 'them' which are rooted in colonial history? Paul Gilroy has observed that

> Old, modern notions of racial difference appear once again to be active within the calculus that tacitly assigns differential value to lives lost according to their locations and supposed racial origins or considers that some human bodies are more easily and appropriately humiliated, imprisoned, shackled, starved and destroyed than others. (2003: 263)

Gilroy argues that fine ethnic distinctions based often on country of origin 'effectively revive a colonial economy in which infra-humanity, measured against the benchmark of healthier imperial standards, diminishes human rights and can defer human recognition' (Gilroy 2003). The non-entrée regime, which is in fact a hierarchical regime, and which allows some to move freely whilst immobilising others, is implicated in this process described by Gilroy. Immobility is not simply about non-movement; the means by which it is achieved involves restricting people's access to human rights, denying them human dignity where for others it would unquestionably be granted and ultimately assigning differential value to the lives of human beings. The lowly status of asylum seekers and others, then, 'underscores the fact that they cannot be reciprocally endowed with the same vital humanity enjoyed by their well-heeled captors, conquerors, judges, executioners and other racial betters' (Gilroy 2003).

The post-Second World War period is only one moment when the relationship between colonialism and the response to refugees has been made starkly apparent. More broadly, colonial histories of racial classification and international political and legal exclusion are deeply implicated in the current mode of operation with regard to asylum seekers within Britain and many other countries. A thorough and rigorous account of the context to the rise of the non-entrée regime, then, would be one which accounts for colonial histories in both the development of the international legal framework for asylum and then the response to more recent cohorts of asylum seekers. In this book I seek to do both.

MOVING FORWARD

The standard narrative, as a generally accepted historical context to contemporary phenomena, has implications for how we critically respond to asylum policy and for the challenges that it is possible to make. Refugees are often described as a 'modern' phenomenon. That is, modern in the sense of being one of the features (or residual categories) of the system of democratic nation states which emerged after the French Revolution, and with it came the idea of the rights of man and then human rights. This is important because the alignment of refugeehood with modern states (those who experienced the enlightenment, adopted democracy, developed and subscribed to human rights and were industrialised in the nineteenth century) means that those displaced people harking from the non-modern world are then not necessarily refugees, they are something else. To be a refugee is to be modern within this context. The association between modernity and refugeehood has been acknowledged, but the fact that colonialism was integral to the development of modernity, and the fact that foregrounding this process immediately shows us that the central dividing line in refugee studies as well as the realpolitik of asylum policy is between the modern and the traditional (the not yet modern world; always spatially, culturally, economically excluded from full modernity, or the ability to fully 'catch up') have not. If refugee studies have not yet dealt with histories of colonialism even though they are entangled with the concept of modernity which underpins so much scholarship in the field, neither have those who seek to explain hostility to asylum seekers as racism without engaging with coloniality/modernity.

The next chapter offers an alternative standpoint from which to approach the politics of asylum. The standard narrative is first discredited as a 'myth of difference' using scholarship from Third World Approaches to International Law (TWAIL), something which I touched upon briefly in this chapter. Next, the inadequacy of theories of 'racism' or 'racialisation' to account for the hostile policy regime is explained in more depth. Instead, hostility to asylum seekers is re-theorised using the work of scholars from postcolonial and decolonial studies including Michel-Rolph Trouillot, Walter Mignolo and Sylvia Wynter. Central to this re-theorisation is the critique of 'modernity' as a worldview, rather than a geographical and temporal phenomena, and an exploration of the entanglement of exclusionary and hierarchical ideas of 'man' and the 'human' with ideas of modernity. The chapter therefore lays the groundwork for reading the substantive, more empirically focused chapters that follow.

Chapter Three

Decolonising the 'Problem'

An Alternative Standpoint for Analysing the Exclusionary Politics of Asylum

The previous chapter described the rise of asylum seeking as something seen to be a problem *in itself* and charted the development of successive laws and policies which have steadily eroded the right to asylum as enshrined in international law. The underlying narrative of asylum policy analysis was identified, and it was argued that this narrative makes the response of Western states to the presence of asylum seekers appear to be a *divergence* from earlier policy approaches, rather than business as usual. It was argued that there are many absences in the dominant story of the history of asylum in the West, particularly the absence of colonial histories from the vast majority accounts. In response, this chapter proposes a new theoretical framework for understanding the policy shift in relation to asylum seekers, one which draws on insights from Third World Approaches to International Law (TWAIL) and postcolonial and decolonial studies.

Though the perspectives drawn on originate in distinct schools of thought which have different foci, all challenge the privileging of European subjects over others and seek to bring to the fore histories of inequality which may have led to contemporary exclusions. They do not see inequality today as the end point in an uncontrollable, natural or inevitable sequence of events but rather as emergent of deeply rooted historical trends. What this provides is an epistemological starting point which is radically different from the literatures discussed in the previous chapter, especially those dominant in refugee studies. Rather than starting from the 'problem' of asylum seekers within the normative framework of human rights, we are required to start from the very idea of 'man' as a supposedly universal, rights-bearing subject.

The chapter starts with what B.S. Chimni describes as the 'myth of difference', a hegemonic discourse within academic and policy circles that views asylum seekers today as fundamentally different from previous cohorts in number and character. Building on this and in dialogue with a range of thinkers including Michel-Rolph Trouillot, Walter Mignolo and Sylvia Wynter, the colonial origins of ideas such as 'man' and 'human' but also modernity and the modern are discussed. Through these discussions the hegemonic epistemology of colonial modernity emerges as the most adequate framework within which one might begin to understand the exclusionary politics of asylum today, as opposed to globalisation, hypermobility or racism. The idea of coloniality/modernity (coloniality and modernity as two sides of the same coin) draws attention to the impasse between the theoretical rights-bearing human and the lived reality of the racially marked 'other'. In subsequent chapters this theoretical perspective is then mobilised to make sense of four inter-related case studies and the final part of this chapter is dedicated to describing how, methodologically, these continuities are traced. An institutional orders approach is employed within the case studies to sharpen the analysis and in order to reveal the shifting discourses of humanity (and inhumanity) over time as well as the justifications for exclusionary measures and the extent to which national policies on these issues have long been entangled with international relations.

THE MYTH OF DIFFERENCE

The previous chapter outlined what I called the standard narrative. The standard narrative is a widely used story which provides the historical context to asylum policies in Western states today. The narrative underpins much literature on what has been dubbed the 'non-entrée regime' (Orchard 2014), and in questioning it I seek to rethink the basis upon which critical reflection on the politics of asylum is made. In a similar vein B.S. Chimni identified in 1998 what he dubbed the 'myth of difference'. The myth of difference, according to Chimni, was pervasive within the discipline of international law, a discipline which he sought to critique from the perspective of the emerging field of TWAIL. Despite being published in the journal *Refugee Studies*, Chimni's article does not appear to have had the level of impact on refugee studies as a cross-disciplinary field of study that such a far-reaching critique might warrant. I seek to partly correct this neglect here.

Between 1950 and 1989 Cold War imperatives were, Chimni (1998) argues, the primary basis upon which the international refugee regime, and individual national responses to asylum seekers, rested. That is, asylum seekers were understood to be European, and it is within that context that asylum policy was made at the national and international level. The arrival in the West, from the 1980s onwards, of the 'new asylum seekers' from the Global South, coupled with the end of the Cold War, led to a policy shift. The refugee 'no longer possessed ideological or geopolitical value' (Chimni 1998: 351) and the response was the development of the non-entrée regime which privileged repatriation over resettlement and sited the causes of refugee flows in sending countries, as opposed to international contexts. Underpinning this policy shift was the 'myth of difference':

> The nature and character of refugee flows in the Third World were represented as being radically different from refugee flows in Europe since the end of the First World War. Thereby, an image of a 'normal' refugee was constructed – white, male and anti-communist – which clashed sharply with individuals fleeing the Third World. (Chimni 1998: 351)

These new refugees were not necessarily different in terms of the legitimacy of their claim to asylum under international law. What was different was that they were from the Global South, usually from former European colonies. This made them undesirable, and the myth of difference was one means by which Western states legitimised efforts to steadily erode their human right to claim asylum. If asylum seekers are represented as not having a legitimate claim to refugee status, they are then labelled 'economic migrants' – migrating by choice for work rather than under duress because of persecution (Mayblin 2016b). The myth of difference thus discredits non-Western asylum seekers through both a blurring and reinforcing of the boundaries between economic migration and forced migration. The boundaries are blurred in that it is acknowledged that voluntary and forced migration are complex and interrelated, facilitating a process of undermining individual claims for asylum. They are reinforced in that migrants must nevertheless be categorised as one or the other. If they fail to meet the criteria defining a refugee as described in the 1951 Convention, in the image of the Cold War asylum seeker, they must be an economic migrant. If this is found to be the case, they are exposed as 'bogus', attempting to 'cheat the system', and can legitimately be criminalised, detained and deported.

Chimni (1998: 356) notes, as I have done, that 'there is constant reference in the [academic] literature to the enormous magnitude and the unprecedented nature of the contemporary crisis'. The myth of difference is of course based on the assumption that there were no non-European refugees in the world at the time of drafting the 1951 Convention and that these refugees appeared only in the late twentieth century. When non-European asylum seekers do appear on the scene there are too many, and they are so different from previous cohorts that the punitive policies directed at them appear to be a reasonable response. For Chimni, then, refugee studies, and the more recent rise of forced migration studies, have contributed to the legitimising of the containment of refugees from the Global South outside of the Global North (Chimni 2009), what Richmond (1994) refers to as the new global apartheid.

While this is an important, and certainly underappreciated, intervention, Chimni does not theorise the myth of difference or trace its emergence in history. The myth is inaccurate, he charges, but on what basis is such a thing possible? The task of the next two sections is to think about how we might theorise the myth of difference, and the task of the remainder of the book beyond this chapter is to seriously engage with the histories which gave rise to it in the late twentieth century, in dialogue with that theorisation. A common refrain is that hostility to asylum seekers is rooted in racism, that this hostility, and by implication the myth of difference, can be theorised as racism. The first task is therefore to explore approaches that use racism as their starting point and use a critique of these as the foundation for a deeper theoretical engagement with the myth of difference in a historical perspective.

Asylum Seeker Hostility: Racism or Racialisation?

Let us look now at the broader discourse surrounding contemporary asylum seekers, a discourse that will go unchallenged on a fundamental level until the myth of difference is thoroughly discredited. The dominant representation of asylum seekers by the popular press and politicians in Britain is that they are unwanted, uncivilised hoards, swarming at the borders and threatening the British way of life. This representation is clearly dehumanising and draws on many of the tropes that have characterised racism more broadly over the past few centuries. For example, when Katie Hopkins, a columnist in the British tabloid newspaper *The Sun*, described asylum seekers crossing the Mediterranean Sea as 'cockroaches' in summer 2015 she was drawing on a well-established semantic association between immigrants and racialised others within (e.g. Jews in Europe) and swarming, invasive, unhygienic insects. A few months later the British Prime Minister himself drew on this semantic field when he described migrants living in the Calais migrant camp known as the 'Jungle' as 'swarming'. Asylum seekers are, in this way, dehumanised discursively and materially (through their treatment) in ways that draw on the modus operandi of racism. In other words, we can observe, as many have (Cole 2009; Fekete 2009, 2001), a clear connection between racism and hostility to asylum seekers.

What this apparently logical observation – noting commonalities between hostility to asylum seekers and racism more broadly – implies, however, is that anti-asylum seeker sentiment *is* racism, that it is one amongst many examples of the different *types* of observable racism that can then be empirically identified. Yet the flaws in this argument very quickly become apparent when placed under scrutiny. If we are to approach asylum seekers as a group that is racialised, there is an implication that it is possible to categorise asylum seekers within a racially based framework. And yet, such an approach is immediately confronted with limitations. The label 'asylum seeker' is a legal term, and does not denote similarity in religion, culture, skin colour, nationality, language or ethnicity. While racism is not only about skin colour but also often about culture (Lentin 2008), neither of these are adequately encapsulated in the slippery domain of hostility to asylum seekers. It is their *generalised* presence, their numbers, their imagined multitude, that is problematic. Racism gets at some of this but cannot adequately explain the phenomena, particularly when one is looking at government policy which is articulated in carefully deracialised terms.

This point is best demonstrated with an example: Cole (2009) argues that contemporary British racism can be divided into various subcategories. He suggests that this process of disaggregation is important because it foregrounds the fact that not all racism is related to skin colour and in doing so helps us to better combat the various types of racism. The types of racism which he identifies are 'non-colour-coded racism', 'anti-gypsy Roma traveller racism', 'xeno-racism' (which he, unlike Sivanandan and Fekete, discussed below, applies only to white Eastern European immigrants) and 'newer hybridist racism', which can be divided into two groups: 'Islamophobia' and 'anti-asylum-seeker racism'. Having disaggregated racism in this way, Cole does not further theorise racism in order to flesh out what is 'racial' about these types of hostility. 'Non-colour-coded racism' is, he argues, a function of class politics. Alluding to the application of eugenics to the lower classes in the nineteenth century, this historical understanding of social Darwinism is, he implies, an explanation of how the hostility experienced by white immigrants today can be conceptualised as racism.

This plethora of racisms as a proxy for types of 'othering' is inadequately theorised and so expansive that it ceases to be analytically useful. If some racisms are non-colour-coded on the basis of social Darwinist beliefs, then homophobia and prejudice against disabled people are also variations of racism. This implies that all prejudice which groups people together on the basis of physical, mental or cultural typologies and targets them in a discriminatory way are therefore 'racist'. Though a coherent argument on its own terms, this expansive understanding of racism does not add any depth to our understanding of these various prejudices beyond noting that they are similar. While I agree that racism exists, even where it is not explicitly observable, I would also argue that in the absence of racialised language charges of racism need to be set very clearly and thoroughly within historical contexts. Certainly, a brief mention of social Darwinism cannot suffice. In short, simply claiming that racism can be 'non-colour coded' does not help us to make sense of hostility to asylum seekers in the current moment, and since it is non-colour coded the charge of racism certainly does not offer critical purchase for challenging the treatment of asylum seekers by the state or by the general public.

Gilroy (2003: 262) observes that ' "race" supplies enabling analogies and legitimising scripts in a host of historical situations where natural differences and social divisions are politically, economically and militarily mediated'. However, he warns that recognising the role of the concept of race in 'specifying what we [academics] might call "the logic of type" and "the nature of difference" should not lead us deeper into an engagement with "race"'. It is possible that expanding the number of categories of racism to better fit the groups in question inadvertently reifies supposed racial differences. If racism is inadequate, then perhaps 'racialisation' – the imposition of racially based stereotypes upon certain groups – is more accurate? Squire (2009) argues that decolonisation encouraged migration towards Europe and was accompanied by opposition to 'coloured' immigration, which rearticulated the political community in racial terms. She rejects a focus on racism in favour of an analytical focus on 'racialisation', a process by which 'certain groups or individuals are marked as "different"' (Squire 2009: 46). For her, ' "undesirable" migrants are marked as different, regardless of their skin colour'. Garner (2013: 504) develops the application of racialisation in the case of asylum seekers further, suggesting that it

> must be understood not exclusively in terms of categorising according to appearance and culture, but also as a more abstract process of attributing innate characteristics to all members of a given group. In the case of asylum-seekers in England, it is the group's social status, rather than shared physical characteristics, that serves as the basis for racialization.

Theoretically, this turn away from racism towards racialisation is interesting but needs to be unpacked. Racialisation is not wholly about being marked as different irrespective of skin colour; otherwise an alternative vocabulary around prejudice would be suitable. Again, being marked as different need not be equated with 'race' difference. Indeed, the now significant body of literature dealing with racialisation suffers at times from a lack of clarity which I believe hinders the concept's explanatory potential (see Carter 2000; Murji and Solomos 2005 for more expansive discussions of this issue).

Banton (1997: 35) has argued forcefully that the concept of 'race' has no meaning and yet that differences between people are 'racialised' 'by the use of words which implied that the differences sprang from biological determinants postulated in racial theories'. Indeed, as Barot and Bird (2001: 601) point out, 'race' still has meaning for many people in terms of their lived experience of the world, and for them 'it is this problem of the lived experience of people on the one hand and uneasiness of [academics] with the concept on the other, that seems to account for the current popularity of racialisation'. Garner (2013: 506), for example, suggests that though race-specific discourse is assiduously avoided by residents (participants in his research) objecting to an asylum seeker processing office near their homes, 'the entire group of diverse people are produced as sharing characteristics. The absence of fixed phenotypical reference points makes asylum-seekers' status all the more significant in their construction as homogenous, and dangerous to the ordinary citizens' (see also Hubbard 2005).

While the deployment of 'racialisation' in an effort to avoid the reification of the contested concept of 'race' is useful to an extent, it nevertheless encounters problems if we apply it to asylum seekers in general. The claim is that race-specific discourse is assiduously avoided, but this is nevertheless racism. In order to make such a claim, theoretical and historiographical labour is required. Yet racialisation in this context is often a very immediate and recent process, rather than something more long-standing. We might say that particular discourses, for example, in a newspaper article, racialise asylum seekers in that they associate derogatory characteristics drawing on themes of 'race' hierarchy with asylum seekers. However, asserting that hostility to asylum seekers *generally* is a case of racialisation does not get at the issue of the hostile policy regime, which is often articulated in terms which are carefully non-racialising (see Garner 2013). In short, racialisation names an action, but it cannot aid in unpacking the historically embedded interconnections between apparently different fields of action, some of which may be very difficult to straightforwardly associate with 'racial' logics. Racialisation, then, is a concept that I am purposefully avoiding. Following Banton's assertion that the language of 'race' has to be present for racialisation to occur, and wanting to avoid either the reification of the concept of 'race' or the ill-fitting inclusion of asylum-seeker hostility into a discussion of 'race', the focus must be a much wider metadiscourse from which both racism and negation of duty to (and infra-humanity of) asylum seekers emerges.

Sivanandan (2001) and Fekete (2001, 2009) deal with this conundrum by introducing a new concept, 'xeno-racism':

> It is a racism that is not just directed at those with darker skins, from the former colonial countries, but at the newer categories of the displaced and dispossessed whites, who are beating at Western Europe's doors, the Europe that displaced them in the first place. It is racism in substance but xeno in form, a racism that is meted out to impoverished strangers even if they are white. It is xeno-racism. (Sivanandan 2001: 2)

Here again is an attempt to establish a link between racism and immigration controls, at the same time as arguing that the poor are being re-racialised.

Not the British poor, however, but the poor from the wider world – the 'Third World'. Sivanandan (2001: 2) writes, 'xeno-racism is a feature of the Manichaean world of global capitalism, where there are only the rich and the poor', while Fekete (2001) argues that poor would-be immigrants are the new communists in terms of being enemies of the West.

Irregular migration is criminalised, Sivanandan and Fekete argue, through international cooperation on migration management between 'First World' governments, which are then imposed upon 'Third World' governments through sanctions and pressure. It is the capitalist principle, therefore, that underpins xeno-racism, making the 'managed migration' agenda a new form of Darwinism. Sivanandan (2001) argues that while xenophobia is innocent, racism is culpable. This is his way of explaining the disjuncture between hostility to asylum seekers – which clearly marks some people as less human than others – and the justifications for such hostility – which are articulated in sanitised non-racial terms around economics and population statistics.

Though a useful contribution, what is problematic for me in this account is the privileging of contemporary capitalist political economy in the analysis to the detriment of histories of colonial domination when what the authors are really trying to account for is the sense that racism is somehow implicated in the process. Both the philosophical and political (eugenicist) agenda of social Darwinism and the differential wealth accrued in Western Europe and the white settler colonies (North America and Australasia) to the detriment of the former European colonies (now labelled the 'Third World' or 'developing countries') are outcomes of the colonial world system. Focusing on the contemporary outcomes of capitalism, then, obscures important political histories which are vital to the story. That is, the hierarchical ordering of people in the world according to geographical location and visible physical characteristics as part of the colonial project. This perspective thus makes the 'xeno' element necessary, while the remaining sense that this contemporary hostility is nevertheless 'racial' in some sense necessitates the 'racism' element. What is needed, again, is a peeling back of the layers of this argument and a focus on the much wider metadiscourses from which both racism and negation of duty to asylum seekers emerge.

There is clearly a 'racial' element to the types of hostility that racialisation and xeno-racism seek to explain, something which allies the racialisation of, or xeno-racism against, asylum seekers with racism, as opposed to homophobia for example. The 'race' element in racism, racialisation and xeno-racism offers a useful shorthand for the kinds of processes of 'othering' which the authors above address. However, my concern here is with digging deeper into the histories which created the *conditions of possibility* for this perception of difference and with the ways in which some bodies are particularly marked as different. We know that the proliferation of hostility to asylum seekers particularly accompanied the arrival of non-European, postcolonial asylum seekers (Mayblin 2014). The aim, then, is to historicise the negative reception of asylum seekers in contemporary Britain and, most importantly, foreground the coloniality which lies beneath prevailing understandings of differential human worth. The process whereby asylum seekers came to be marked as different in line with a narrative of unwanted, alien 'others' from the 'underdeveloped, non-modern world' is one which is very specifically informed by histories of 'race' science but endures today because of the continued logics of coloniality – the legacies of the justificatory discourses of colonialism. Thus it is not the fact that *they* are marked as different, as a consequence of *their* difference, but that colonial discourses marked them as such and that rationales of inequality and civilisational incommensurability remain. The only way to make sense of this is through acknowledging the spatial and temporal logics of modernity (Bhabha 2005 [1994]). Ideas of progress, civility and modernity are, as Bhabha (2005 [1994]: 347) points out, 'negotiated within the "enunciative" present of discourse' and over time the site of enunciation is transformed (e.g. deracialised), concealing 'the fact that the hegemonic structures of power are maintained in a position of authority through a shift in vocabulary in the position of authority'. This analysis, developed further below, allows for a more complex understanding of racialisation as a historically grounded, denaturalised, non-inevitable process.

I propose, then, that racism and racialisation are replaced as the basis for analysis with a coloniality/modernity frame. The key to making sense of hostility to asylum seekers – socially and politically – is not, then, 'race' but the category of 'man', which is rhetorically universal and yet exclusionary in practice. Within this framework we no longer need to claim homogeneity or engage with questions of biological or cultural similarity. Hostility to asylum seekers is not an issue of 'race' per se (though racial ideas are linked) but can be understood through the analytical framework of coloniality/modernity. Asylum seekers are therefore people out of place in the spatial organisation of modernity. In the remainder of this section I explain how a coloniality/modernity perspective drawing on postcolonial and decolonial theory refocuses away from 'race' and towards the coloniality which lies beneath prevailing understandings of differential human worth. In incorporating an account of coloniality into my analysis, I turn to decolonial thought. The starting point is to conceptualise Britain principally as a postcolonial society, not simply within the context of past historical events. This is about understanding the relationship between Britain and asylum-seeking 'others' as rooted in the coloniality/modernity duality, and conceiving of coloniality as epistemic, rather than simply an empirical, and historical, occurrence.

Asylum Seekers and (un)Modernity

The concept of modernity is the predominant frame through which much work in the social sciences is undertaken. Modernity has both temporal and geographical dimensions. The temporal concerns rupture – the idea that at some point in time something happened to Western societies which transformed them from pre-modern societies into modern societies. The Renaissance, the French Revolution and the Industrial Revolution form the key pillars of this story, together facilitating the Age of Enlightenment, the emergence of democracy and the rise of capitalism in the West (Bhambra 2007). For sociology, anthropology, political science and international relations, this rupture is pivotal because it is the basis for the disciplinary division of labour. Politics and sociology have traditionally been concerned with modern societies (liberal capitalist democracies), and the story of how Europe came to be modern is fundamental for understanding the world in which we now live. International relations then is concerned both with how modern states interact and also how they interact with the non-modern world, as well as if/how the non-modern world might become/is becoming modern. The role of anthropology has historically been focused exclusively on the non-modern world, though this has changed in recent decades.

The geographical dimension establishes difference – not everywhere in the world experienced an Enlightenment-style transition away from religion in favour of scientific reason, and many places are neither democratic nor capitalist. This reaffirms the idea that some places in the world today are modern, while some are not. Combined with the temporal variable, this logically means that some societies are 'behind' Western societies, existing in their past rather than in a global present. A basic distinction is thus made between Western societies in the present, and other societies which are seen variously as 'pre-modern', 'traditional' or perhaps 'transitional'. Bhabha (2005 [1994]: 344) describes this as a time lag; modernity took/takes place in some locations and for him 'this insistent and incipient *spatial* metaphor in which the social relations of modernity are conceived' introduces 'a temporality of the "synchronous" in the structure of the "splitting" of modernity'. Despite challenge from post-modernism, modernity remains the central framework of the social sciences and a key signifier of the specialness of Europe. The post-modern turn is after all located in the West, maintaining the idea that these societies lead the rest. To be postmodern, 'we' first had to become modern. Modernity is therefore most commonly theorised as simultaneously distinctive and European in its origins. For example, Giddens (1990: 174) writes that modernity has its 'roots in specific characteristics of European history' and that this has 'few parallels in prior periods or other cultural settings' (see also Wagner 2001).

For Walter Mignolo (2000, 2007, 2011), a leading scholar of decoloniality, the hidden agenda (and darker side) of modernity as a foundational concept for interpreting the world is coloniality. Coloniality 'names the underlying logic of the foundation and unfolding of Western civilization from the Renaissance to today of which historical colonialisms have been a constitutive, although downplayed, dimension' (Mignolo 2011: 2). In other words, echoing Bhabha, what has come to be understood as 'modernity' is in fact a narrative which frames the way we understand world history and the present. This narrative incorporates primarily European experiences – such events and processes as the French Revolution, the rise of representative democracy, secularisation, the Industrial Revolution and the success of capitalism. These events and processes are then seen to explain how and why particular societies in the world might be considered 'modern' while others are relegated to the 'traditional'. They may progress towards modernity (via 'development', for example), through following the path laid by those already existing in modernity. Mignolo and others (Quijano and Ennis 2000), however, point out that a key feature of world history, and the attendant success of some countries to the detriment of others, was colonialism. Without colonialism the fruits of modernity would not be possible.

Coloniality and modernity are therefore 'two sides of the same coin' (Mignolo 2007: 464). This means that as the idea that some parts of the world are modern while others are premodern or traditional rose to prominence, with it rose the idea that Europe and Europeans were superior to others. This justified colonial activities from the fifteenth to the twentieth centuries and, according to decolonial theorists, many of the underlying assumptions remain. Coloniality, then, is a way of thinking about the world in civilisational terms, a way of thinking which allows us to ignore those aspects of British history which were dependent upon the exploitation of others through colonial activities and in service of domestic economic aims. Within this frame, racism of course flourished. Understanding the world in terms of hierarchically ordered groups of people was fundamental both to the project of colonialism and also to the success of projects which led Britain to become 'modern'. Coloniality allows for a tacit understanding of the hierarchical ordering of human bodies that some are more worthy of respect, labour rights, migration rights, access to healthcare and education than others – that some are more or less corrupt, more or less enlightened. The coloniality/modernity dialectic explains the impasse between the theoretical rights-bearing human and the lived reality of the 'other' who struggles to access the right to asylum.

When modernity is viewed, as in this perspective, as an epistemological frame that is inseparably bound to the European colonial project, this has clear implications for the theorisation of border crossing and thus links into issues of asylum and refugee policy. While in the modernity frame some societies are designated as premodern, so too are their inhabitants (Hall 1996). Certain human bodies exist in the past, while others inhabit a modern present and embody the future. The former can be found fighting for entry into modernity through access to the territories of the modern states. In other words, some categories of migrants, including asylum seekers, are assigned non-modern status, thus making them undesirable to modern states. We see this sense-making process taking place when asylum seekers from poor countries are described as economic migrants. Contradictions emerge when the harbingers of modernity claim universality in their value systems, such as human rights, while at the same time depicting a vast gulf between the modern West and those existing outside of modernity. Suddenly we see that access to fundamental rights is not universal but earned through promotion into the ranks of the modern.

This theoretical position thus underpins the idea of 'coloniality'. Colonial ideologies are fundamental to the idea of European modernity and are therefore central in understanding contemporary hostility to asylum seekers. Decolonial scholars dub such ways of thinking 'epistemic violence' and charge that 'there is a history of epistemic violence in every geographical location, including the geographical West' (Vázquez 2011: 28). The designation of the asylum seeker as infrahuman – as distant, different, less valuable – in contrast to the civilised modern British citizen is an act of epistemic violence. But to dig deeper into this we need to look at the very idea of 'man' through the lens of coloniality/modernity.

Modernity and 'Man'

At the present juncture all people are in principle (the principle of human rights) born equal and yet do not remain equal for the rest of their lives, including the extent to which they are able to access 'basic' and 'universal' human rights (Mignolo 2009). In order to understand why this spirit of universal human equality is rarely lived as such by large swathes of the world's population, we must remember that from their first declaration, human rights were exclusionary; they did not originally apply to everybody. 'Man', therefore, is not a simple descriptive term referring to human beings which has historically been gendered. It is a politically loaded term which has only recently been used on an international scale to refer to all human beings. What I am arguing is that in order to understand the non-entrée regime, we must first acknowledge that the concept of 'man' underpinning human rights cannot be taken for granted. Rather than being viewed as a universal concept applicable to all, 'man' and 'human' should be located historically and geographically. In order to fully comprehend this, we must turn to the history of the concept of 'man'.

For both postcolonial and decolonial theorists, the idea of 'man' is rooted in European modernity as an idea and a worldview (as opposed to a time period). The Middle Ages saw the rise of the descriptor 'black' to refer to people with dark skin; by 1750 'black' also meant bad. What happened in the meantime, Trouillot (1995) points out, was the expansion of African-American slavery. Trouillot (1995: 75) suggests that what we now call the Renaissance ushered in a new set of philosophical questions: 'What is beauty?' 'What is order?' 'What is the state?' But also, and above all, 'What is "Man"?' As the latter was being discussed, (European) men were 'conquering, killing, dominating, and enslaving other beings thought to be equally human, if only by some' (Trouillot 1995: 75). Within the melee of ideas being developed at that time there were multiple schemas for classifying human beings, always hierarchical, always based on physical characteristics, always 'scientific'. The role of enlightened science in this process will be discussed further in the next chapter.

There were degrees of humanity and therefore degrees of civilisation. In these early battles over ideas, the idea of human hierarchy supportive of colonial enterprise won out – Man was primarily European and male, and 'on this single point everyone who mattered agreed' (Trouillot 1995: 76). We should not be surprised by this outcome; philosophical questions about the nature and specialness of humankind perpetually rubbed up against practices of violence and domination which were extremely profitable. In order to make sense of this without undermining the accumulation of wealth amongst Europeans and European settler colonials the fact of white superiority, rooted in scientific reason, was an epistemological necessity. So, as Walter Mignolo has acknowledged, 'the figure of the colonized did not qualify for the "right of Man and of the citizen" ... The rights of Man and of the citizen were not meant for black and enslaved people' (Mignolo 2011: 239).

Sylvia Wynter deconstructs the Western episteme of the human as 'man' and looks at the contemporary implications of this for black African heritage peoples around the world. She writes, '"man" is not the human, although it represents itself as if it were. It is a specific, local-cultural conception of the human, that of the Judeo-Christian West in its now purely secularised form' (Wynter 2003: 260). Wynter charts the development of the secular idea of 'Man' from Christian roots in Medieval Europe and argues that the Christian/Other dichotomy was transmuted into Man/Other as secular rationality rose to prominence:

> in the wake of the West's reinvention of its True Christian Self in the transumed terms of the Rational Self of Man ... it was to be the peoples of the militarily expropriated New World territories (i.e. Indians), as well as the enslaved peoples of Black Africa (i.e Negroes), that were made to reoccupy the matrix slot

of Otherness-to be made into the physical referent of the idea of the irrational/ subrational Human Other to this first degodded (if still hybridly religio-secular) 'descriptive statement' of the human in history, as the descriptive statement that would be foundational to modernity. (Wynter 2003: 265)

The idea of 'races' then

would enable the now globally expanding West to replace the earlier mortal/ immortal, natural/supernatural, human/the ancestors, the gods/God distinction as the one on whose basis all human groups had millennially 'grounded' their descriptive statement/prescriptive statements of what it is to be human, and to reground its secularizing own on a newly projected human/subhuman distinction instead. (Wynter 2003: 264)

'Man' is not therefore 'human', and yet 'human rights' were for man, not for humanity. The Man versus Human struggle is, for Wynter, the struggle of our time. The 'usually excluded and invisiblized' are 'defined at the global level by refugee/economic migrants stranded outside the gates of the rich countries' (2003: 261). The conceit was clearly articulated by Frantz Fanon when he wrote 'you are making us [the colonised] into monstrosities; your humanism claims we are at one with the rest of humanity but your racist methods set us apart' (Fanon 1967: 8). The 'other' to man is not therefore woman, as noted above, but those categories of humans who are negatively marked 'within the terms of man's self-conception, and its related understanding of what it is to *be* human' (Wynter 2000: 25). It is Fanon's (1967) *damned of the earth*. Yet this otherness, this liminality, according to Wynter, makes possible the Western concept of the human in that man is defined by what he is not. The racially marked person, therefore, is 'the deviant other to being human within the terms of *man*' (Wynter 2000:25). And yet, despite this provincial history, 'man' as a concept is made to seem natural and not at all the product of human actions and decisions (Headley 2005).

While Wynter's account of the radical otherness of the African vis-à-vis the European is so totalising that it does not leave room for hybridity and the more complex entanglements which colonialism gave rise to, her intervention is nevertheless an important one. What it gives us, alongside Chimni, Mignolo and Trouillot, is an account of the idea of 'humanity' as a place-specific (not universal), historically emergent (not eternal) concept which has its origins in European colonial activities and philosophies. Equally, coloniality/modernity – the historical process through which Europe and her settler colonies became modern through colonisation and therefore through constant reinforcement of the hierarchical ordering of the world's people – has produced, at least in part, the predicament of today's asylum seekers. What we can also see from this is that to simply label the non-entrée regime as 'racist' prevents us from taking full account of these historically contingent processes.

Tracing Histories of Continuity

The aim of this book is not just to theorise the continuities between past and present, it is also to empirically map those continuities. One of the main criticisms of work in postcolonialism is the preoccupation with theory, cultural and literary analysis and consequently the apparent remoteness of many analyses from concrete events and political processes. This is a valid criticism and in evidencing the kinds of large-scale processes that were discussed above we need not just a theory of coloniality/modernity, nor even the observation that the rights of man were exclusionary. Trouillot (1995) is highly successful in this regard in his study of the Haitian Revolution as indicative of colonial historical silencing. We need, then, to look in depth at concrete historical events – political debates, campaigns, laws and institutional norms. In order to do this a methodological approach is required which will allow for an analysis of several hundred years of history. As such, I turn to a diachronic analysis of institutional orders at three critical junctures and one contemporary case study.

Historical institutionalists focus on institutions as one means of accessing the role of ideas, deployed by actors within institutional settings, in enacting political change and use this perspective to investigate the adoption and deployment of ideas through time. In this case, that means looking at ideas of human hierarchy in institutions influencing political change in Britain at particular points in history. That politics is not limited to the realm of institutions such as Parliament is well established (Offe 1985; Helmke and Levitsky 2004). Following Orren and Skowronek (2004), institutions are defined here as organisations that (a) have broad but discernible purposes, (b) establish norms and rules, (c) assign roles to participants, and (d) have boundaries marking those inside and outside the institutions. There are many actors and institutions involved in seeking to influence policy makers or enact legislative change, often from a broad range of positions, with varying degrees of power and articulating their viewpoint in a variety of ways. This presents challenges for social scientists in understanding how particular policy choices were made. Some have dealt with this complexity by conceptualising the relevant actors in terms of state versus non-state actors (Omi and Winant 1994; Wacquant 2002). Yet, within a democracy, policy choices are not solely the domain of senior members of the government, and even within the ruling party there may be contestation. In many policy areas this process involves a complex web of interactions between actors in government departments, those working in third sector organisations, activists, legal professionals, politicians, business interests and academics, to name but a few. Therefore, the implication that policy making occurs within a singular institution, 'the state', is problematic.

Historical institutionalists have responded to this problem by conceptualising political change in terms of the outcome of conflict between multiple institutional orders. Institutional orders are conceptualised as 'coalitions of state institutions and other political actors and organisations that seek to secure and exercise governing power in demographically, economically, and ideologically structured contexts that define the range of opportunities open to political actors' (King and Smith 2005: 75). These are not state agencies or political movements; they are coalitions of actors striving for the same ends but with varied motives. Institutional orders are therefore both 'more diversely constituted and loosely bound than state agencies' and 'more institutionalized, authoritatively empowered, and enduring than many political movements' (King and Smith 2005: 75).

This approach gives a useful methodological roadmap for researching the dialogue between coloniality/modernity, ideas of man and human and often but not always racially articulated understandings of human hierarchy. King and Smith's work (2005) is an interesting example of how this has been done in the case of US politics in order to draw attention to the role of ideas of 'race' in structuring political life there. They focus on racially defined institutional orders, and while they have not made the jump from 'race' to coloniality/modernity, in part because the US political context has for so long been dominated by explicit discourses of the black–white divide, their interest does have overlaps with the project of mapping ideas of differential humanity over time that is the focus of this book. Their racial institutional orders thesis 'elaborates how the [American] nation has been pervasively constituted by systems of racial hierarchy since its inception', thus rejecting claims that racial injustices are anomalies in an otherwise egalitarian country. Importantly, the perspective 'captures how those injustices have been contested by those they have injured and by other political institutions and actors'. Thus, King and Smith argue that American politics has historically been constituted in part by two evolving but linked racial institutional orders: 'a set of "white Supremacist" orders and a competing set of "transformative egalitarian" orders' (King and Smith 2005: 75).

The coalitional nature of institutional orders means that 'their unifying aim must be power for many purposes', not for the benefit of a few narrow interests (King and Smith 2005: 75). Some members' alignment will inevitably be tentative and alterable, while some actors will choose not to be aligned with a particular (or dominant) order. Leaders hold these varied motives together 'by gaining broad agreement on the desirability of certain publicly authorized arrangements that predictably distribute power, status, and resources along what are seen as racial lines' (King and Smith 2005: 75). This means that racial change is not seen in the racial institutional orders framework as the product of interactions between racially based activists, NGOs, social movements and the state but 'as a product of opposing racial orders ... all of which include some state institutions and some non-state political actors and organizations' (King and Smith 2005: 76).

As institutional orders are plural and competing they may be defined in opposition to each other. In the US case, the authors identify two main orders, as outlined above: 'white supremacist' and 'transformative egalitarian'. These orders are not static and have changed over time to adapt to the circumstances of the day, but they must always be seen within their historical context and as emerging from what might now be seen as outmoded opinions. For example, while the white supremacist institutional order in the United States is no longer defined by its support for chattel slavery, King and Smith argue that contemporary beliefs have nonetheless developed from this perspective. It therefore follows that while white supremacist racism now takes the form of anti-immigrant sentiment, it remains racially motivated. This argument is at risk of falling into the same traps as the racism and racialisation debates vis-à-vis asylum seekers. It is the perception of people 'out of place' on the map of modernity which is at work here, which at points involves racialisation but is best understood, I would argue, as a function of the coloniality of power.

This broader conceptual framing notwithstanding, King and Smith's approach nevertheless provides useful methodological directions in terms of the functioning and interaction between competing institutional orders dominated by different understandings of humanity. For example, they suggest that meaningful development, or change, occurs when one dominant order gives way to another, or when the dominant order's goals, rules, roles and boundaries are significantly revised. This maps well on to story of the abolition of slavery (see chapter 4), when the colonial institutional order felt compelled to abandon slavery in a revision of racial goals (expanding the British Empire in terms of trade and cultural imperialism, in place of the previous slaving focus), rules (enslaving black people was now illegal, and their humanity, though 'primitive', was enshrined in law) and roles (the end of the master–slave relationship, to be replaced by coloniser–colonised or civiliser–civilisee). I will add in to this framing a broader observation that the rise of racial science went hand in hand with practices of colonialism and ideas of modernity, but the route to researching this empirically is nevertheless aided by the insights of historical institutionalism.

Therefore, while their focus has primarily been on the United States, and on 'race' as an orienting conceptual compass, I wish to argue that the racial institutional orders framework has methodological applications beyond this original geographical and conceptual focus. Racial institutional orders are those in which a range of actors adopt and adapt racial ideas, aspirations and commitments in coming together to form coalitions (sometimes to structure governmental institutions). Support is likely to be the result of varied motives: economic aims, the desire for political power, to quiet social anxieties or to further ideological goals.

The racial institutional orders framework has several characteristics that are useful for the analysis of the UK asylum regime. First, it offers a way of understanding political decisions which are not economically defensible, which is the case for asylum policy in the United Kingdom. Second, it offers a framework for making sense of long periods of history, in both their continuities and their discontinuities. I manage this historiography through focusing on three moments in history which represent 'critical junctures' when racial institutional orders were in conflict (more on this below), and then a contemporary example. Third, it offers a unifying frame in which to manage empirical findings which span centuries, facilitating the important work of taking the long view. Fourth, this view of politics and policy making, as organised around support for or against particular agendas across institutional forms (as opposed to social movements versus the state, for example), is sensitive to the complexities and contradictions within the process of legislative change (or indeed continuity).

Aside from the issue of the conceptual focus on 'race' at the expense of coloniality/modernity, which facilitates a broader analysis of human hierarchy historically and in the present, there are two other issues to be addressed in relation to this approach. First, the racial institutional orders approach is, by design, methodologically nationalist. The racial institutional orders identified in King and Smith's analysis are not contextualised as emergent of a wider system that the United States is a part of. This wider system is colonial. The racial hierarchies established at the founding of the United States emerged from the colonial context: the subjugation of indigenous peoples already living on the land when European settlers arrived and the importation of enslaved people of colour to work on that land not as migrant workers but as private property to be owned and traded – 'things' rather than human beings. These activities were not exclusive to the United States; they were a part of a global colonial and slaving system which existed in service of white Europeans to the detriment of others. Underpinning the activities of political institutions, then, was an ideology of racial hierarchy which went hand in hand with colonial projects around the world. The history of US political development is therefore certainly one of racial institutional orders, but, more fundamentally, it is one of colonial ideology.

Second, bringing in the colonial aspect raises a further problem: the racial institutional orders approach focuses on the level of the nation state, while colonial histories are international. A significant aspect of any political analysis which looks at racial hierarchy in political development, with an eye on Empire, must by necessity incorporate international politics into the account. But the institutional orders framework still works when we pan out to the international; coalitions of actors working in collaboration need not necessarily originate in the same territory. Indeed, political aims are often aligned across nations and states, and as the power of large empires waned, international organisations such as the United Nations (UN) and European Union provided for alliances (Tarrow 2001). Activists and NGOs also work across borders, proving that it is not only in the domain of inter-governmental activities that politics can be approached in an international frame (Keck 1998; Santos 2008). As will be seen in subsequent chapters, the international dimension has tended to strengthen institutional alliances rather than undermine them. Furthermore, at the international level the division between governmental and other actors becomes more well defined. The governments of states, for example, might be aligned in an order against racial equality (see chapter 4), strengthening both the legitimacy of this position and the power to act upon it.

It is now clear that in analysing the ways in which racial institutional orders have been influential in shaping both US and British politics over the past few centuries, and in particular the response to racially marked 'others', colonialism as a theoretical concern must be addressed. Similar problems therefore present themselves in racial institutional orders as in racialisation and xeno-racism: namely, the focus on 'race' at the expense of a deeper understanding of the coloniality of power which gives rise to racism but also to carefully de-racialised discourses in relation to immigration. The aim of this conceptual move is not to diminish the enduring importance of racism and ideas of 'race' to contemporary political, social and economic life. As I laid out in the previous section, it is rather to make sense of the differential humanity afforded to asylum seekers within institutional politics in the United Kingdom as not exactly the same as racism but as part of the broader context of coloniality/modernity from which racism also emerged.

In order to investigate those histories which have led to differential access to refugee rights – to exclusionary asylum policies – the next four chapters present a diachronic analysis. This means that a number of snapshots, or historical cases, are used to demonstrate developments over a long time frame (Hay 2002). I call these 'critical junctures'. These snapshots in time have more of a 'panning' effect than a 'moving picture', such as that offered by a historical narrative approach which uses process tracing (George and Bennett 2005). The benefit of using a diachronic approach, as opposed to synchronic (a single historical snapshot), or comparative statics (two cases which are compared and contrasted) is that it allows for building a picture of both continuity and change without losing the complexity present in historical case study research (Hay 2002; Amenta 2009).

The chapters are all based on archival research and the use of secondary sources. I draw on British government documents, including those held at the National Archives: the minutes of Cabinet meetings in conjunction with Cabinet papers and departmental sources, Hansard records of parliamentary debates and official submissions to, as well as preparations for, the UN negotiations. In chapter 6, evidence is also drawn from the UN archives, from the negotiations surrounding the Refugee Convention, as well as from the Declaration of Human Rights, where relevant. Specifically, transcripts of the negotiation meetings, including the UN Ad Hoc Committee on Refugees and Stateless Persons and the UN Conference of Plenipotentiaries on the Status of Refugees and Stateless Persons, are used. This is then supported by reference to secondary sources. Four snapshots are provided, and all address the evolution of ideas of humanity refracted through the lens of colonialism. They are:

1. The campaigns for the abolition of the slave trade and slavery in the early nineteenth century.
2. The discussions around the proposal by Japan for a race equality clause to be included in the League of Nations covenant in 1919.
3. The debates leading up to the establishment of the human (and by consequence, refugee) rights conventions in 1951.
4. The contestations over the levels of asylum support provided to destitute asylum seekers in the United Kingdom from 2012 to 2015.

What we see over the course of the book is the way in which the coloniality of power develops, initially with an explicit discourse of racial hierarchy and later against that discourse but with consistent logics. This is what Bhabha (1994: 344) described as the 're-inscription of the sign ... without a transformation of the site of enunciation'. There is the danger, he points out, that the contents of the discourse will conceal the fact that the hegemonic structures of power are maintained. Vocabulary shifts, but the nature of power and the exclusionary logics of modernity continue. Uncovering this 're-inscription of the sign' is the task of this book.

Conclusion

Starting with B.S. Chimni's 'myth of difference', this chapter has drawn on postcolonial and decolonial theory to develop a theoretical framework for analysing the continuities between historical ideas of differential humanity and the treatment of asylum seekers by Western states today. The starting point for the analysis developed in subsequent chapters is therefore radically different from the literatures discussed in the previous chapter, especially those dominant in refugee studies. Rather than starting from the 'problem' of asylum seekers within the normative framework of human rights, we are required to start from the very idea of 'man' as a supposedly universal rights-bearing subject. This idea of man must be understood as rooted in coloniality/modernity.

Over the next four chapters a story will emerge which evidences the theoretical claims. In order to discipline the analysis over four historical case studies an institutional orders approach is used. Drawing on the work of King and Smith on racial institutional orders in American political development, but introducing the missing colonial aspects to the approach, these case studies are methodologically rooted in well-established approaches of political studies. By contrast, the story which emerges is at odds with almost every other account of the politics of asylum. Starting from 1833 and ending in 2015, I will follow a core set of ideas over time and place, and in doing so I will disrupt and denaturalise the way that we approach the exclusionary impulse towards those seeking asylum today.

Chapter Four

Slavery and the Right to Be Human

In the introductory chapters I argued that ideas of racial hierarchy, rooted in histories of colonialism, are relevant in developing a deeper understanding of asylum policy choices today. In this chapter, I begin to flesh out this argument by focusing on the first of three critical junctures. These critical junctures are analysed at the political institutional level. The first critical juncture, the focus of this chapter, is the campaigns for the abolition of slavery and the slave trade in the early nineteenth century. It is my intention to use this critical juncture to highlight the role that slavery played in influencing early conceptions of humanity and differential rights – the 'rights of man' which would pave the way for human rights. Public debate on the topic of slavery was augmented by the campaign for abolition, and it is through the interaction between these two perspectives that changing ideas of both 'rights' and 'man' can be observed.

Two institutional orders are identified: the colonial institutional order and the transformative order. Here, I methodologically follow King and Smith (2005) in identifying the vital challenge presented by actors seeking transformative change and pursuing this change within an institutional context and, indeed, within a wider institutional order. However, my analysis of the British situation at this point in time (the abolition period), and through the other critical junctures investigated within this study, identifies an opposing set of institutional orders which I label 'colonial'. In doing so I seek to highlight the vital role that coloniality played in the development and deployment of ideas of racial hierarchy within these institutional settings.

In the eighteenth and early nineteenth centuries the humanity of enslaved people was at best ambiguous, and they were often consequently excluded from the suite of rights being promoted by philosophers and politicians of the day (Drescher 1990b; Fischer 2004). The call for abolition was therefore a public debate around the humanity of black bodies. If black slaves were human, they might be entitled to rights; it might be the duty of the government to recognise those rights and protect them in courts of law. The implications for Britain, economically, socially and politically, of this expansion of the human category cannot be overstated.

The reason for focusing on the issue of the Atlantic slave trade, slave labour and its abolition is that this was the first fundamental legislative reframing of Britain's understanding of 'others' from outside of Europe. This reframing happened at the same time that the seeds of what would come to be called 'modernity' were sown. The legislation which abolished slavery is the first critical juncture that I will focus on, and it is part of a long series of connected histories which have contributed to the framing and understanding of the deserving and the undeserving, the familiar and the 'other' in Britain. I contend here that the key political orders of this period, which would later have a significant impact on attitudes towards immigrants and non-whites in Britain and its Empire, were those which coalesced around the abolition of slavery.

This history is pertinent for two key reasons. First, the abolition debate was occurring at the same time as new ideas around the rights of man were being proposed, discussed and debated. This sowed the seeds of the human rights agenda in the twentieth century, an agenda which provided for the right to asylum. The historical example therefore foregrounds the entanglement of 'rights' with colonially informed rationales of differential humanity and demonstrates that the parameters of humanity (and exclusion from it) have been matters of contention since the inception of the very idea of rights. Second, it serves to highlight the colonial origins of British national identity in relation to a wider world which consisted, for several centuries, (largely) of European settler societies and colonial territories. This is an important reminder that despite histories of 'otherness' within and beyond Europe, there have been groups, such as black enslaved people of African origin, who have not simply been considered different or inferior, but rather inhuman, in British legal history. This example therefore demonstrates the significant potential for overhaul in taxonomies of humanity, rights and duty, at the same time as setting the stage for a discussion of the present – when de facto access to human rights is hierarchically organised on the basis of country of origin.

The chapter begins with a discussion of slavery and the links between the practice and ideas on differential humanity. This leads to a deeper discussion around the debates which culminated in the abolition of slavery. The final part of the chapter addresses some key themes raised by this critical juncture and some of the legacies of this period for future conceptions of human hierarchy in terms of geographical location and racial classification.

ATLANTIC SLAVERY

Around ten million enslaved people were transported in the transatlantic trade from the mid-fifteenth to the mid-nineteenth century (Curtin 1969). Between 1741 and 1810, 60,000 enslaved people were traded annually, despite this being a period of significant agitation against the trade and one in which ideas of rights and liberties exploded in European politics and philosophy (Rawley and Behrendt 2005). None of this was possible without the salience of the idea that some people were human while others were either not human or in some way sub-human. With the trade coming to be dominated very quickly by the trading primarily of Africans, an association developed between certain coloured bodies originating in certain parts of the world and sub-humanity.

Many history scholars have suggested that racism developed as 'principle handmaiden to the slave trade and slavery' (Lawrence 1970: 3; Morton 2002). What transformed black people from exotic curiosities to sub-human commodities to be traded as private property was therefore first and foremost slavery (Walvin 1986). For Trouillot (1995: 77), the logic was flawed but clear: 'blacks were inferior and therefore enslaved; black slaves behaved badly and were therefore inferior'. Over a short period of time anti-black racism formed the foundation of planter ideology in the Caribbean and justification for the trade in the metropole. Enslaved people were not simply denied access to basic rights; they were denied even their humanity: 'they were things: chattel and property, comparable (in law and to some extent social practice) to other inanimate material objects' (Walvin 1986: 22).

Yet opinion did not at some point solidify around a homogenous story accepted throughout metropolitan society. Debate and discussion characterised an age in which British and other European philosophers, scientists and theologians were grappling towards a bounded definition of 'man' and European man's relation to others. Were these 'others' animal, sub-human or human and therefore possibly disposed to Christianisation and civilisation? Anthropologists and travelling scientists provided 'facts' about non-Europeans through a growing body of travel literature, though these texts were themselves mostly framed by the structures of contemporaneous knowledge production (Strack 1996). Travel writing nevertheless 'became a source of moral and political examples for European philosophers and hommes des lettres ... generating theories ranging from cultural relativism to a full confirmation of traditional values' (Strack 1996: 287). At the same time, the late eighteenth century saw early forms of scientific categorisations of the 'races' and 'species' of man, including debate around poly versus monogenesis – accounts of the origins and development of human beings (Bernasconi 2001). Vitally, the ambiguity of these scientific, theological and philosophical debates offered sufficient openings for the discrediting of slavery and the trading of enslaved people on religious and moral grounds.

This ambiguity is the crack through which the movement for the abolition of slavery emerged in Britain. The following section provides an institutional orders analysis of the battle for the abolition of slavery. This allows for a number of key debates to be raised around early ideas on humanity and 'race' as linked to the ideas of Christianity, science, philosophy and law.

Abolition: An Institutional Orders Analysis

The slave *trade* was abolished in 1807, and slavery in 1833. This change happened after more than two hundred years of expansion, peaking in the late 1700s. Only twenty years before 1807, abolition remained unimaginable to many. Yet in the 1780s an oppositional alliance began to emerge in the United Kingdom led by Quakers. By the early 1800s a mass movement of people in Britain seeking transformative change had developed. From industrial workers to middle-class women's groups, freed slaves to Parliamentarians, all used what means they had to push for the abolition of the slave trade. Existing alliances between those directly involved with the trade – planters, merchants and colonial agents – galvanised against this threat to their wealth and, in some cases, their livelihoods.

This section provides an institutional analysis of abolition. Two key institutional orders emerged for and against slavery. It is these that the analysis focuses on, addressing their ideas and actions around the key legislative changes of this period: the 1807 Slave Trade Act and the 1833 Slavery Abolition Act. The analysis is divided into three parts: a discussion of the transformative order, a discussion of the colonial order and finally an outline of how the transformative order was ultimately victorious.

The Transformative Order

Table 4.1 outlines those included in the anti-slavery order and by what means they voiced their objections. These include formalised institutions – coalitions of actors committed to acting together with leaders, rules and some resources attached to them – as well as non-formalised coalitions of actors acting together but without a formal structure that is identifiable in the historical records. Something to note about this order is that it was dispersed, that there were many informal groupings and connections as well as a more focused group of leaders and that a very large number of people were involved. Members were relatively politically powerless, with the majority being unlikely to have the right to vote in local or national elections owing to their gender and/or lack of property. This was in stark contrast to the much

Table 4.1. The (Anti-Slavery) Transformative Order

Level	Who?	How?
1. Leaders	Committee for the Abolition of the Slave Trade *Representative in Parliament*: William Wilberforce *Key Player outside of Parliament:* Thomas Clarke	*In Parliament:* Proposing bills. Initiating debates. Presenting petitions. *Outside of Parliament:* Meetings to discuss tactics and plans. Writing and publishing abolitionist literature. Researching the slave trade (including finances, conditions of enslaved people). Gathering petitions. Encouraging the initiation of local abolitionist groups. Networking local groups.
2. Abolitionists – other	Black radical groups Industrial workers groups Local groups around the country Women's groups Christian institutions (mostly non-conformist) Missionaries Political philosophers High-profile freed slaves (e.g. Equiano)	Attending meetings. Attending/participating in debates. Attending protests. Signing petitions. Producing abolitionist literature, including poetry. Preaching. Pamphleteering. Preaching to enslaved people, encouraging education and self-expression. Supporting enslaved people in the colonies. Writing accounts of the treatment of enslaved people for the British audience. Publishing abolitionist material.
3. Objectors	Consumers (especially women)	Sugar boycott.
4. Indirect participants – resistors not necessarily subscribing to the order but contributing to their cause	Self-emancipated slaves in Britain Self-emancipated slaves in the colonies Plantation slaves involved in organised revolt Theologians Political philosophers	Resistance to the system of the slave trade and slavery through running away and participation in revolt. Ideas contribute to the abolitionist cause (sometimes against the author's intention).

smaller number of people with a high degree of concentrated financial and political power involved in the pro-slavery order.

The first attempts to bring about the end of slavery were made by enslaved people themselves in the Caribbean colonies (Midgley 1992). From the first substantial slave revolt in the British West Indies, in Barbados in 1675, to the culmination of the Haitian revolution (1804), resistance was continuously present. Such events were present in the European consciousness as part of the connected international political, economic and social milieu of the time (Buck-Morss 2009). However, my concern here is the coalitions of actors working together to enact change within British politics. The enslaved people of the Caribbean formed an alliance of resistance, but only in indirect ways could they be said to be a part of the political order of which I speak here. They were, in a sense, fighting a parallel battle – socially embedded in overlapping, but independent, sets of relations to those institutional orders in Britain. At times, plantation resistance supported the abolitionist arguments and at others, it incited fear amongst the powerful in Britain and made them less inclined to emancipation.

As noted above and shown in table 4.1, the abolitionist movement was indeed a movement – dispersed across the country in local communities, social clubs and workplaces. According to Ogborn, it was the first mass mobilisation of British people on an issue that reached beyond their own immediate interests: 'new global geographies of sympathy and connection were beginning to form that were based upon more than trade and profit' (Ogborn 2008: 270). This was also an inclusive movement, as it developed between the 1780s and 1830s, increasingly 'welcoming adherents who were otherwise remote from the political process by reason of gender, religion, race, or class' (Drescher 1990b). For this there is significant evidence. For example, Liverpool Member of Parliament (MP) General Isaac Gascoyne complained in the House of Commons:

> every measure that invention or art could devise to create a popular clamour was resorted to on this occasion. The Church, the theatre, the press, had laboured to create a prejudice against the slave trade ... There had never been any question agitated since that of Parliamentary reform, in which so much industry had been exerted to raise a popular clamour and to make the trade an object of universal detestation. In every manufacturing town and borough in the kingdom all those arts had been tried. (House of Commons, 10 February 1807)

The abolitionists at level 1 in the table above utilised the new technologies of print media and publishing through sympathetic publishers. The abolitionists 'inundated their country with propaganda, newspaper advertisements, lectures, mass meetings, petitions, lawsuits, and sugar boycotts, presenting ever more radical abolition agendas as moral and political imperatives' (Drescher 1990b). Texts were produced to suit every age, class and taste. Works were distributed in North America and translated into French, Portuguese, Danish, Dutch and Spanish (Ogborn 2008). Visual images were used to full effect with a branding campaign featuring a design by Wedgewood on cups, plates, snuff boxes, brooches and hair pins. Images depicting the slave ship 'Brookes' with enslaved people squashed in so that no space was spared horrified people and the abolitionists sought the widest possible distribution (Clarkson 2006 [1808]). In Parliament, William Wilberforce gave long and emotive speeches, often noted for their rhetorical power, in presenting petitions and proposing bills (Carey 2005).

For white women, who could not vote or legally sign petitions (though some did anyway), the writing of prose and poetry, attending debates in debating clubs and boycotting sugar (the first mass consumer boycott) provided pathways to action (Midgley 1992). The abolition campaign was initiated by non-conformist Christians, notably Quakers, but also Methodists and Baptists, and only later expanded with a wider support base. The religious wing of abolitionism typically 'belonged to interlocking networks of organizations devoted to temperance, women's rights, penal reform, peace, hydropathy, in fact to benefiting mankind in almost every way imaginable' (Midgley 1992: 97).

Enslaved people living in the United Kingdom regularly deserted their masters and by the mid-eighteenth century 'there is evidence of cohesion, solidarity and mutual help among black people in Britain' (Fryer 1984: 67). Bogues (2003: 26) goes as far as to suggest that the period 'was one in which black abolitionism was a significant plank on the world's political stage'. Fryer notes that 'the mob' 'saw black people as fellow victims of their own enemies, fellow-fighters against a system that degraded poor whites and poor blacks alike. With their help, London had by the 1760s become a centre of black resistance' (Fryer 1984: 72). Coupled with the abolitionist drive to turn the tradition of petitioning into a tool of mass protest, black–white worker solidarity garnered some significant results. For example, in 1788 one hundred petitions were sent from working class radical groups all over Britain to Parliament in favour of the abolition of the trading of African enslaved people (Hudson 2001).

As discussed in the previous chapter, a crucial concern for historical institutionalists is the interplay between institutions and the ideas supporting, linking and emerging from them. So how did this institutional order achieve such widespread support? What were the ideas underpinning the movement? The rhetoric of anti-slavery was full of 'nuances and shades of meaning, the affinities associated with particular terms at particular times, the occasional ambiguity of language, deliberately or not, at the service of political ends'

Table 4.2. Transformative Order Discourses

Metadiscourse	Original Focus	Use for the Transformative Order	Key Interpretations (by all or some of the order)
1. Political philosophy	Understanding society and politics in Europe	When applied to slavery it delegitimises the practice	The rights of man as incompatible with slavery. Individual liberation from tyranny and tradition. Normative morality: slave trade and slavery immoral. Worker solidarity: black and white, slave and free all part of the same fight for civil, political and economic rights.
2. Christianity	Understanding man's role in the world and provision of a moral code to live by	When applied to slavery it delegitimises the practice	Black enslaved people as human. They therefore have souls and it is wrong to enslave them (risk of eternal damnation). Europeans have a duty to educate enslaved people in Christianity. Salvation of immortal souls of enslaved people requires their release from physical bondage – enslaved people must first become men (i.e. be free) before they can become Christians. Evangelism: need to bring politeness back into politics, re-moralise the upper classes. Abolition a part of this.

Slavery and the Right to Be Human 59

		When applied to slavery it delegitimises the practice	
3. International political economy	Framework for enabling maximum individual and national wealth	When applied to slavery it delegitimises the practice	To end the trade would decrease the risk of slave revolt. Concern about autonomy of colonies, Caribbean island authorities becoming too powerful: if free slaves then there will be greater metropolitan control over colonies. It would subject slave owners to metropolitan law. Could make enslaved people more British in language, culture, etc., and more loyal. Moral superiority: If British lead in abolition, the world will follow. Slave trade not sustainable in long term for trade with Africa, freeing enslaved people and initiating trade in goods with Africa will be economically beneficial for Britain. Slave trade as less profitable than widely believed to be. Free men work harder than enslaved. They are less likely to die, healthier and more likely to breed. Hence, greater profitability.
4. (British tradition of) law and justice	Framework for protection of society and the individual within the community of the nation from harm	When applied to slavery it delegitimises the practice	Slave trade unjust. Black enslaved people have Habeas Corpus.

(Kriegel 1987: 434). In this regard, Kriegel argues, the inner motives of the abolitionist spokesmen and women is unimportant; 'what is crucial is to recognise the manner in which spokesmen, in Parliament and outside of it, justified their political goals and actions' (Kriegel 1987, emphasis added). These justifications drew on a variety of fields of ideas, as shown in table 4.2.

Discourses (or fields of ideas) drawn on in the debate around abolition, as so often in politics, came from a variety of sources. They were taken from contemporary emerging ways of making sense of the world and deployed by the abolitionists to delegitimise the existence of slavery. A review of the Commons and Lords debates around abolition, petitions presented to Parliament at the time, the secondary literature on the period of abolition and other relevant literature, such as publications produced by abolitionists, reveals four fields of discourse or metadiscourses present in the justifications used in the anti-slavery campaign.

The most striking thing about table 4.2 above is the diversity of opinion. The question of why to end the slave trade, or slavery as a whole, received a chorus of answers. Walvin (1986) asserts that philosophy, theology and literature were the origins of the ideas of abolition. He argues that 'at certain crucial junctures, ideas from these particular "disciplines" spilled over, often in transmuted form, into a wider, more politicised arena' (Walvin 1986: 101). Drescher's (1990a) analysis of Parliamentary rhetoric around the abolition of the slave trade found that the abolitionists were more than twice as likely to draw upon moral as upon policy considerations, with the opposition countering with the opposite approach. Similarly, he also found that petitions presented to Parliament all demanded abolition first on grounds of humanity, with the overwhelming majority not raising the issue of policy at all, and 'of the minority which did address policy, most described it as irrelevant compared with moral considerations' (Drescher 1990a: 567). It is in morality that the religious and philosophical ideas coalesced.

Walvin (1986: 98) argues that 'there is a clear, direct and unbroken line of descent from anti-slavery as an abstract intellectual issue to anti-slavery as the substance of practical politics and reform'. He finds evidence that very quickly the ideas of eminent philosophers were 'transmuted into the stuff ... of everyday political argument' (Walvin 1986: 98). These were not simply intellectual abstractions. The fundamental contradiction between ideas of rights, liberty and freedom on the one hand and the presence of slavery on the other were both philosophical and practical.

For ex-slave abolitionists, writing narratives of their experiences and political texts on slavery provided both a broader audience for their abolitionist message and a means of demonstrating membership of the human community. Gates (1988: 128) writes that they are 'testimony of defilement: the slave's representation and reversal of the master's attempt to transform a human being into a commodity, and the slave's simultaneous verbal witness of the possession of a humanity shared in common with Europeans'. However, the expression of a common humanity was not the limit of the ambitions of slave narratives; some were sophisticated political texts drawing on the famous philosophers of the day. For example, the prominent concept of 'reason' in Enlightenment philosophy was taken up by writers such as Quobna Ottobah Cugoano. Cugoano used the language of radical political thinkers (for example, Thomas Paine) who saw slavery as robbery of natural liberty (see Paine 1775). He suggested that slavery was evil not only because it went against natural rights (Paine) or because it contradicted divine laws (senior white abolitionists in the institutional order), but he declared that it was evil on both of these measures with the added charge that it contradicted reason (Bogues 2003; Cugoano 1825).

For some, particularly upper-class white abolitionists, Enlightenment philosophy contributed to the idea of human perfectibility. If men are perfectible, then underdeveloped humans were, theoretically, perfectible too. For example, Lord Sidmouth invoked the opinion of Burke in the Lords second reading of the Slave Trade Abolition Bill:

> With respect to the West Indies themselves, he [Sidmouth] would recommend the advice of that great man (Mr. Burke), viz. that churches should be built for the negroes in the islands, and that they should be instructed in the morality and doctrine of the Christian religion; he would also have them united by the ties of matrimony, as the first step towards civilization, and the future improvement of their condition. (House of Lords, 5 February 1807)

Thus, though radical and transformative, few in the transformative order were making an equality argument. Many of the abolitionists believed in the inferiority of black people but crucially believed that it was possible for them to develop and civilise under the tutelage of white Europeans. Evidence of this was thought to be the greater civility and higher culture of those regions of Africa, particularly the interior, which were not affected by the trade. Drescher writes,

> it was precisely because the abolitionists linked negative characteristics [of the black slaves] so causally and so completely to the African slave trade and to colonial slavery that they could assure their contemporaries of a more rapid civilizing of blacks than of any other 'backward' people on the globe. (Drescher 1990b: 420)

Thus, abolitionist initiatives led to an upsurge of writings on the possibility of improvements in Africa and the Americas, whose rebirth would begin with the ending of the slave trade (Drescher 1990b: 420). Though there was a rising black population in Britain, it was still very small (and essentially dictated by slave owners) and as such the problem of slavery remained largely a remote problem of the overseas territories (Fryer 1984).

It is here that the overlap between philosophically based ideas and emerging Christian theology can be seen. The possibility of perfectibility was compatible with a Christian mission. Indeed, these were the seeds of the missionary movement which came of age in the mid- to late nineteenth century. More specifically, in the late eighteenth and early nineteenth century the teachings of Christianity, which had long supported the slave trade, were being re-examined by non-conformists and evangelists, and again a fundamental contradiction between theory and practice was identified. In the realm of religious ideas, it was 'sin' that formed the origins of abolitionism (Davis 1966). It was therefore a change in theological thinking around sin that paved the way for the passionate abolitionism which some, notably the Quakers, espoused. As Davis points out, 'men could not fully perceive the moral contradictions of slavery until a major religious transformation had changed their ideas of sin and spiritual freedom' (Davis 1966: 292). Added to this was the recent fashion for religious philanthropy or the idea that good Christians have a moral duty to help those less fortunate than themselves. For some Evangelists, society, and particularly political society, needed 're-moralising'. Bringing morality and politeness back into politics would feed into the amelioration of any number of social ills as the upper classes provided an example for the rest of the population. Abolition was a part of this project.

The opinion of God was, in a sense, the abolitionist 'trump card', providing retorts to most arguments in defence of the trade. This is indicated in the following extract from a political pamphlet by Peter Peckard (Peckard 1788: 2):

> the advocates for this traffick ... say that neither Religion, Morality, nor Humanity is concerned in transactions of Beings that are not of the Human race. This too, is indeed a grievous error; for even supposing the Negroes to be Brutes, the benevolent spirit of religion teaches us that a truly righteous man is merciful to his beast, and that they are entitled even in this view to a treatment far different from that which they receive at our hands.

Similarly, Robert Boucher Nickolls, Dean of Middleham, wrote in a letter (which was later published and widely distributed due to the force of its message) to Samuel Hoare, treasurer of the Society Instituted for the Purpose of Effecting the Abolition of the Slave Trade:

> And why, upon the foot of humanity I ask the question, are these poor people to be excluded from those comforts of our religion which its founder commanded to be tendered equally unto all? They are under no incapacity which they do not owe to us ... The people in our islands not only neglect, but object to the

conversion of their slaves, upon pleas, which, if admitted originally, would have annihilated Christianity at its first appearance. (Nickolls 1788: 20)

The civilising project fed in to the abolition debate for both moral and economic reasons: 'the Westernised other looked increasingly more profitable to the West, especially if he could become a free labourer' (Trouillot 1995: 80). Abolitionists, extolling the ideas of Adam Smith, argued for the superior profitability of free over slave labour. International connections mediated by political economy therefore had to be addressed by the abolitionists. They argued that to end the trade would decrease the risk of slave revolt, securing the profitability of the colonies. The slave trade, it was claimed, was less profitable than widely believed and was not sustainable in the long term for trade with Africa; freeing enslaved people and initiating trade in goods with Africa would be more economically beneficial for Britain. Furthermore, for those concerned about the increasing autonomy of the Caribbean island authorities, the abolitionists said that if the enslaved people were freed then there would be greater metropolitan control over the colonies. Slave owners would become subject to metropolitan law while enslaved people could be made more British in language, culture and religion and therefore more loyal to what would later be termed 'the motherland'.

International competition, though, was of great concern to opponents of abolition. To this, the transformative order forthrightly suggested that if the British led in abolition, the world would follow and Britain would gain from such moral superiority. On this, the pro-slavers were less than convinced. The abolitionists were on safer ground invoking the British tradition of law and justice. Drawing on religious and philosophical arguments, they argued that the slave trade was unjust and that Habeas Corpus clearly applied to black enslaved people as much as whites. Yet these ideas only stood up if the humanity of the enslaved people was accepted. Law and justice were not seen to be applicable to all creatures.

This was the transformative egalitarian institutional order of its day. It was also the first in the history of the United Kingdom seeking transformation on the basis of the rights of 'others' both *within* and *without*: within the jurisdiction of the British Empire and without the rights to which British subjects (and human beings) were entitled. This humanity was largely conceived not as one of equality, however, but as one of potential for improvement.

The Colonial Order

Table 4.3 shows those involved in the fight against abolition. These include formalised institutions – coalitions of actors committed to acting together with leaders, rules and some resources attached to them. As with the

Table 4.3. The Colonial Order

Level	Who?	How?
1. Leaders	The West India Committee (main committee plus sub-committees, most notably the Sub-Committee of the West India Planters and Merchants Appointed to Oppose the Abolition of the Slave Trade) Members were the most powerful planters in the colonies absentee planters living in Britain merchants in Britain industrialists in Britain agents for the colonies Governors in the colonies The monarchy (King George III and sons)	*In Parliament:* Resisting bills proposed by abolitionists in the House of Commons. Resisting bills proposed by abolitionists in the House of Lords. Presenting petitions. *Outside of Parliament:* Writing and publishing anti-abolitionist literature. Gathering petitions from merchants, planters, ship owners and industrialists. Meetings to discuss tactics and plans with rich and powerful interests.
2. Associate members of the order	Lesser planters, merchants, agents and industrialists in Britain	Petitions to Parliament. Financing Members of Parliament to represent interests in Parliament.
	Planters and colonial administrators	Petitions to Parliament. Dissemination of pro-slavery pamphlets, tracts, paintings, local histories, poems, plays and other literature.
3. Indirect participants – supporters not necessarily subscribing to the order's agenda but contributing to continuation	Consumers	Buying slave-produced sugar – consumer demand.
	Wealthy British residents	Owning enslaved people as domestic servants.

transformative order, this includes non-formalised coalitions of actors acting together but without a formal structure that is identifiable in the historical records. However, this order had few (if any) disorganised and dispersed elements. Compared to the transformative order there were fewer people involved but members were much more powerful, financially and politically.

Up until the 1832 Reform Act a large number of constituencies, county and borough (and especially those with small electorates), were under the control of rich male property and land owners (see Phillips and Wetherell 1995). Both the Houses of Commons and Lords were populated by landed gentry and a small but growing class of industrialist 'nuevo riche' who aspired to be like them (Phillips and Wetherell 1995). An Oxbridge education and inherited or awarded peerage were common, and the majority had direct or indirect interests in the Atlantic slave trade. Prior to the attack from the anti-slavery transformative order, the West Indian interests were already well organised as an alliance in formal institutions serving their economic and political interests (Penson 1921). This 'West Indian Interest' included the Planters Club and the Society of the West India Merchants. With the attack from abolitionism these formal institutions coalesced around resistance to the changes being proposed and mobilised their political capital. This was done in print, through petitioning and in Parliament.

The strength of this network of wealth and privilege was expressed by artist, naturalist and abolitionist Katherine Plymley in her journal following a visit from Thomas Clarke (one of the most prominent and active abolitionists in the transformative order), which is worth quoting at length:

> The King is not with us and all the Princes are against us. They are all brutes, except the Prince of Wales ... he I believe has some tenderness in his disposition. But he is persuaded to think favourably of the Slave trade. Fox has got his ear now. // I ... am entirely convinced [Mr Pitt] is hearty in the cause but the divisions in the Cabinet were so great that it was impossible for him to do more than an individual, for he cannot issue out a treasury letter unless the Cabinet are unanimous, cou'd he have done that we shou'd have carried it, for many of the members wou'd have voted, had be pleas'd, that black was white. // Very many members having been brought to promise the West India planters to vote against the abolition, perhaps over a bottle, and had never read the evidence, when they ... heard the arguments on the other side ... wou'd have wished to have voted contrary to their engagements ... but the planters were at the bar reminding them of their promise. They were therefore desirous to wipe off the stigma ... and voted in favour of ... the Sierra Leone Company. (cited in Gibson Wilson 1996: 69–70)

The high levels of absenteeism amongst West Indian plantation owners facilitated their high levels of representation in the British Parliament in London. Combined with the significant number of London merchants trading to the West Indies and the colonial agents (who represented the resident planters), the West India Committee was able to 'exert an influence over British politics far greater than that of its contemporaries' (Penson 1921: 374). Records of the meetings of the Committee show that in response to the attacks from the abolitionists, the work of the West India Committee was dominated by the project of opposing the attacks on the slave trade. There was even a specialist 'Sub-Committee of the West India Planters and Merchants Appointed to Oppose the Abolition of the Slave Trade', and in 1788 the charge paid by members increased sixfold to meet the demands of this urgent work (West India Committee 1785–1792).

King George III was on the throne for the whole period of the abolitionist campaign. He opposed ministerial support for abolition during William Pitt's tenure as Prime Minister (1783–1801 and 1804–1806) with the support of his sons, who were conspicuous in their canvassing against the bill in the Lords (Drescher 1994). In addition to this force at home, planters and administrators formed what Lambert (Lambert 2005) terms a 'counter-revolutionary Atlantic'. Working in defence of slavery, they sent petitions to Parliament and disseminated pro-slavery pamphlets, tracts, paintings, local histories, poems, plays and other literature. In this way, West Indian planter networks sought to penetrate metropolitan culture and reinforce the bonds of interest between colony and metropole which would support their activities in the Atlantic region.

A review of the Commons and Lords debates around abolition, petitions presented to Parliament, the secondary literature on the period of abolition and other relevant literature, such as publications produced by planters, merchants and agents, reveals the discourses listed in table 4.4 as present in the colonial order. These are the ideas underpinning, linking and emerging from this institutional order. It should be noted that in the popular means of distribution – newspaper columns, petition meetings, pamphlets and merchandising – the abolitionists vastly out-produced their antagonists. Consequently, this section relies much more heavily on debate transcripts from the Houses of Commons and Lords than the section above on the transformative order. The Parliamentary arena was the one space in which both sides of the debate had equal voice (and therefore ideas as espoused in public could be accessed) due to the convention of turn taking.

As discussed above, metadiscourses (or fields of ideas) drawn on in the debate around abolition were, as so often in politics, not originally focused on slavery. They were taken from contemporary ways of making sense of the world and deployed by the colonial order to legitimate the practice of enslaving and trading in human beings. The same four discourses are present in the justifications used by the pro-slavery order as by the anti-slavery campaign, but this time with the opposite aim and very different interpretations.

The first major attack on slavery by the abolitionists produced 'a surge in racially justified defences of the institution' (Drescher 1990b: 421). However, tactics and argumentation quickly became both more sophisticated and more diverse. It was common to produce texts which sought to directly counter and ultimately discredit the arguments espoused in anti-slavery texts. For example, Gordon Turnbull (1786) wrote in a patronising tone that most abolitionists, though meaning well, had never even visited the West Indies and were misinformed by ignorance. George Hibbert, MP for Seaford, spoke in the House of Commons in 1807 of his relief that he had not suffered such brainwashing:

> I will not say that I knew many of these abolitionists who, with the exception of their prejudices on this subject, were much like other men; and that, had I been, as, thank God I was not, like them, misled by delusive theories, deceived by false, exaggerated, or partial accounts of what has passed, and is passing in Africa and the West Indies; instigated by popular clamour (itself artificially and enthusiastically excited); and fascinated by oratory, I might with them, have given my voice for a measure which has proved destructive of its object, and has sacrificed one main source of our national prosperity. (House of Commons, 10 February 1807)

Drescher (1990a) notes the scant reference to religion or morality in the pro-slavery Parliamentary argumentation, in comparison to that of the abolitionists. He describes how the anti-abolitionists 'sneered at their opponents for being quixotic "emperors of the world," who refused to recognise the ultimate futility of their plans in the face of history, geography, and economics', suggesting that 'implicitly, abolitionists sensed the advantage of their opponents in this "international" frame of reference' (Drescher 1990a: 575). Twenty years after Hibbert spoke in the Commons the same tactics were favoured, with Alexander Barclay, a planter recently returned to Britain from Jamaica, writing in 1827:

> Never perhaps, were mistakes more prevalent upon any subject than they are at present upon that of West India slavery. There are many in this country, and by no means in the lowest stations, who never hear the subject mentioned but they have before their minds chains, dungeons, scourging, maiming, wounding and death. To their terrified imaginations it appears the land of horrors, where cruelty sits in brief authority, and the oppressed drag out a gloomy life in groans and tears, without any of the comforts of existence, and of course, without any signs of enjoyment. (Barclay 1827: i–ii)

He placed the blame for this negative propaganda in the hands of 'authors and orators in the mother country' whom he accused of being less interested in making accurate representations of the condition of the 'negroes' 'than to give an aggravated and frightful description of it, in order to obtain for themselves the praise and favour' (Barclay 1827: i–ii). He went on to argue that colonists did not hate the 'negroes', and there was merely a difference in intellect. The 'negroes' are described as 'rude and ignorant pagans', and their enslavement to more civilised masters meant that they

Table 4.4. Colonial Discourses

Metadiscourse	Original Focus	Use for the Colonial Order	Key Interpretations (by all or some within the order)
1. Political philosophy	Understanding society and politics in Europe	When applied to slavery it legitimates the practice	Stages of human civilisation, impact of climate on human development – race could be the basis of political rights and imperial control. Black enslaved people as commodity and private property.
2. Christianity	Understanding man's role in the world and provision of a moral code to live by	When applied to slavery it legitimates the practice	Black enslaved people are not human and cannot therefore be Christian, making slavery defensible. Black people as sub-human, an 'unholy' mix of man and animal, making slavery defensible. If the slave trade, or slavery in general, were wrong then God would not have allowed it to continue, and for so many to become so rich as a result of it. Miscegenation wrong – to raise slave's position in society would be to risk inter-breeding. Laws are made by the King in God's name and to challenge them is blasphemy. To challenge slavery is blasphemy.

Slavery and the Right to Be Human 69

3. International political economy	Framework for enabling maximum individual and national wealth	When applied to slavery it legitimates the practice	Slave trade as essential for British international imperial competitiveness (especially with France). The slave trade as a 'nursery for seamen', therefore vital in maintaining military strength against enemies. Increasing the numbers of slaves in plantation colonies facilitates social stratification amongst them and decreases the risk of revolt. Ending the trade would mean a decrease in slaves, less class structure between them and risk of revolt. Slave trade as essential for British international economic competitiveness (especially with France). Abolition would have damaging effect on commerce of cities such as Bristol and Liverpool, and on the British economy as a whole. (earlier) Ending the trade will mean a decrease in slaves on the plantations and decrease in profitability – they breed at insufficient rates and have high mortality.
4. (British tradition of) law and justice	Framework for protection of society and the individual within the community of the nation from harm	When applied to slavery it legitimates the practice	Black slaves do not have Habeas Corpus. Rights of planters to private property trump rights of enslaved people to liberty. The treatment of the enslaved people may be cruel and immoral, but justice dictates that it must therefore be improved, not the trade ended (comparisons with treatment of animals).

were 'advancing to civilization, under the government of an enlightened people, to whom they look up as so greatly their superiors, that subjection to their authority is scarcely felt as a hardship, and certainly not at all as a degradation' (Barclay 1827: viii).

The image of African cultural inferiority was therefore approached by the pro-slavers as irreversible, rendering abolition pointless, even harmful to the enslaved people (Barker 1978). Like the abolitionists, black people living in Britain provided proximate evidence for their arguments. For example, James Tobin, a planter from Nevis, wrote in a response to a tract by Reverend James Ramsay, a prominent abolitionist writer, that it was unheard of to see a free black man working in a respectable position such as porter, ditcher or ploughman. He put the fault for this with the freed slaves. He wrote, 'those who are not in livery are in rags; and such as are not servants, are thieves or mendicants' (Tobin 1785: 118). This was seen as evidence of the inability of black people to civilise and improve themselves, a direct challenge to the abolitionist belief that a civilising project was possible. The same people who were against abolition were therefore also those who were concerned about the black presence in Britain, as indicated by the words of James Tobin above (Walvin 1986).

In the earlier years of the abolition debate Edward Long published two texts, *Candid reflections upon the judgement lately awarded by the Court of King's Bench, in Westminster-Hall, on what is commonly called the negroe-cause* (1772) and the influential book *The History of Jamaica* (1774). The former urges that 'some restraint should be laid on the unnatural increase of blacks imported' due to the social problems that they are causing (Long 1772: 48). Long writes that 'the lower class of women in England, are remarkably fond of the blacks, for reasons too brutal to mention; they would connect themselves with horses and asses, if the law permitted them' (Long 1772: 48–49). He was an influential and wealthy member of British society, as well as an established Jamaican planter and slaver, described by Fryer (1984: 70) as 'the father of English racism'. Walvin (1986) refers to Long as 'the most acerbic of anti-black writers in the 1770s', while Drescher (1990b: 422) describes *The History of Jamaica* as 'the most extensive racially grounded argument in defence of slavery written before the age of abolition'. The three-volume history linked 'negroes' to the animal world through designating them as an intermediate species between white Europeans and orangutans. He wrote of their 'bestial and fetid smell'; affirmed that their children, like animals, matured more rapidly than those of whites; and stated that they embody 'every species of inherent turpitude' and imperfection that can be found scattered among all other races of men (Long 1774: 353–357). Drescher (1990b: 422) observes that Long was widely read and 'accepted as an empirical authority by naturalists and anthropologists for generations', while Fryer (1984: 161) suggests that Long's 'opinions were shared by many and [indicate] that racism had more than a foothold in England'.

This is related to the fact that despite the central ideas on the rights of man, and the perfectibility of humanity from a state of nature, the Age of Enlightenment was nevertheless the golden age of the slave trade and the West Indian plantation (Davis 1966; Mayblin 2013). Famous philosophers such as Hume, Burke, Locke, Rousseau and Hobbes 'had shown that a defence of slavery could be reconciled with belief in abstract natural law and natural rights' (Davis 1966: 391). For example, rightly or wrongly, apologists for slavery took from Montesquieu that 'one could not apply European notions of liberty and justice to Negro bondage without resorting to fanciful metaphysics' (Davis 1966: 395). Kant was the author of the first theory of race, beginning with his *Of the Different Human Races* in 1775 (Bernasconi 2002). His theory, based almost exclusively on a typology of mental attributes derived from skin colour, had a significant impact on the sciences of the period (Strack 1996; see also Morton 2002 on Hume).

The handling by philosophers of the gap between their thoughts on the question 'what is Man?' and the practice of slavery and slave trading grew in the eighteenth century, and the arguments in support of slavery in an age of rights accordingly became ever more sophisticated. Drawing on the work of such philosophers, Gordon Turnbull wrote in a pamphlet in 1786 that enslavement and the use of slave labour is a natural occurrence in human society and that

> Those real, but mistaken, philanthropists (or pretended zealots in defence of, what they call, *the natural rights of mankind*) who maintain that, because all men are born equal, all should enjoy an equal degree of liberty, might as well contend that the people of every climate, should be clothed in the same manner; or as they are born naked wear no clothes at all. (Turnbull 1786: 9)

He argued that the trade was 'consistent with justice and humanity as well as sound policy', and ultimately that 'negro slavery'

> appears, then, to be as far as reason can judge, one of those indispensable necessary links in the great chain of causes and events, which cannot and indeed ought not to be broken ... *part* of the stupendous, admirable, and perfect *whole*. (Turnbull 1786: 34–35)

Abolitionist writers such as the French writer Bernardin de Saint Pierre complained of this, writing in 1818, 'I am sorry, that philosophers who combat abuses with so much courage, have hardly spoken of Negro slavery except to joke about it' (cited in Cook 1936). Yet, as Trouillot (1995: 78) points out, 'that the material wellbeing of many of these thinkers was often indirectly and, sometimes, quite directly linked to the exploitation of African slave labour may not have been irrelevant to their learned opinions'.

Christianity had long been 'one of the pillars upon which the slave system rested' (Ogborn 2008: 261). Black enslaved people were viewed by many as not being human, meaning they could not therefore be Christian, which made slavery as morally wrong as enslaving animals to work on farms. For some, black people were sub-human, perhaps an 'unholy' mix of man and animal, again making slavery defensible. 'Unholy' as this mix was, further miscegenation must be prevented and to raise the position of enslaved people in society would be to risk inter-breeding (Fryer 1984).

If black people were considered human, their enslavement remained defensible on the grounds of original sin. Christians were universally bonded and should be free but pagans deserved to be enslaved people. Furthermore, 'if physical labour was the penalty for man's rebellion against God, the most severe form of punishment had been inflicted on the Africans' – in other words, they deserved their punishment (Davis 1966: 174). Further proof of this reasoning was the lack of punishment afforded to those benefitting from slavery, George Hibbert pointed out in the House of Commons in 1807. The MP noted that Jamaica had been free from hurricanes for twenty years yet 'that period no way marked by a forbearance as to the purchase or labour of slaves' (House of Commons, 10 February 1807). As hurricanes were viewed as the manifestation of God's anger with human beings, this was a sure indication that slavery did not displease the divinity. Furthermore, in four successive years 'hurricanes have visited that island, and have specially desolated one of its districts – that district and those years not chargeable with any extraordinary concern with the slave trade' (House of Commons, 10 February 1807). And finally, he observed that no 'judgment has, at those periods, fallen upon British legislators and statesmen, the authors and promoters of the slave trade, who, as I shall shew, did not make their acts of Parliament in ignorance, but knew well what they were doing' (House of Commons, 10 February 1807). Not only were those involved in slavery and the slave trade not punished by God, 'but, on the contrary, the era in which the slave trade was authorised and encouraged by the British legislature was one of distinguished prosperity in that country, one in which she became the envy of the world' (House of Commons, 16 March 1807). If this was not evidence enough of the morality of slaving, laws were in fact made by the King in God's name, and to challenge them was blasphemy. Therefore, to challenge slavery was nothing short of blasphemous.

In Parliament the main concerns were the threat to the economic and political competitiveness of Britain in relation to other European countries, particularly France. This encompassed both economic concerns regarding the lost revenues to be incurred if the trade were to be abolished and the inevitable loss of international power and symbolic capital, again particularly in relation to France. The inevitable ruin (a word used frequently in relation to the issue of abolition) to be brought to Britain and its empire was spoken of in apocalyptic terms. Even the war effort would be hindered as the slave trade as a 'nursery for seamen' would cease to train young soldiers.

In debates around the abolition of the slave trade pro-slavers argued that to end the trade would mean a decrease of slaves on the plantations and a corresponding decrease in profitability. The enslaved people apparently bred at insufficient rates and had too high a mortality rate to maintain the working population. Furthermore, increasing the numbers of enslaved people in plantation colonies was said to facilitate social stratification and decrease the risk of revolt. The logic followed that ending trade would mean a decrease in enslaved people, less class structure between them and greater risk of revolt (House of Commons, 16 March 1807).

Later, when slavery itself was at stake the primary weapon in the pro-slavery order's economic arsenal was that of free versus slave labour. Were free workers more productive than those enslaved due to the wage incentive and improved health, or did the cost of wages cancel out any potential benefits? Predictably, the colonial order was in favour of forced labour as the only economically viable solution to labour force requirements in the colonies. They referred to many of the same economies as the abolitionists, only interpreting them differently. In one of their last reports against the abolition of the slave trade, the slavers of Jamaica wrote,

> Whether tried on the Principles of the mercantile System, or on those of the Economists, as developed to the English Reader in the Writings of Mr. Hume and Doctor Adam Smith, this important Commerce [the Afro-West Indian trade] will be found equally beneficial. (Jamaica Assembly, 1805)

In this line of reasoning the colonial order was always at an advantage – what could be more lucrative than producing profitable goods without labour costs? The opening up of basic rights for enslaved people was fraught with dangers and hidden costs as yet unforeseen. Of this the colonial order, a business focused organisation since its inception, was acutely aware. Drescher (1990a: 580) writes, 'far from forming a consensual and reassuring ideology, the argument over slave vs. free labour generated an enduring vein of pessimism about abolitionist policies which endured in Parliamentary debates right down to British slave emancipation in 1833'. It was a line of reasoning against abolition that the transformative order could not win, which is why they put so much effort into shifting the debate onto their terms.

The rights of planters as property owners were discussed in an entirely different language to that of the rights of the enslaved people. While enslaved people were often denied agency, planters were very much rights-bearing citizens and British subjects, and the violation of their rights would be fundamentally counter to the British tradition of law and justice. Their right to property was established and had historical precedence; the right of enslaved people to liberty was a new idea and legally uncertain. Importantly, black people were exempt from the rule of Habeas Corpus, which prevented people from being unlawfully detained without authority. They, quite literally, did not have the legal right to their own bodies.[1] This left open the possibility for the amelioration of their conditions, as opposed to abolition, once pressure from the transformative order forced the widespread acknowledgement that enslaved people were often cruelly treated. This would tend to changes in the moral framework of society without having to alter its legal articulation. The planters had entered into slaving with sanction from the King on an entirely legal basis, and to disregard their rights as property owners simply because of this recent reappraisal of the status of their property would be wholly unfair.

In the early days of the campaign for abolition the inevitably ruinous consequences of such reform were stated repeatedly in Parliament in an effort to prevent the change from occurring. However, as it became clear that abolition was inevitable, attention turned to diminishing its impact. Planter compensation preoccupied Parliament considerably in the final stages of the abolition debates, with numerous ministers feeling compelled to speak on the behalf of what they felt to be a persecuted group (slave owners). Ultimately they were successful; a fund of £20 million (£1.2 billion in today's money) was given to the Treasury 'from time to time to make grants for the compensation of the planters' (House of Commons, 31 July 1833).

Victory for the Transformative Order

Though the abolitionists formed a truly mass mobilisation of people, the gatekeepers to change were the men sitting in the Houses of Commons and Lords. As previously stated, the West Indian lobby was powerful in both houses, not least due to their personal financial interest in the colonies. Yet a number, gradually growing between 1800 and 1833, were moved to support abolition.

There is an important distinction here between the abolition of the slave trade and the abolition of slavery. First the 1807 act made the trade in African enslaved people illegal. This occurred through a combination of tactical manoeuvring on the part of the abolitionists in Parliament and a growing sense of unease at the force of popular support for abolition amongst the population of the country. In 1806 the abolitionists successfully played on nationalist sentiment and rivalry with the French by passing the Slave Importation Restriction

Bill, which outlawed the involvement of British subjects with French slave traders (Ogborn 2008). Some objected, such as the Marquis of Sligo, who opposed the bill in the House of Lords on the grounds that it was 'pregnant with infinite danger to the very existence of the West-India islands' (House of Lords, 16 May 1806). He was in the minority in spotting the ulterior motives of this covert measure which eradicated two-thirds of the British slave trade with little resistance.

The abolition of the slave trade in 1807 garnered support for what might be seen as counter-intuitive reasons, mostly related to the continuation of slavery (albeit in a less cruel form) and the prevention of revolt in the colonies. The following extract from a speech by Lord Grenville in the House of Lords on the second reading of the Abolition of the Slave Trade Bill illustrates this. Grenville firstly argues that abolition is a matter of justice, though he is careful to note that this is not a justice between equal human beings but is a matter of legal justice nevertheless:

> Had it been, my lords, merely a question of humanity, I am ready to admit that it might then have become a consideration with your lordships as to how far you would extend or circumscribe that humanity ... Justice, my lords, is one, uniform and immutable ... you are called upon by this measure not only to do justice to the oppressed and injured natives of Africa, but also to your own planters. (House of Lords, 5 February 1807)

Thus, even if the trade was found to be morally defensible, there were nevertheless important reasons to outlaw it. Yet the fact was that the trade had been found to be

> the most criminal [enterprise] that any country can be engaged in tearing the unhappy Africans by thousands and tens of thousands, from their families, their friends, their connections, and their social ties, and dooming them to a life of slavery and misery ... surely there can be no doubt that this detestable trade ought at once to be abolished. (House of Lords, 5 February 1807)

Arguments made by Wilberforce in 1789 (when the campaign for abolition was in its infancy) that the enslaved people were treated with cruelty and lived in poor conditions were no longer disputed by 1807; they were accepted as facts. The transformative order had infiltrated the debate with its ideas to such an extent, and forced the issue in Parliament for so many years, that previously disputed assertions about cruelty and injustice were conceded by the opposition. The question for Grenville was twofold: Would the continuation of the slave trade ultimately harm the British economically, and does the trade run counter to the norms of justice and fairness which he and his contemporaries hold to be an intrinsic value of British society and one of the rationales for their superiority in the world? These questions implicitly assume enslaved people to be human beings (albeit inferior, underdeveloped human beings) as opposed to simple property.

By the early 1820s British abolitionists had become dispirited. The lack of progress towards abolition of the African trade worldwide and the realisation that ending the trade to the British West Indies had not led to amelioration of the condition of enslaved people there frustrated many within the order (Davis 1975). In 1823 there was a high-profile case in Demerara of a missionary being imprisoned for his work with enslaved people who had been treated cruelly and his support for them in an uprising which saw three white planters killed and 250 enslaved people put to death in response. The cruelty taking place in Demerara, a relatively new plantation colony, outraged the British public (Walvin 2007). The key actors in this story were the missionaries, who were becoming increasingly active in the plantations, converting significant numbers of enslaved people and reporting the cruelties taking place back to Britain.

Later that year the Society for the Mitigation and Gradual Abolition of Slavery was formed by Wilberforce's successor in Parliament, Thomas Fowell Buxton.[2] He brought to Parliament a motion to abolish slavery in May 1823 and a resolution was moved in the House of Commons to improve the conditions of enslaved people and gradually pursue abolition. The ideological ground shifted and economic arguments grew in prominence on the abolitionist side, though humanity, morality and justice remained stalwarts of the campaign. These economic arguments focused on the availability of sugar sold on world markets which was produced by free workers and was cheaper than that produced by enslaved people largely in the East Indies. The colonial order was left with little to dispute. Walvin writes, 'despite a rearguard opposition in the House of Lords, black freedom no longer divided the British, but had instead, become an issue which united the British as no other' (Walvin 2007: 125).

However, in Parliament the strength of the colonial order and its political and economic power stalled abolition for another ten years. It was only after a series of events in 1832 that the opportunity to successfully pass a bill in Parliament came: First was a cholera epidemic which killed tens of thousands of people, coupled with massive Jamaican plantation revolts. These were both viewed as divine punishment for national sins, with slavery representing quite a significant sin. Growing instances of slave revolt in the colonies, a significant drop in the slave population and the decreasing profitability of plantation slavery also meant that the government was less likely to want to pay 'the considerable political and financial costs of continuing to defend slavery', while planters were 'more willing to consider a compensated abolition of slavery' (Blackburn 1988: 436). In addition, the 1832 Reform

Act significantly extended suffrage, vitally increasing both the number and importance of middle-class voters, many of whom supported the transformative order, and significantly reduced the strength of the West Indian interest in Parliament. In the general elections of 1832 the abolitionists made candidates declare their support for slave emancipation, which two hundred did (Walvin 2007). This combination of circumstances and the abolitionist infiltration of the seat of power allowed for the passing of the Abolition Bill in August the following year.

Enslaved People, 'Blacks' and the Legacy of Differential Humanity

Following discussion of this first critical juncture, this concluding section looks at the significance of the abolition of slavery in terms of its legacy and relevance for asylum policy today. First, there are three key points to take from the case study:

1. The legislation which abolished the slave trade and then slavery throughout the British Empire represents the first major positive change in the way the British government officially viewed its non-white subjects.
2. The legislative change was not achieved on the basis of equality but only by its possibility through European civilisation.
3. Abolition subsequently buttressed ideas of British moral superiority and paved the way for the codification of the world's population in terms of geographical location and 'race'.

Woven through the chapter is one constantly recurring theme: conceptions of humanity and the status of non-white bodies in relation to it. Contestations over the meaning of the category 'human' were initially biological but quickly moved in to the trickier territory of culture and civilisation. The colonial worldview is therefore, as Mignolo points out in his work on coloniality/modernity, deeply entwined with rise of self-conscious European modernity. While Europeans were busy becoming modern, they were also busy deciding where others might be placed in relation to this modernity, and if indeed anyone who was not white could be viewed as even capable of entering into the category of the rights-bearing 'man', the baseline of modern civilisation.

A long-standing current of hostility towards those perceived to be outside 'others' was temporarily interrupted by the campaign for abolition, a campaign which sought a complete reappraisal of the parameters of humanity, justice and duty (Walvin 1986). Yet, following 1833, there was a reversion to more disdainful racial attitudes, strengthened significantly by the imperialist surge in the second half of the nineteenth century. While the outpouring of support for black freedom from bondage and the tremendous support garnered for the anti-slavery order were unprecedented, the debates laid the groundwork for what was to come. Supporting King's and Smith's (2005) depiction of institutional orders, the orders identified reveal a wide variety of discourses bringing the coalition together, which left room for racist views of black inhumanity even within the transformative agenda. Though some of its followers were, in today's terms, racist, and most were only moderately egalitarian, many nevertheless opposed the white supremacy which underpinned the slave trade and slave labour, if not that which supported a hierarchical view of humanity.

Of the US context, King and Smith (2005: 77) write, 'at the nation's founding, a political coalition of Americans formed that gained sufficient power to direct most governing institutions, and also economic, legal, educational, residential, and social institutions, in ways that established a hierarchical order of white supremacy'. Yet, the existence of the Atlantic slave trade, of course, was the reason that enslaved peoples lived in the country at the founding of the United States, just as the colonial rationales which accompanied colonial activities (including slavery) provided the ideology behind the hierarchical order of white supremacy. The picture that I am drawing, then, is one of international interconnections, not nationally or territorially bounded historical contexts.

King and Smith (2005: 77) write that their transformative order 'had its governmental institutionalisation in legal guarantees of equal rights that were sometimes implemented in judicial rulings and legislative statutes, often under the pressure of religious groups, black and white'. As this chapter has shown, this was also the case in Britain. The authors also point out that the transformative order in the United States was initially far weaker than white supremacist actors and institutions, and that 'conflicts between proslavery and antislavery forces, not white supremacists and racial egalitarians, formed the central axis of, especially, late antebellum politics [1781–1860]' (King and Smith 2005: 77). They therefore argue that while the transformative order which formed around anti-slavery was not necessarily in favour of racial equality, it was nevertheless a force for egalitarian racial transformation. This was also the case in the British context, where the triumph of the transformative order in terms of abolition strengthened the position of more racially egalitarian actors and the institutions they occupied.

Nevertheless, for many in the transformative order, a civilising project delivered by the Christian missionary movement was always an ambition of abolition. They believed black slaves to be inferior but had faith that they could develop, particularly through religious education. The triumph over slavery therefore gave them a mandate to pursue the mass conversion of Africans and former West Indian enslaved peoples to Christianity as the

Empire expanded through the nineteenth century. Those who had been deeply involved in the campaigns for abolition simply continued this mission, with the successor to the Society for the Mitigation and Gradual Abolition of Slavery Throughout the British Dominions, 'The British and Foreign Anti-Slavery Society',[3] being formed in 1839. 'The African Civilization Society' was also started by Thomas Fowell Buxton in 1840, which had Thomas Clarkson, one of the leading abolitionists, as vice president.

That a racially transformative agenda could accommodate ideas of racial hierarchy into the ideology of emancipation is consistent with historical institutionalist perspectives on political change. When political change occurs, it is rarely supported by as radical a change in ideas as the popular remembering of the events might have us believe. In the case of contemporary asylum policy, while the most radical campaigners for change argue for an end to borders and immigration controls as the only means to equality of access to human rights, the majority of those who have a public voice on the issue (charities such as the Refugee Council, for example) argue not for an end to the principles underpinning the system but for less punitive policies. The idea of freedom of movement and free and equal access to a safe haven, or to the prosperity offered by economic stability, then, has its limits.

Many of those involved in the colonial order remained defenders of slavery to the last, adjusting to a new way of working after abolition while still holding their old views. Indeed, abolition was implemented gradually, which eased the transition. Planters had access to the £20 million compensation fund, which both legitimated their rights as property owners and supported the belief that enslaved peoples were property – property that had been lost and required compensation. Catherine Hall's work on the legacies of this compensation scheme for investment within and beyond Britain shows that the money enriched wealthy families for generations as well as laying down significant infrastructure from which Britain continues to benefit (Hall et al. 2014). Some flipped and supported abolition in the final debates, though never on the basis of equality, more often on economic grounds, seeing financial opportunities in trade within the burgeoning Empire. The weakness of moral arguments in the face of economic priorities is perhaps one of the most striking aspects of the long campaign for abolition. In the face of mass protest, the powerful men in Parliament moved only when the economic viability of slavery was under threat.

Nascent racial thought from the abolition period, with its early efforts at categorising human beings into hierarchically organised group types, was to pave the way for fully fledged scientific racism in the latter part of the nineteenth century (discussed further in chapter 5). These early practitioners 'sought to delineate bio-cultural boundaries, coinciding with innate and inheritable mental and moral differences', a project which lost none of its fascination in the post-slavery British Empire (Drescher 1990b: 418). In many ways, then, as much as the fifty-year abolition campaign transformed the politics of racial domination, it also ushered in a new age in which the orders forged around and against abolition were able to develop their ideas and act upon them in new contexts. While the campaign described above was large-scale and ultimately successful, it was not fully transformative of the global racial order. This is because the transformation was primarily legislative. It focused on a legal category of person and on outlawing the practice of owning and trading in enslaved people. What the order was only very partially successful in doing was enacting transformative change in wider social practices, beliefs and prejudices, as well as imperial and colonial activities. There are parallels here with the situation of asylum seekers today; despite legally binding international agreements signed over sixty years ago proscribing the right to asylum and the duty upon host states, this act alone did little to transform wider social practices, beliefs and prejudices which support the differential treatment of human beings on the basis of country of origin, language, religion and culture.

The abolition debate was occurring at the same time that new ideas around the rights of man were being proposed, discussed and debated. The rights being explored in theory by philosophers of the day (and realised in revolutionary France and Haiti) sowed the seeds of the human rights agenda in the twentieth century. This was an agenda which of course included the right to asylum. The historical example therefore foregrounds the entanglement of rights talk with colonially informed rationales of differential humanity and demonstrates that the parameters of humanity and exclusion from it have been matters of contention since the inception of the very idea of rights. Indeed, rights talk always entails discussion of entitlement – who is included, and who excluded? Where everyone is, at least in principle, entitled to make rights claims, it should be no surprise that pre-existing prejudices and old hierarchies would play a role in the disruption of access to those rights.

The critical juncture further serves to highlight the colonial origins of British self-conception in relation to the wider world. For several centuries this wider world was a colonial world consisting largely of European settler societies and colonial territories. The history recounted in this chapter is an important reminder that despite histories of 'otherness' within and beyond Europe, there have been groups, such as black enslaved people of African origin, who have been considered not only different or inferior but also inhuman in British legal history. This example therefore demonstrates the significant potential for overhaul in taxonomies of humanity, rights and duty. At the same time, exploring these histories sets the stage for a discussion of the present response to asylum seekers in Britain as part of a much longer history of ideas of differential humanity.

Abolition was a moment of rupture in prevailing conceptions of humanity, but the debates around it, accessible through the plethora of material available from the time, provide insights into early conversations on the nature of humanity – who belonged and who did not. This is the birth of coloniality/modernity, and while at this point there was clearly an explicitly racial element to the hierarchical ordering of human worth, we can also see the organisation of human beings around ideas of place of origin, religion, civilisation and culture, which is so much more than the biological essence of racial ascription. These are the ideas which, tangled together, we will see interpreted, reinterpreted and revised over time for new circumstances, but at their core many of the rationales and assumptions are around the inherent modernity ('equal' humanity) or unmodernity (infrahumanity) of particular bodies in particular places. This has profound implications for the level of violence that can be tolerated against certain bodies and when the moral duty of protection applies. In this sense, the debates around the abolition of slavery are not directly related to contemporary asylum policy in a linear manner. Rather, they are historically entangled, with slavery and abolition quietly implicated in the genealogy of the idea of common humanity and its failings. In the next chapter the racial articulation of these systems of classification following the abolition of slavery are investigated in more depth.

NOTES

1. There were a small number of exceptions to this general rule. The most famous is the Somerset case of 1772. James Somerset, represented by Granville Sharpe, prominent defender of slaves in the courts, successfully won the right to not be removed from England by his owner in Virginia. News of this case spread, and by 1774 the view was prevalent amongst slaves in America that if they ran away to England, they would be free there (see Shyllon 1974; Fryer 1984).

2. An evangelical Christian, Fowell Buxton was also the main organiser of the African Civilization Society, which gives some indication to his ideological inclinations.

3. This continues today as 'Anti-Slavery International'.

Chapter Five

Colonialism, the League of Nations and Race Equality

This chapter is concerned with the rise of conceptions of racial hierarchy in the nineteenth century and the ways in which these taxonomies influenced international relations in the twentieth century. More specifically, it investigates the Japanese proposal in 1919 that race equality be included in the Covenant of the League of Nations. The chapter draws on analysis of original archival documents from the negotiations and secondary literature on the period in analysing the case. The proposal was rejected, twice. Leading the resistance was the British Empire delegation, strongly supported by the United States. The evidence presented in the chapter shows that their resistance can be understood clearly within the context of contemporaneous ideas of racial hierarchy derivative of the colonial experience but which had begun to be expanded well beyond biological identifiers. Ideas of civilisational inferiority, incommensurability and the self-conception of Europe as singularly modern facilitated the domination of colonial subjects, understanding their place in the world as being below that of the European 'race' in a world hierarchy of humanity. This chapter shows that these powerful ideas had an enduring impact in world politics into the twentieth century.

In 1919, at the Paris Peace Conference, Japan was invited as one of five 'great powers', 'the only power in the non-Western world which could possibly make any impact on the conference and the world thereafter' (Shimazu 1998: 1). The Japanese delegation proposed for the first time on the international stage that race inequality be legally abolished. Shimazu (1998: 4) describes this as 'the first major stage of the development of racial equality as a general principle of national importance'. As noted above, the proposal was rejected twice with particular resistance from the British Empire delegation and the United States. Their resistance, as this chapter will show, can be understood clearly within the rubric of coloniality/modernity and was articulated as a concern that though Japan had become wealthy and powerful, it had not become modern in civilisational terms.

Racial hierarchies and their articulation in 1919 are important in the story of the history of asylum. At the present time some people are granted better access to human rights than others, as outlined in the introductory chapters. In pursuing restrictive, punitive asylum policies while internationally recognised refugee-producing situations take place (contexts in which persecution is likely to occur), the British government sends out an implicit message that certain levels of violence are more tolerable if they happen to people from certain places. Such ideas are not new, they did not spring into being in the late twentieth century, and they have a long lineage. Tracing this lineage through three concrete historical moments in which the salience of ideas of human hierarchy have appeared provides an explanatory lever in understanding the actions of the modern state. Indeed, that the British Empire led the rejection of the concept that all people are equal regardless of 'race' in 1919 is highly relevant in understanding that country's efforts to exclude the colonised from human rights in 1951, as discussed in the next chapter.

The first section of the chapter outlines the rise of conceptions of racial hierarchy in the nineteenth century and their enduring resonance in the twentieth century. Following this is an examination of the second critical juncture, the Japanese proposal for a race equality clause to be inserted in the Covenant of the League of Nations. The proposal was rejected and the rejection was articulated within a discourse of white supremacy, 'coloured' inferiority and fears over a possible race war – the 'yellow peril'. Again, two institutional orders will be identified: the colonial order and the transformative order. Having looked at the perspective of the transformative order, led by the Japanese delegation at the conference, the analysis turns to the institutional order which they were in conflict with. The colonial order included the British Empire delegation leading the resistance, and the United States in support. Here, Britain's white settler colonies articulated their solidarity in the language of blood, culture and 'race'. This left the Japanese always in the position of alien 'others', despite their newly acquired 'great power' status. The final section entails a discussion of human hierarchy, the case study and the enduring relevance of this event in the history of differential conceptions of humanity, which, I will argue, have such an important place in the politics of asylum policy today.

THE RISE OF 'RACE' HIERARCHY IN THE NINETEENTH CENTURY

This section will outline the rise of scientific and popular ideas of 'race' hierarchy, overlapping with concepts of civilisation and the civilising mission, in the nineteenth century. The purpose of this discussion is to frame the case study in the following section. That these ideas of 'race' difference and hierarchy were of enduring relevance in understanding the rejection of the race equality clause at the League of Nations in 1919 will become clear. However, these ideas are not only important in understanding this one case study of international politics. They are also part of a much broader history in which human bodies have been, and continue to be, granted differential access to purportedly universal human rights.

The idea of 'races', of human beings in different parts of the world being mentally and physically different from each other, and the origins of such difference preoccupied scientists for much of the nineteenth and well into the twentieth century. Discussion around the origin of human beings, as one (monogenesis) or a series of separate races (polygenesis), had been going on long before Charles Darwin published his *On the Origin of the Species* in 1859. The main aim of the popular Ethnological Society of London, for example, was to investigate the 'races of man' to determine whether they were 'of one blood' (cited in Stocking Jr 1971: 372). The question was whether 'the "distinguishing characteristics" of different groups were simply modifications of one original type, or whether they represented differences in original hereditary make-up' (Stocking Jr 1971: 372). Authors on the subject were most commonly naturalists, botanists and those undertaking medical research. They were connected through pan-European networks of letter writing and publication. Within Britain, institutions such as the Ethnological Society, the Anthropological Society and the Royal Academy provided a focus for interaction through meetings, debates and lectures.

Swedish botanist Carl Linnaeus was one of the earliest and most widely recognised authors to propose a taxonomy of humanity. His regularly updated pamphlet *Systema Naturae* grew into a large encyclopaedia by the late 1700s. In later versions, he presented a mode of categorising the world's people which proposed four distinct groups: European white, Asiatic yellow, American red and African black. Around the same time Georges Louis Leclerc comte de Buffon (1776) and Johann Friedrich Blumenbach (1969 [1779]) proposed their own typologies. They again described a territorially based typology equating geographical location with physical appearance, cultural practices and psychological disposition.

In the early nineteenth century, works on the natural history of mankind began to be produced in greater number, often drawing on the typologies devised previously and hypothesising on their basis. Founded upon the principle that the races were separate and fundamentally different, questions arose about both their origins and their potential. Scientists such as William Lawrence (1822: 424), for example, asked, 'Why have the white races invariably, and without one exception, raised themselves to at least some considerable height in the scale of cultivation; while the dark, on the contrary, have all almost universally continued in the savage or barbarous state?'

James Prichard (1847) proposed an explanation: that the primitive stock of men were all negroes, suggesting that whites were a highly developed form of human and that people of colour were a relic of their long distant past. In 1850 Robert Knox published his influential *The Races of Man* based on a series of public lectures that he had delivered across the country. The preface states, 'race is everything: literature, science, art, in a word, civilization, depend on it' (Knox 1850: 7). Whether labelled 'races', 'species' or 'permanent varieties', Knox, like most of his contemporaries, was certain that man could be divided into distinct groups and that human history was founded upon their separation.

When Darwin's theory (suggestive of monogenesis, though not directly applied to humans) was published, it was hotly debated and contested within the context of ongoing discussions of 'race' difference. The Anthropological Society of London, formed by polygenesist James Hunt in 1863, opposed Darwinism, as it promoted human unity. The society grew rapidly in the 1860s and became extremely popular in an age when 'Darwinism made the nature of man a matter of general public intellectual concern' (Stocking Jr 1971: 377). Hunt and his associates presented copious amounts of evidence for the separateness of the 'races' and, according to Bressey (2007), gained many followers (see Hunt 1863). Phrenology (the study of the shape of human skulls in determining personality traits) was very popular at this time and was used as proof of fundamental biological and psychological difference between various racial categories (see Verity 1839). When skulls failed to prove sufficient difference, writers often found the evidence to be inadequate rather than the hypothesis wrong (Verity 1839).

The typologies developed in the nineteenth century all mix nationality, territory, physical appearance, personality traits, language and biological 'science'. They also all differ in their categorisation of humanity. However, two categories always remain, and their status at top and bottom, civilised and savage, is constant. These are white/European – the two words are often used interchangeably – and black/African/negro, the latter accounting for the complexity introduced by the dislocation of slavery. Where European 'others' appear, it is in the problems they pose for the purity of European racial whiteness (for further discussion on this, see Bonnett 1998). Where non-European 'others' appear as 'negroes' and other 'backward' indigenous peoples, they are entirely 'other' and indisputably inferior in every way.

Such classifications were political in that scientific ideas were intertwined with the activities of the Empire. They provided justification for the oppression of non-white peoples across the globe. Three key fields of knowledge were infused through the politics of this period and through the rationales of classificatory systems. They were the fields of science, civilisation and religion. First, scientific reason and method (particularly phrenology) lent legitimacy through claims of objectivity to an ideologically driven project. Confirming the 'facts' of racial groups as distinct, mentally and physically, was hugely powerful and the language of 'race' in scientific texts bled into non-scientific discourses relating to the various nations and 'races' of the world.

This was the case even for scientists who did not develop a theory of race. The primary example is Darwin. Darwinism, despite posing a challenge to the mainstream of science on racial difference, was itself taken up and developed in support of ideas of racial hierarchy. The idea of the survival of the fittest suggested that theories of inequality 'could be shown to have a basis in natural history, the result of a long and painfully slow evolutionary battle for supremacy between naturally emerging human groups' (Lentin 2008: 13). Political and social life, including wealth creation, thus became 'natural' and biologically determined. Of importance here is the fact that in the nineteenth century, as Bernasconi (2010: 144) points out, 'the boundary between scientists and philosophers was not fixed as it is now'. This made a marriage between philosophical justifications for colonial subjugation and scientific research possible.

First applied to individual and family behaviour, social Darwinism was later extended to the international scale. The biological metaphors of 'advanced' and 'backward' derived from Darwin's ideas on 'fitness'. This was then applied to global racial and, by extension, national relationships. Consequently, the idea of 'advanced' and 'backward' nations and 'races' became a frequently used device for understanding the world in Victorian times. It, in effect, extended British class politics to the realm of inter-state relations (Rich 1990). Social Darwinists believed that the competition for survival which ultimately led to the 'fittest' winning out was also a battle for racial supremacy. Less 'fit' members of white society, such as the poor or disabled, should not be helped, as their propagation would ultimately damage the racial stock. Such ideas even appeared in Parliamentary debate (House of Commons, 25 March 1867). Ultimately, one 'race', most probably the superior whites, would win, but they would have to fight to defend their supremacy. The idea of 'race wars' is one which we will see again in the section below discussing the study's second critical juncture.

This 'science' might not be recognised as such today, especially since the idea of 'race' is generally viewed as a social and political construct as opposed to a biological category. And yet in the context of the time, as Bernasconi (2010) points out, such ideas and practices as detailed above were seen as both scientific and objective. Bernasconi (2010: 141–142) writes that 'leading scientists of the nineteenth century embraced the concept [race]'; it had significant status 'for some years in the consciousness of many ordinary people who believed that it had been given scientific legitimacy'. The popularity of such ideas is expressed through the frequency with which nineteenth century texts refer to racial lineage as common knowledge.

Related to the ideas of the racial sciences were ideas around the concept of 'civilisation'. This was the popularisation of a European consciousness about the Age of Enlightenment, and what the appearance of this revolution in thinking meant for the British (and European) place in the world. Britain was a country of rights, equalities, liberties, technological development, fine art and political progress towards democracy – a place where morality and virtue were of the utmost importance. Such factors were combined with the new sciences which suggested that some 'races' of the world were inferior and some superior, as outlined above, always coming to the conclusion that those categorised as 'whites' (and particularly the English) were superior. This was both biological (in the form of 'races') and geographical (where 'races' were to be found). For example, scholar and humanitarian Gilbert Murray stated in 1900,

> There is in the world a hierarchy of races ... those races which eat more, claim more, and earn higher wages, will direct and rule the others, and the lower work of the world will tend in the long-run to be done by the lower breeds of man. This much we as the ruling men of colour will no doubt accept as obvious. (cited in Banton 1998)

Nationalism was therefore an intersecting variable on the axis of race and civilisation. The British had abolished slavery because they were more civilised than their neighbours and, importantly, clearly superior in civilisation to those of other continents. Walvin (1986: 19) observes an almost instantaneous amnesia on the part of the British following abolition 'despite the fact that the British had carried perhaps 2.5 million Africans into bondage, and had established some of the most successful slave colonies in the Americas'. The subsequent 'unflinching persistent emphasis upon British liberties, and the British love of freedom ... become a regular decant in all sorts of mid-nineteenth-century literature', he observes (Walvin 1986: 19).

Patterson (2007: np) points out that 'the superiority of British institutions and customs was rarely publicly questioned, at least not by those who served in an official capacity'. Thus, uncivilised peoples were incapable of governing themselves at present, but with tuition from the British, who had emerged from Roman and Norman bondage to become a conquering 'race', they could be shown the way. Unfortunately, the point at which they were deemed capable of equal civilisation, and by extension self-government, was always far off on the horizon. When a 'race' appeared to be advancing towards the European standard, as was the case with Japan in the early twentieth century (discussed below), deeply held ideas of 'race war' and threat to the white civilisation were invoked.

Clearly linked to developments in science and civilisational thinking, Christian teachings added to the idea of trusteeship. Bearing in mind that 'whites' were superior on the civilisational scale, they had a duty to educate the 'darker races' of the world and facilitate their development up the scale. This was the duty of trusteeship, with British colonisers represented as the shepherds of the earth (Porter 1992). 'Christian duty' was an idea of enduring resonance in the nineteenth century. It was raised in Parliament in relation to all manner of issues from prison reform to policy in the Ionian Islands and East Indian opium revenue (House of Commons, 7 May 1861, 10 May 1870, 24 April 1850). The idea of 'Christian duty' was used in a loose and inconsistent sense to refer to anything that was right, honourable, charitable and fundamentally not for one's own selfish benefit. More concretely, Christian duty for many included the missionary duty of spreading the religion around the world. Van der Veer and Lehmann (1999: 22) write,

> one can only wonder about the extent to which Christian imagination in Britain was fuelled by the imagery of the poor Hindus, Muslims and others being lost for eternity ... [but] there can be little doubt that the simultaneous Evangelical activities of Bible societies, missionary societies, and Sunday schools, created a public awareness of a particular kind of world and of an imperial duty of British Christians in the Empire. (van der Veer and Lehmann 1999: 22)

Thus, Indian students living in Britain in the latter half of the nineteenth century commonly reported people trying to convert them to Christianity (Visram 2002). Even if they were already Christians, many were assumed to be heathens on the basis of their appearance. Evangelism had of course been a driving force behind abolitionism, and the Christian mission in this period was very much a continuation of this.

Having briefly discussed the rise and popularisation of race science and ideas of racial difference, hierarchy, competition and relative 'civilisation', the scene is set for a more specific analysis of such ideas in action on the world political stage. The next section looks at the 1919 Paris Peace Conference, where Japan for the first time put the issue of race equality on the international political agenda. Many of the ideas outlined above can be observed being operationalised by the British Empire in objecting to the proposal.

The Race Equality Proposal at the 1919 Paris Peace Conference

This section provides a case study institutional analysis of the race equality proposal at the 1919 Paris Peace Conference. The case study provides an illustration of the kinds of ideas outlined above at work in international politics, in a forum which was the precursor to the United Nations (UN). The Paris Peace Conference of 1919 met with the aim of determining the peace settlement with Germany and the Austro-Hungarian Empire following the First World War. In addition, the leaders of the United States, the British Empire and France were all also committed to forging a league of nations which might help to preserve world peace in the future. A second aim of the 1919 Conference was therefore to agree upon a covenant for the new League of Nations, which was ultimately included in the Treaty of Versailles, the peace settlement (Goldstein 2002; Burkman 2008).

In January 1919, ahead of the start of the conference, Britain, France, Italy and the United States met and decided that decision making on major issues would be kept in their hands, with the addition of Japan as a newly appointed 'great power' (Goldstein 2002).[1] However, by March Japan had decided that the discussions in the Council of Five were Eurocentric and opted out. Japan was nevertheless still a great power, the only non-Western 'power' in the world, and had a delegation at the conference who took part in all other discussions. All of the states involved in shaping the outcome of the First Wold War were invited to the conference, excluding Russia and Germany.[2]

On 25 January 1919 the Preliminary Peace Conference established the League of Nations Commission, whose task was to draft the covenant of the League of Nations. The commission comprised two representatives each from the five great powers. In addition, it was decided that 'the commission shall have power to invite to any of its meetings the representatives of other allied, associated or neutral nations in order to elicit their views' (Cabinet Office 1919: np). Nine countries were selected for this task on the commission, each having one representative present. They were Belgium, Brazil, China, Czechoslovakia, Greece, Poland, Portugal, Romania and Serbia. Fifteen meetings took place between 3 February and 11 April 1919, during which the Japanese delegation made two (unsuccessful) attempts to insert 'race equality' into the covenant. US President Wilson insisted on a consensus on the issue of race equality, giving the British Empire the power of veto, despite other powers acquiescing on the issue.

My analysis of this second critical juncture shows that there were again two identifiable institutional orders at work: the transformative order and the colonial order. Continuity from the previous chapter is apparent in the ideas underpinning the colonial (white supremacist) order. This confirms that it is not so much 'race', the relations between 'races' or physical or mental difference that are at stake in combating racial hierarchy, but the motivations of racists and the obstacles they impose. The colonial/modern mindset was well established by 1919, as we shall see.

Japan and the Transformative Order

Table 5.1 below shows the individuals and organisations which I have identified as being part of the transformative order. This is an order in the sense that all involved were, like the slavery abolitionists, fighting for the same thing – the abolition of racially based discrimination in the League of Nations. However, a diversity of opinion existed around the reasons for pursuing this agenda, the appropriate extent of the ambitions pursued and the most suitable methods to be used.

The Japanese delegation at the Paris Peace Conference was led by Saionji Kimmochi (elder statesman and former prime minister) and Nobuaki Makino (ambassador plenipotentiary to the Paris Peace Conference), with Chinda Sutemi (ambassador in London), Ijūin Hikokichi (ambassador in Rome) and Matsui Keishirō (ambassador in Paris) supporting them. Makino and Chinda (as he was known) were the Japanese representatives on the covenant drafting commission. Though this was the official face of Japan for the purposes of the conference, there were a large number of people within Japan and the Japanese diaspora lobbying for the race equality clause. Often these activists were highly critical of the efforts of the delegation in Paris in articulating the problem and fighting for the cause. In addition, the Japanese proposal attracted the attention of a wider constituency of people involved in anti-colonial and anti-racist struggles, particularly in the United States.

Discourses (or fields of ideas) drawn on in the campaign to have race equality accepted at the League of Nations were similar across all levels, but with varying degrees of radicalism. While the official Japanese delegation sought to limit the scope of their demands and minimise the wider implications of race equality in order to increase their chances of success, others were able to make those links more explicitly. A review of the transcripts of the discussions around the proposal, petitions presented to the various delegations, speeches made and newspaper articles published in Japan, as well as the secondary literature on the topic, reveals the four discourses shown in table 5.1 present in the justifications used in the race equality order.

Each delegation went to Paris with one or a number of primary aims. The main aim for Japan at the conference was making efforts to secure suitable guarantees against the disadvantages to Japan which arose out of racial prejudice (Colonial Office 1919). If they were to join the League, they did not want to be at a disadvantage. The Japanese delegation made the proposal that a race equality clause be inserted into the League covenant because though considered a great power on economic and military grounds, the Japanese perceived that they were not treated equally to the other great powers. All of the other great powers had Western European origins and Japan considered the root of the prejudice to be grounded in a belief that

Table 5.1. The Transformative Order

Level	Who?	How?
The official Japanese delegation	*Key negotiators for race equality:* Nobuaki Makino and Chinda Sutemi *Other members of the delegation:* Saionji Kimmochi, Ijūin Hikokichi and Matsui Keishirō	Meeting with members of the US and British Empire delegations for 'behind the scenes' negotiations. Making proposals to the drafting commission. Supporting speeches to the drafting commission.
Organised Japanese lobbyists	*Within Japan:* Society for the Abolition of Race Discrimination (SARD; an amalgamation of organisations, individuals and social movement representatives) Sympathetic journalists *Outside of Japan:* Japanese ambassadors (particularly in the United States) Japanese diasporic organisations	Mass meetings. Letters/telegrams to the commission and commission president. Printing articles, letters and the declarations of the SARD. Public speeches. Newspaper interviews. Letters to hostile delegations (British Empire and the United States).
Anti-racists and anti-colonials	Particularly in the United States For example, Booker T. Washington, Marcus Garvey, W.E.B. Du Bois NAACP	Newsletters. Speeches. Visits between the United States and Japan for attendance at anti-racist meetings.

the Japanese were racially and culturally inferior (Shimazu 1998; Bennett 2001; Horne 2004).

Part of this perception related to policies across the British Empire and in the US state of California which discriminated against Japanese immigrants. Some places, such as the Canadian state of British Colombia, sought to exclude Japanese immigrants from entering, under the remit of 'white Canada'; others such as California sought exclusionary property, employment and education laws (Bennett 2001). Strained relations with the other powers during the First World War, uneven trading agreements and a general diplomatic sense of suspicion also fuelled the perception of discrimination. Japan's reaction was part of a broader racial discourse ('Jinshuran') popular at that time in Japan and emerging in response to the Western 'yellow peril' discourse. Within ten years it would become part of mainstream Japanese foreign policy. Young (1997) writes that 'the Japanese appropriated European vocabularies of racial fear (yellow peril) and racial mission (the white man's burden) and turned them against the West, calling on Asians to join forces against the 'white peril' and proclaiming their intent to liberate Asia from the shackles of white imperialism'.

For now, however, senior ministers saw the League of Nations covenant as an opportunity to enshrine in an international document a statement of equality. Not equality of all, but of the Japanese in relation to the Europeans (Shimazu 1998). Japan's primary motivation was preventing 'itself and its nationals as a state from suffering the humiliation of racial prejudice in the League of Nations' (Shimazu 1998: 113). The Japanese delegation initially proposed four different draft proposals to Mandell House of the US delegation and President Wilson in private, therefore arriving at something less than ideal but perhaps acceptable to the United States. House presented this to Balfour of the British delegation on 10 February, again in private. Unable to find agreement with the British, Japan made the initial proposal to the League of Nations Commission on 13 February. This was dismissed. Following intensive interactions with the British Empire delegation to find a mutually acceptable compromise, they presented a new, heavily watered down version. This was again blocked, with the Australian Prime Minister offering the most resistance. He did suggest a possible formulation but one which withheld the rights of Japanese to enter Australia, an option which the Japanese rejected.

As mentioned above, the official Japanese delegation were seeking the equality of the Japanese amongst the great powers only, in accordance with their recent turn to 'Western facing' policies; they were not fighting for global racial equality. Such narrow self-interests, however, proved unpalatable to many Japanese. On 5 February 1919 a meeting of five hundred people took place in Tokyo. The objective of the meeting was seeking the abolition of racial discrimination through the League of Nations. Twenty-seven Japanese

Table 5.2. Transformative Order Discourses

Discourse	General Focus/Argument	Use for the Transformative Order	Key Interpretations (by all or some of the alliance)
International relations	Maintaining harmonious relations between the great military and economic powers in the world	Delegitimises great power status and the League of Nations	Membership of the League of Nations has no meaning without official recognition of race equality of powerful members.
Race hierarchy	There is a world hierarchy of 'races'	Delegitimises the League of Nations	Japan as most 'civilised' of the non-Western 'races', culturally equal to Western powers. Must be recognised as such within the League of Nations.
Anti-colonialism	Colonialism as oppressive regime which must be ended in order for peace to truly exist	Delegitimises the League of Nations	Without a recognition that colonialism is unjust and itself undermines world peace, the League of Nations is rendered meaningless. In order for colonialism to be brought to an end, the League must recognise race equality.
Race equality	All 'races' are equal	Delegitimises the League of Nations	Denial of race equality unveils Japan's 'great power' status as meaningless, undermining the League of Nations project.

societies and organisations were represented and attendees included 'statesmen, scholars, newspaper men, and other Japanese from various walks of life' (Foreign Office 1919c). This was 'a fair representation of intelligent Japanese', according to a Japanese newspaper, or 'a large proportion of unbalanced thinkers ... [and] chauvinistic societies ... not furnishing a representative group of the solid and sober thinkers of Japan', according to a British Embassy official (Foreign Office 1919c). A committee with forty-one members was formed to bring the demand to the notice of the Japanese Foreign Office and to send a telegram to the Japanese delegation at Paris and to Monsieur Clemenceau (French Prime Minister and President of the Council).

An English language newspaper article in Japan recounted many of the speeches made at the meeting (Foreign Office 1919c). All speeches emphasised the fact that racial discrimination should be abolished, with many of the speakers drawing special attention to the existing 'race feeling' in the United States and Great Britain. For example, Kenichi Otake, a member of the Imperial Diet, opened the meeting, expressing his support for a league of nations, but said that it could not be formed unless race discrimination was first eliminated. He said,

> Because of the difference of colour or skin, there should be no discrimination, and now that the peace delegates from different nations are working to reconstruct the world, it is a good opportunity for Japan to present this issue of the abolition of race discrimination. The government officials cannot be trusted to take care of the interests of Japan by themselves. They need the united support of the people. (Foreign Office 1919c: np)

He went on to declare that 'the world does not belong to the Europeans alone'. Mr. Tanabe, a 'noted publicist', spoke of 'a dark current running through the hearts of the coloured races of the world, in India, China and elsewhere' (Foreign Office 1919c: np). The movement, which was started in Japan, would 'surely be re-echoed throughout these lands of coloured races'. He said, 'it will moreover lead to a formation of public opinion in the world regarding the abolition of race discrimination ... the coloured races will join and rise in revolt' (Foreign Office 1919c: np). Such utterances drew on global linkages between the Japanese and others outside of the West who sought to oppose European white colonial hegemony.

At least two speakers, including Otake, insisted on the abolition of racial discrimination as a necessary condition for the formation of the League of Nations. Vice Admiral Hamiidzumi, representing sympathisers among naval reservists, paid tribute to President Wilson but said that if a league of nations was really desired, 'racial discrimination must as the premier question be first abolished' (Foreign Office 1919c: np). Doctor Yasoroku Soejima of the Indo-Japanese Association was said by a British official to have used practically identical language. Mr. Tanaka, representing Buddhists, 'emphasised that in philosophy Japan and the Orient had all that Western philosophers would tell us'. This begged the question, 'why is it that Japan has been reduced to a state today of being obliged to cry for abolition of race discrimination?' He found the answer to be not in Western traditions of race hierarchy, as I am arguing, but in the hands of the diplomats: 'it is because the Japanese diplomats have been too backward and self-humiliating' (Foreign Office 1919c: np).

Indeed, a recurring theme at the meeting was the inadequacy of the political establishment in fighting for this issue at the international level. General Sato (a writer of anti-British military articles) was quoted by the newspaper *Jiji* as stating at this meeting that 'not only the government but the various political parties also are extremely indifferent to this question neither Viscount Kato of the Kenseikwai, nor Mr Inukai of the Kokuminto is here, while as for the Seiyukwai, the Premier Hara likewise has not come' (Foreign Office 1919c: np).

Using the language of 'race' hierarchy, Vice Admiral Maiizumi, representing the reservist navalists, 'said that the Japanese are not treated so badly [as some], but as elder brothers to these oppressed coloured races, Japan cannot keep silence' (Foreign Office 1919c: np). Mr. Ando, of the *Asahi Shimbun* newspaper, reminded the audience 'of the Kaiser's Yellow Peril instructions to Marshal Waldersee, at the time of the Boxer Trouble', while Mr. Shimado, of the Kenseikai political party, said that

> the western people have been unconsciously committing wrongs against coloured races. But they are awakening to their mistakes. Germany's attempt at the time of the Sino-Japanese war to oppress Japan failed, for Russia and France which were Germany's partners realised their mistake in joining hands with Germany against Japan. That broke down the race barrier ... Now it is time for England and America to awaken.

He recounted the history of the treatment of the Hindus across the British Empire and the United States and suggested that the British are 'coming to realise that they cannot treat coloured races badly and maintain the British Empire in a good state'. As 'Whites are now against Whites' ('witness Germany'), this was the perfect time to push for race equality.

The association unanimously passed a resolution stating that discriminatory treatment because of 'race' difference should be abolished by the peace conference and cabled it to French Prime Minister Clemenceau. It read, 'The Japanese nation is in hearty support of the plan of the Allied Powers to establish at the Peace Conference a league of nations for the purpose of maintaining permanent peace in the world, and wishes for its successful formation'.

> But the discriminatory treatment of different races hitherto prevailing in international relationships was not only against the great principle of liberty and equality, but it is likely to be the cause of future international conflict. If it is allowed to remain all the alliances and treaties will be only castles on sand. The general peace of the world will not be secured. Therefore in order to firmly establish the peace of the world as well as to seek in the carrying out of the principle of justice and humanity at this moment we appeal to the public opinion of the world, and hereby resolve:
> That the Japanese nation expects to see the discriminatory treatment, because of race difference, now prevailing amongst the nations, shall be abolished at the peace conference.
> Society for the Abolition of Race Discrimination in Mass Meeting
> (Foreign Office 1919c: np)

However, rather than expanding them to cover all peoples, as the negotiations unfolded, the Japanese delegation in Paris increasingly watered down their proposals. On 13 February Baron Makino made a speech to the League of Nations Commission stating that the intention of the proposal was not to realise full racial equality in the world and proposing that the insertion in the covenant applied only to discrimination against members of the League. This remained unacceptable to the British Empire delegation, and Australia particularly had strong objections. Eventually, the Japanese delegates suggested a sentence insertion into the preamble (as opposed to an article), which was totally unrecognisable from the initial proposal (Shimazu 1998).

Japanese Ambassador Viscount Ishii, speaking at the annual dinner of the Japan Society in New York on 15 March 1919, made a strong plea for including some provision against racial discrimination in the proposed covenant of the League of Nations. He pointed out that this question had long been a cause of international discord in the past and would continue to be so in the future unless steps were taken to eliminate it. Seeking to distance the proposal from issues of immigration, upon which the British Empire and US delegations seemed fixated, he asked that the issue be seen 'independently of questions of labour or emigration' (Foreign Office 1919c). The Japanese nation would, he said,

> calmly though anxiously await time when by gradual process of evolution this difficult matter would be finally settled to the mutual satisfaction of both countries and it would not be the policy of Japan to force hastily the cause of Labour question should a new article be inserted in the Covenant against racial discrimination. (Foreign Office 1919c)

The speech 'attracted great attention' in the United States, according to Lord Reading, a British representative (Foreign Office 1919c).

Again, on 20 March 1919 the Secretariat General received a telegram, which found its way to the British Foreign Office, urging that the League of Nations covenant should make provision against racial discrimination, this time from officials from the Japanese of the Hawaii Islands. It read, 'Japanese in Hawaii American earnestly pray that League of Nations from its principle of justice, righteousness and humanity will abolish racial discrimination in all high contracting nations' (Foreign Office 1919c: np). Despite watering down the proposals, Baron Makino was not prepared to back down completely and undermined Australian Prime Minister Hughes by appealing directly to the Australian people for sympathetic treatment, through national newspapers. He warned them that if they continued to resist race equality Australia would be held accountable for discrimination. When Prime Minister Hughes returned home he was pressured into a U-turn, and he became a supporter of the Anglo-Japanese alliance (Bennett 2001).

There is evidence that many in Japan were using the language of 'race' hierarchy around this issue but, as indicated in the speeches at the public meeting recounted above, this was not necessarily a binary of white against 'other'. Often, the Japanese, a colonial power themselves, were presented as above other 'coloured races' within and outside of Asia. For example, a Japanese newspaper report from the period (undated) predicted that after the European war, Asia would become the 'field of international rivalry among the Powers, and the future destiny of the world will be decided by the awakening of the myriads who throng this great arena' (Cabinet Office 1918a: np). As 'Japan was the first among the nations of the East to receive enlightenment; it is her duty to help and guide those nations which are akin to her' (Foreign Office 1919c). Ultimately, it would be the enlightened, civilised Japanese who would lead Asia into the modern world.

Clearly the vision presented above has echoes of the British civilising mission. However, some were less convinced of their country's leadership capabilities. In July 1919 Professor Kanokogi Kazunobu from Kyushu Imperial University wrote in *Ajia Jiron*, a national journal, that 'when Japan brought forward the proposal for the abolition of racial discrimination at the peace conference she threw into Europe and America a bomb of high explosive power' (Foreign Office 1919c: np). The failure was on the part of Japanese officials – in fact throwing a 'dud – as effective as a coconut ... it had about as much effect as a rubber ball' (Foreign Office 1919c: np). Professor Kazunobu suggested that the abolition of racial discrimination

> is a question affecting the welfare of the whole of mankind excepting a small number of white races in Europe and America, and the sole object of the proposal

brought forward was to break down the almost impassable barrier blocking the road to progress for these numerous peoples. (Foreign Office 1919c)

'The diplomats in Paris should never have let the other Great Powers decide the fate of the proposal', the professor said. He invoked racial solidarity, writing that it was 'deplorable that the Japanese people, obsessed with greed for petty but immediate gain, with no thought of their racial and international position or their hereditary mission, should have missed such an excellent opportunity' (Foreign Office 1919c). Though unimpressed with the performance of the delegation at Paris, Kazunobu nevertheless here invokes the Japanese 'hereditary mission', a racial bond with other non-white peoples and some kind of responsibility as the most developed of the group.

Though the Japanese delegation were working primarily towards *Japanese* equality with the other great powers, their actions and the wider Japanese anti-racist movement had the attention of anti-racists and anti-colonials in other countries. Black activists in the United States had already been inspired by the Japanese defeat of Russia in 1905, seen as signalling a crisis of white supremacy (Horne 2004). W.E.B. Du Bois, Booker T Washington and Marcus Garvey all expressed solidarity with and admiration for Japan. The NAACP's[3] James Weldon Johnson praised Japan for 'throwing a wrench into the machinery that is grinding out the League of Nations ... by raising the race issue and forcing it right up to the point where it must be met and met squarely' (cited in Gallicchio 2000: 23–24). Onishi (2007: 193) writes that following the race equality proposal, African-American leaders 'projected the image of Japan as a race rebel and a racial victim and helped construct the iconography of the Japanese as the New Negro of the Pacific'. There was a growing sense, then, that Japan provided a new promise of hope for non-whites globally in the face of centuries-long white supremacy and imperialism. Indeed, this perception of solidarity was not one-sided; Garvey's writings were published in the Japanese press and scores of Japanese activists visited the United States and spoke at anti-racist meetings (Onishi 2007).

These solidarities did not go unnoticed by the British Empire and US establishment. However, as we shall see in the next section, invocations of transnational racial solidarities, uprisings and 'race wars' did little to convince these objectors that the race equality clause should be accepted. On the contrary, it played into their greatest fears.

The Colonial Order

Having outlined the Japanese position and approach at the conference in the previous section, this section looks at the colonial (white supremacist) institutional order with whom the Japanese were seeking to insert their race equality clause. Just as many of the themes of racial hierarchy discussed in the first section could be observed in Japanese discourse on the topic, this order was deeply imbued with the ideas and language of 'race'.

As table 5.3 below indicates, this order was one of powerful state representatives from the white Anglophone world. In blocking attempts by Japan to have racial equality pursued as a keystone value of the League of Nations, a disparate array of supporters and social movements was not necessary.

The British Empire delegation at Paris was made up of representatives of Britain, its Dominions and India. The key individuals in the delegation were David Lloyd George (Prime Minister), Arthur Balfour (Foreign Secretary), Andrew Bonar Law (Lord Privy Seal and Leader of the House of Commons), George Barnes (Minister without Portfolio), and one representative (rotating) from the British Dominions (Canada, South Africa, Australia, New Zealand and India). The Dominions, excluding India, played a prominent part in the race equality negotiations despite playing a lesser role in League of Nations negotiations more broadly. This is reflected in the fact that the main British representatives for the race equality negotiations were Lord Robert Cecil, Arthur Balfour, Jan Smuts (South African Prime Minister), Billy Hughes (Australian Prime Minister) and Robert Borden (Canadian Prime Minister).

The reasons for including the Dominions in the conference are not certain. That they were represented in the Imperial War Cabinet and pushed for inclusion in that context played a part (see Cabinet Office 1918b). That Britain was keen to show that it took seriously the commitment to Dominion status and the decision-making powers which went with it was another factor. There is also evidence that significantly increasing their voting power in the League of Nations was appealing. For example, a Foreign Office official wrote during the conference,

> I need not dwell on the very significant fact that for the first time the British race is represented collectively by Empire Representatives instead of by delegates from Great Britain only. In the ways which matter most the British Empire can exercise a stronger influence over the course of the present negotiations than any other of the Great Powers ... it does not follow that the need for exercising either of these faculties will arise, but the fact that they exist lends an almost irresistible and unconscious weight to any views expressed by the British Empire Plenipotentiaries. (Foreign Office 1918–1919)

Table 5.3. The Colonial Order

Level	Who?	How?
Leaders	The British Empire Delegation (Great Britain with the Dominions Canada, South Africa, Australia and New Zealand) The United States of America	Imposing a consensus condition on decisions relating to race equality. Refusing to concede any concession to race equality proposal in the negotiations.

For this order, the chance of the proposal being successful was minimal at best as it represented something beyond the horizon of contemporaneous knowledge about the world and the various people in it. This is reflected in the discourses which the order drew on in constructing their objections, shown in table 5.4 below. These will be further elaborated in the discussion that follows.

Table 5.4. Colonial Order Discourses

Discourse	Original Focus	Application for the White Supremacist Order	Key Interpretations (by all or some of the alliance)
Racial hierarchy (based in race science)	The justification of colonial activities	Delegitimises any claim to racial equality on the part of non-white peoples	All races are distinct, separate and hierarchically organised. The white race is at the top of the global hierarchy, the Japanese are below them. They cannot be equal because they are not white.
Civilisation	The justification of colonial activities	Delegitimises any claim to race equality on the part of non-white peoples	No non-European heritage society (racially and culturally) is as developed in civilisational terms as European and European settler societies. This cultural inequality delegitimises any claims to racial equality.
Race war / 'yellow peril'	Military threat posed by non-white states exists due to inherent differences. 'Race war' inevitable.	Delegitimises any claim to racial equality on the part of non-white peoples	Even if the Japanese develop on a par with Europeans, there will never be equality and peace, only inevitable war as they compete for global power.
Immigration	Non-white immigration to 'white states' endangers the biological (through miscegenation), social, cultural, and moral condition of the nation	Delegitimises any claim to race equality on the part of non-white peoples	Racial equality among League of Nations members would imply equality of migration rights, particularly for Japanese, which would have a detrimental effect on host societies – biologically, socially, culturally and morally.

What is perhaps more important for the purposes of this analysis is both the centrality of colonialism and the conceptions of 'race' to decision making around the conference. The retention of the German colonies acquired during the war, and acquisition of more if possible, was a primary aim of the British Empire delegation at the Peace Conference (Foreign Office 1919a). Lloyd George convened a sub-committee on 'territorial desiderata' whose aim was to find ways of securing as much overseas territory from the settlement as possible (Goldstein 1991). This was perhaps one of the main reasons for having Dominion representation – to make it appear as though Britain was not unfairly benefitting. Even the Australian Prime Minister recognised this fact:

> As regards ... the question of the former Colonies, I understand that the attitude of the British Empire is to stand firm for their retention, but I certainly do expect a great deal of difficulty ... I think the course suggested, namely, that those Dominions who are primarily interested should put their case forward, is the best course ... I do not think that America regards the Dominions as being synonymous with Great Britain, although she may do so and may say 'with all parts of the Empire'. At the back of her mind she says: 'These are as we were, and, by increasing their territory, does not necessarily mean that it is increasing the territory of Great Britain'. (Cabinet Office 1917)

Speaking of the type of league which might emerge from the conference, Hughes invoked the enduring relevance of ties of blood and 'race', saying that a 'great Anglo-Saxon Empire' would 'assure the peace of the world' (Cabinet Office 1917). It would work, according to Hughes, because members would be bound together 'not by any Utopian scheme but by ties of blood, of common history and of common purpose' (Cabinet Office 1917). He suggested that American, Englishman, Canadian and Australian all think alike 'and we are all cousins' (Cabinet Office 1917). Indeed, a league which would ensure world peace would be one 'whose history and traditions and ideals are nearly alike' (Cabinet Office 1917). The British Empire delegation consistently spoke in racial terms – of their white alliance and natural affinity with the Americans above all others. For example, Robert Borden suggested in the Imperial War Cabinet,

> Whether the establishment of a League of Nations is possible or not, there is at least possible a league of the two great English-speaking Commonwealths, and, with a view to arriving at such a league, I should like again to urge that the United States should be invited to undertake world-wide responsibilities in respect of undeveloped territories and backward races. (Cabinet Office 1917)

The salience of ideas of racial affinity was of course linked to those of racial hierarchy and a belief in the unbridgeable difference between the different 'races'. Some were seen to be simply incapable of running their own societies. On 7 February Professor Oppenheim of Cambridge University wrote, upon request, to Mr. Baker at the Foreign Office with his expert opinion on the League of Nations proposals. The provisions concerning the 'tutelage' of former German colonies 'which are inhabited by peoples not yet able to stand by themselves under the strenuous conditions of the modern world' concerned him (Foreign Office 1919b). Tutelage was to be exercised by the new mandate system which Oppenheim found to be a dangerous proposal 'in so far as they are to apply to African and other territories populated by natives of whom it cannot be expected that they will be able within measurable time to govern themselves' (Foreign Office 1919b). Surely, he mused, 'these territories must sooner or later become colonies of some established civilised state' (Foreign Office 1919b).

Regarding the Japanese, the British delegation certainly held the view that this 'race' of people was, though economically and militarily powerful, incommensurably *different* and certainly inferior. The British Paris Peace Conference handbook on Japan stated that 'it would be difficult to find a nation more affected by sentiment than the Japanese ... though there is much which is sincere in this sentiment, there is also a good deal which is artificial' (Foreign Office 1919a: 107). Popular writings likening the imperial dynasty to the sun were described as 'Oriental hyperbole'. The booklet goes on:

> The pride of the race in its achievements is, like its loyalty and patriotism, exaggerated. The astonishing progress the country has made in the past fifty years ... [has] to some extent turned the heads of the Japanese, and made them think themselves superior to Western nations, and look down with contempt upon other peoples of the East. (Foreign Office 1919a: 108)

The Japanese did not apparently 'perceive their own lack of creative talent', or that everything they had in terms of development and civilisation had been borrowed from the West 'at no cost to herself, without expenditure of time or thought, labour or money, she plucked the fruit of generations of toil in Europe and America' (Foreign Office 1919a). This is a fact which in their arrogance the Japanese 'are inclined to overlook' (Foreign Office 1919a).

Yet these borrowings were 'material rather than moral' and modernisation (Westernisation) was in fact only partial in Japan (Foreign Office 1919a: 107). 'New ideas imported from abroad exist, for the most part, side by side with the old' (Foreign Office 1919a: 111), which was seen negatively. For example, the Georgian calendar was used for official purposes but 'counts for little in other respects a few miles from the capital' (Forcign Office 1919a). Furthermore, the Emperor, 'who, on certain State occasions, performs the functions of a European monarch in accordance with a ceremonial borrowed from the West', on other state occasions acts 'as high priest in the chapel attached to the palace', conducting a Shinto service 'according to a ritual so antiquated as to be almost unintelligible, and quite out of keeping with the modern ideas which the nation has adopted' (Foreign Office 1919a: 112). It is clear from this that the writer assumed Japanese traditions to be inferior and 'backward' and Western traditions superior and modern. That the Japanese combined the two indicated that the country had not yet fully entered modernity. This demonstrates the entanglement of coloniality and modernity.

Echoing wider fears over a 'race war', the author suggested that it was not surprising 'that the Japanese should regard with jealousy and irritation the rule of Western peoples over Asiatic "races," wherever it is found' or that she 'should sympathise with the native populations of Egypt and other parts of Africa where the governing authority is in Western hands; and should resent as an offence to their dignity the anti-Japanese attitude which exists in certain British colonies, and especially in America, where the right of naturalization is denied to them' (Foreign Office 1919a: 110). There were a number of barriers to progress for Japan, the booklet said, but the greatest was this: 'the reluctance of some of the leading Powers to treat the Japanese in all respects on an equality with Western races' (Foreign Office 1919a). This, the writer concludes, 'in view of the prejudice in which it has its origin, will be the hardest to remove' (Foreign Office 1919a: 113).

Lake and Reynolds (2008) note that Japan's victory over Russia in the 1904–05 war not only was a source of surprise on the part of the Western powers but also incited suspicion and fear. Symbolically, this was a victory of the East over the West. Where next for Japan? Valentine Chirol, Foreign Editor of *The Times*, observed that Japan's triumph had brought the problems of the relations of all the races of the East and the West 'to our very doors' (cited in Lake and Reynolds 2008: 166). Alfred Zimmern wrote in *The Third British Empire* (1926: 82) of a lecture he gave at Oxford where he set aside the topic of the day and told his students 'about the most important historical event which has happened, or is likely to happen, in our lifetime, the victory of a non-white people over a white people'. At this time, the victory was a sign of the reality of the so called 'yellow peril' – the race war which was inevitable if the Japanese became wealthy enough.

It was within this context that the British Empire delegation responded to the race equality proposal. Baker wrote in an internal memo to Cecil on 10 February 1919, 'the League of Nations is not based on the principle of Equality of all its members, and it is most desirable that this phrase should in no form be introduced into the Covenant' (Foreign Office 1919c). Balfour met with US representative House on the same day, stating that he did 'not believe that any of the English-speaking communities would tolerate Japanese flow of immigration' (Foreign Office 1919c: np). Indeed, despite the emphasis of the Japanese delegation, and the broader Japanese lobby for the race equality clause on the issue of race equality broadly, there is no recognition of this in the British Empire documents from the period. For the British Empire, and the United States, the issue was solely immigration. It was as though race equality was beyond the horizon of their imagination. In the same meeting, as Balfour mused that Japan's threat not to join the League if their clause is not included is 'very much like an attempt at blackmail on the part of our Ally', House proposed that 'the unexplored wastes of Siberia might perhaps provide the best outlet for Japanese immigration' (Foreign Office 1919c: np).

Upon reading a British Embassy dispatch and news article on the public meeting recorded in the previous section, Mackay requested copies of the American, Canadian and Australian immigration laws which affected Japanese migrants, leading to a search amongst all relevant delegations and the Foreign Office library for the documents (Foreign Office 1919b). Though the British Empire used the rhetoric of equality between all imperial subjects, the reality was much more problematic. The Dominions all followed a practice of racially discriminatory policies against other imperial subjects as well as those not from the British Empire. More importantly, engaging with the speeches recounted above only in terms of immigration legislation suggests a blinkered understanding of the issue and the possibilities for abolishing racially based discrimination. The Foreign and Colonial Offices were certainly aware of the strong feelings being expressed in Japan and the Japanese diaspora for the race equality proposal. Not only were there official declarations such as that sent by the Tokyo-based Society for the Abolition of Race Discrimination to Monsieur Clemenceau, but British Embassy officials in Japan were sending home regular reports and press clippings on the situation (Foreign Office 1918–1919). Yet universal racial equality was simply not on the agenda as an international issue in 1919; it could be dismissed as completely impractical. As Shimazu (1998: 120) points out, 'the pejorative idea of racism as such was not really existent before the interwar period because Anglo-Saxon society was so deeply imbued with what we would consider today to be racist values'.

Embassy reports were generally disparaging of the activities of activists and described them as 'unrepresentative', even 'chauvinistic' and including 'unbalanced thinkers', as noted above (Foreign Office 1919b: np). Alston at the British Embassy in Tokyo wrote on 10 April 1919 that the opinion of the Japanese press regarding the League of Nations had distinctly hardened, primarily in light of the unfolding race equality debates. He wrote that 'it is difficult to understand what is at the bottom of the sudden ebullition of feeling on this subject, how far it is real, how far artificial' (Foreign Office 1919b). Though he did concede that race equality 'is practically the one topic of discussion, and great dissatisfaction is expressed on all sides at the failure so far of the Japanese Delegates at Versailles to obtain the insertion in the Covenant of a clause abolishing this discrimination' (Foreign Office 1919a: np). He also notes that Viscount Iagil and Baron Makino had both distinguished between the race equality question and immigration. Although a recent report in the *Sichi Sichi* newspaper had said that 'no arms are needed, if the Asiatics combine to break down the barriers of the white races', which somewhat fuelled British fears of a 'race war' (Foreign Office 1919b).

Though the focus for the British delegation was immigration to the British white settler colonies, this was often discussed by them and the United States as being problematic in explicitly racial terms. Writing to Balfour on 24 March 1919, American officials Mr. Murray and Mr. Gould outlined their case as follows:

> The object of the League of Nations is to prevent war. It is not to compel social recognition of equality, -especially if such equality does not exist, -nor is it to compel association by all classes and grades of civilization on the face of the earth. (Foreign Office 1919c: np)

They used the exclusion of Japanese children from schools in the state of California to explain their case:

> lines exist, and no doubt necessarily exist, and if so, they must be drawn, and nowhere more faithfully than in regard to our *young children in our public schools*. If our children, or Australian children, are better trained in their habits and ways – if more moral – it cannot be expected that we or the Australians, will for one moment tolerate the proposition that they be exposed to contaminating influences ... social equality, if not really equal in character, training, behaviours, morals or propriety, they cannot expect, nor should they have. Only association will be denied them until they have become sufficiently trained at home to behave properly. This is an evil to be eradicated by *training*, not by association which would *not train them*, but *only contaminate others*. (Foreign Office 1919c: np, *emphasis in original*)

They continue that America has no grudge or prejudice against Japan and, invoking the idea of civilisation through Western tutelage, write that in the future, 'whatever association we are according the other nations of the earth, we will gladly, when she is fitted for it, accord her'. Until then 'she must not be permitted to deteriorate our own. It is not for her interest, or the interest of the world that she do'. Invoking the threat to their nation's (white) children, the officials 'trust that nothing will induce you to insert any provision which will not have our citizens free to protect their young and susceptible children from contamination from any source. They will not stand for it' (Foreign Office 1919c).

The Australians had similar fears. Writing of the 'white Australia' policy in 1929, Billy Hughes said,

> The idea of a 'white Australia', and one peopled in the main by men and women of British stock, reflects the traditions and achievements of our race. Racial purity pays in the long run ... we cannot assimilate these coloured peoples; their ways are not ours ... we cannot marry their women nor they ours without producing a race of half-castes at which both races would spit contempt. (Hughes 1929: 366)

Such impossibilities of integration overlapped with other fears of racial competition and the possibility of 'race war' internationally. Just after the conference Britain decided to build an imperial base at Singapore irrespective of the renewal of the Japanese alliance. The justification was the likely possibility of 'race war':

> The most likely war was between the white and yellow races. It was no longer possible to rely upon a treaty about to be terminated at far shorter notice than the period for providing adequate defences ... It would be disastrous to the prestige of Great Britain if she were to abandon the Pacific by neglecting to take steps necessary to permit of the Fleet operating there. (Cabinet Office 1912–1923)

Reflecting in 1921 on the race equality proposal, a senior Foreign Office official predicted that there was 'no cure' for the matter. He wrote that the racial equality question primarily concerned Japan, China, British India, the United States, Canada, Australia, New Zealand and South Africa. 'The first three countries demand the right of free immigration and freedom from discriminatory disabilities for their nationals in the territories of the last five countries' (Cabinet Office 1912–1923: np). While 'the question can be regarded from an economic or from a political point of view ... in its essence it is a racial one'. The bottom line was that

> The white and the coloured races cannot and will not amalgamated. One or the other must be the ruling caste; and countries where the white population is in power have determined from a sure instinct for self-preservation that they will never open their doors to the influx of the coloured race, which might eventually become dominant. In this policy the United States of America, taught by the Negro trouble (and especially California, where the Asiatics are most numerous) have taken the lead, and have been closely followed by the British Dominions of Canada, Australia New Zealand, and South Africa. In varying forms and degrees all the countries have excluded and will exclude Oriental immigration.
>   On the other side, only one of the aggrieved coloured races has acquired sufficient material strength to demand a hearing, and that is Japan ... Japan is the only non-white first-class Power. In every respect, except the racial one, Japan

stands on a par with the great governing nations of the world. But, however powerful Japan may eventually become, the white races will never be able to admit her equality. If she can enforce her claim she will become our superior; if she cannot enforce it she remains our inferior; but equal she can never be. There is, therefore at present in practical politics no solution to the racial question. (Foreign Office 1921)

Reading these words makes success for the Japanese proposal appear almost impossible. The worldview of the British Empire delegation was one in which, commensurate with the racial hierarchies outlined earlier, white peoples were superior to others. While Japan had been promoted to the status of great power, asking for freedom from racial discrimination was a step too far. The Japanese may be above the black Africans, but there remained a hierarchy and Japan should know her place. Furthermore, what of the wider implications in the Empire and the global balance of power if such a clause were included?

This discussion has provided a case study of 'race' hierarchy in action at the world political level. It has also demonstrated the strength of coloniality/modernity as the dominant epistemic framing of international politics ninety years after the abolition of slavery. The next and final section addresses the links between ideas of racial hierarchy and the case discussed in this section in more detail, bringing in subsequent histories of differential humanity through uneven access to the right to asylum.

'Race' Hierarchies in Action

This second critical juncture, the case of the race equality proposal at the 1919 Paris Peace Conference, has again been analysed in terms of two competing institutional orders: the colonial and the transformative. In contextualising the critical juncture, the first part of this chapter concerned the popularisation of ideas of racial hierarchy in the nineteenth century. While this agenda was lent legitimacy by scientists, such ideas had their origins in colonial ways of viewing the world and the various people in it. As a political project in a Christian society increasingly influenced by the new rationalism of science, 'race' hierarchy in its various guises provided justification for colonialism. The role of this chapter, then, has been to demonstrate the ways in which these ideas influenced international relations in the twentieth century.

Japan was invited to the 1919 Paris Peace Conference as one of five 'great powers'. The Japanese delegation proposed for the first time on the international stage that racially based inequality be legally abolished. As the only non-Western 'power' at the conference, the Japanese had long faced discrimination in international politics, but also in travelling and migrating to Britain and the British white settler colonies. The Japanese delegation therefore led the transformative institutional order. Their proposal was rejected by the British Empire delegation and the wider colonial institutional order. This resistance can be understood clearly within the rubric of racial hierarchy. The analysis shows how, despite being designated a 'great power' on the basis of its military strength and rising economic power, the Japanese were nevertheless seen by the British Empire delegation as an inferior 'race'. Using language which echoed the racial scientists discussed in the first section, politicians legitimised their rejection of the race equality proposal on the basis that the Japanese were not their equals and should not be treated equally as migrants to any white majority society. Their morality was called into question, and their demands for equality received as pretentions.

The kinds of views expressed in the Foreign Office handbook on Japan for the conference particularly encapsulate the view that though aspiring to be like modern Western states, Japan was still below the British (including those living in the Dominions, excluding India) in a global civilisational hierarchy. When the work of modernising (Westernising) would be sufficiently complete was unclear as all developments were dismissed as stealing the spoils of progress which took Europe hundreds of years to achieve. This is where the discourse of modernity meets that of 'race'. The British delegation saw their affinity with each other (metropole and Dominion) and the United States as one based on ties of blood and 'race' which were as immutable as the inherent difference ascribed to the Japanese. Whatever Japan achieved, their claim to modernity would always be problematic.

This chapter has built on the previous one which looked at slavery and ideas of humanity, showing again that such ideas are not new, that they did not spring into being in the late twentieth century. The institutional orders have again been labelled as 'colonial' and 'transformative'. Though clearly not including the same actors, many of the ideas seen within the institutional orders in the abolition period can be observed at this juncture. Yet there was also transformation in the time elapsing between the two. While in the early 1800s the controversy was around the humanity of black bodies, in 1919 it was around the hierarchical ordering of bodies all considered human. Again, the transformative order was more dispersed and less powerful, but just as in the case of the abolitionists, there was a core of more powerful actors (abolitionists in Parliament in the early 1800s, the Japanese delegation in 1919) who were able to set the agenda, if not determine the outcome.

Racial hierarchies and their articulation in 1919 are important in the story of the history of asylum. That such ideas held sway in matters of international significance at that time not only reveals their enduring appeal into the twentieth century as historically interesting but outmoded ways of understanding the world; it will also be seen in the next chapter that thirty years later, at the birth of the human rights regime, such ideas continued to resonate. Indeed, the existence of exclusionary asylum policies at the present time, when there is no evidence to suggest that asylum seekers are less persecuted than before, suggests that the logical human hierarchy, in which some people are granted better access to human rights than others, continues to resonate with legislators. In pursuing restrictive and punitive asylum policies, the British government indicates, in this analysis, that certain levels of discrimination are more tolerable if they happen to people from certain places.

This critical juncture therefore leads us further along the path from past to present. It demonstrates the enduring resonance of ideas of human hierarchy and how they might be operationalised by international institutional orders in resisting transformative change. However, as the previous chapter on the abolition of slavery and the forthcoming chapter on the Geneva Convention show, even when change occurs, the transformation is rarely complete. While in 1919 the colonial order was successful in resisting calls for equality, at other moments in history a transformative egalitarian agenda has overridden the dominant conceptions of racial superiority amongst powerful actors in powerful states. What this case epitomises, then, is the salience of those dominant prejudices when mobilised by powerful actors. The League of Nations was an alliance formed, like its successor, the UN, to preserve world peace. Its members were those same states that later founded the UN, both times forming an alliance following a world war centred in Europe, and both times seeking a way of balancing the prerogatives of world peace with systematic inequality maintained through colonial apartheid. But the question of course is 'peace for whom?', just as the question in the next chapter will be 'rights for whom?' It is the exclusion of some, on the basis of old ideas of human hierarchy, which endures through time despite the creeping forward of progressive transformative change.

NOTES

1. According to Chaudhary and Chaudhary, the term 'great power' was first used in 1815 by a British statesman and is European in origin, later being sporadically applied to states outside of Europe. The term refers to a state 'that has the ability to exert great influence on a global scale. Great powers characteristically possess economic, diplomatic, military, and cultural strength, which may cause other smaller nations to consider the opinions of great powers before taking actions of their own' (p. 98). 'Great power' status appears to be granted by influential states in a tacit understanding

of international politics at key moments of internationally important decision making. Japan was included in 1919 because of her recent victory over Russia, her growing empire and political influence in Asia and rising economic strength. Chaudhary, M.A. and G. Chaudhary (2009). *Global Encyclopaedia of Political Geography*. New Dehli, Global Vision Publishing House.

2. In addition to the great powers these were the following: Belgium, Brazil, Republic of China, Cuba, Czechoslovakia, Greece, Guatemala, Haiti, Hejaz, Honduras, Liberia, Nicaragua, Panama, Poland, Portugal, Romania, Siam and Yugoslavia.

3. US-based organisation: 'National Association for the Advancement of Colored People'.

Chapter Six

The United Nations and the Right to Be Human

Colonially derived conceptions of human hierarchy are important, but under-recognised, factors in accounting for the current asylum regime in Britain. As outlined in previous chapters, my analysis in this book focuses on three key moments – critical junctures – at the political institutional level. While the previous two chapters have provided historical context for the development and deployment of ideas of human hierarchy, this chapter is concerned with the institutionalisation of human rights, which includes the right to asylum, in the middle of the twentieth century. The right to asylum is enshrined in international law – in the Geneva Convention – and is the primary basis upon which asylum seekers make their claims to Western host states today. Since 1967 it has applied, at least in theory, to all human beings. As a key text of the human rights framework, the Geneva Convention has come to be associated with the very idea of the universalised rights-bearing human being. However, despite the rhetoric of universalism, this was not from its inception a right to which all human beings had access. The world in 1951 was still a colonial world, and consequently many people were excluded from the new human rights conventions.

The human rights agenda was pursued both within European institutions and at the United Nations (UN) with the primary objective of putting in place safeguards against a repeat of the atrocities committed in Nazi Germany, as well as the resulting population displacements. My focus here is on the 1951 UN Geneva Convention on the Status of Refugees, one part of the international legal framework for human rights. This convention defines refugeehood; it proscribes the parameters of 'persecution' in law and as such provides the right to asylum.

Much scholarship on the founding of the right to asylum focuses primarily on the political landscape of Europe in the middle of the twentieth century and on European refugees as *the* refugees of the period. However, the period in question was also one of the dismantling of colonialism and a profound reshaping of the world order which involved mass displacements *outside* of Europe. Colonialism and decolonisation, as epistemic as well as empirical phenomena, are largely missing from work in this area. This omission is problematic because it allows for an analysis of the negation of duties to asylum seekers on behalf of states such as Britain, in the late twentieth century, as explicable on the basis of the sudden arrival in the world of non-European asylum seekers. Connected colonial histories, in this analysis, are obscured, as are historical attempts to systematically exclude large portions of the world's population from rights and justice. The themes addressed in chapters 4 and 5 are of course of vital relevance here. By using this founding moment of contemporary asylum rights as a case study, I am able to consider the entanglement of colonialism and decolonisation with the institutionalisation of asylum policy and thus call for a reconsideration of the bases for critical analysis. In other words, if colonially derived conceptions of differential humanity are vital in understanding the history of the right to asylum, contemporary critique of exclusionary and punitive asylum policies must also include some consideration of these histories.

It is important to highlight this history in the genealogy of asylum because consideration of such issues facilitates a rereading of the present. This rereading sees measures to deny rights to non-European asylum seekers in recent years as entirely unsurprising. In fact, the curtailment of asylum seeker's rights, in this view, is consistent with the types of unequal treatment traced through this study and with the history of coloniality/modernity. That the human rights conventions represented a transformative moment in the history of human society should not distract from the exclusions present at their founding. Indeed, nor should it distract from those exclusions which continue today.

The chapter begins with an overview of the 1951 Geneva Convention on the Status of Refugees, including how this convention fits into the broader human rights framework. Following this is an analysis of the institutional orders within Britain seeking to influence the convention text. Two key orders are identified, again labelled the 'colonial' and the 'transformative'. Having discussed both, including their membership and the discourses employed, the concluding section addresses the legacies of colonial epistemologies in the post-war asylum rights regime.

THE 1951 GENEVA CONVENTION ON THE STATUS OF REFUGEES: SILENCES IN HUMAN RIGHTS

What has now come to be known as the International Bill of Human Rights consists of the Universal Declaration of Human Rights, the International

Covenant on Economic, Social and Cultural Rights and the International Covenant on Civil and Political Rights, plus its two Optional Protocols. The Universal Declaration of Human Rights (UDHR) was, in 1948, the first international articulation of rights *to which all human beings are entitled*. It consists of thirty articles which have been elaborated in subsequent international treaties and laws. Article 14 of the UDHR states that 'everyone has the right to seek and to enjoy in other countries asylum from persecution' (United Nations General Assembly 1948). This was the first international document to recognise the universal right to seek and enjoy asylum from persecution. The right to asylum was then bolstered by the 1951 Convention on the Status of Refugees, which was the first in a succession of legal instruments enshrining the rights of particular groups in international law.* The Geneva Convention on the Status of Refugees was agreed at a special UN conference on 25 July 1951 following three years of discussion. The right to asylum is therefore a human right, and the convention specifically dealing with this topic was being negotiated at the same time as the broader human rights declaration (Hathaway 1990).

The first international legal standards for protecting asylum seekers and refugees emerged in Europe in the period following the First World War, but it is the mid-century UN Convention that has endured and been taken up by countries on every continent. Largely unaltered in sixty years, the Geneva Convention remains the primary basis upon which asylum seekers make their claims to the British state today. Negotiations around the Refugee Convention, specifically around the refugee definition and the territorial applicability of the Refugee Convention, heavily drew upon the UDHR, as well as the already existing rules governing the European-focused International Refugee Organisation (IRO). It is therefore necessary to analyse the Refugee Convention with reference to these broader discussions.

The human rights framework was based on the idea that some legal constraints on a (non-colonised) state's sovereignty might be necessary in order to prevent a repeat of the atrocities committed in Nazi Germany. Refugee rights were prominent in this agenda. This would involve the setting up of a comprehensive system in international law for the purpose of protecting future refugees in the image of those fleeing the Nazis. The Geneva Convention on the Status of Refugees was thus agreed at a UN conference on 25 July 1951

---

* Subsequent conventions: Convention on the Elimination of All Forms of Racial Discrimination (adopted 1966, entry into force 1969), the Convention on the Elimination of All Forms of Discrimination Against Women (adopted 1979, entry into force: 1981), the Convention Against Torture (adopted 1984, entry into force: 1984), the Convention on the Rights of the Child (adopted 1989, entry into force: 1989), the Convention on the Rights of Persons with Disabilities (adopted 2006, entry into force: 2008), and the International Convention on the Protection of the Rights of All Migrant Workers and Members of their Families (adopted 1990, entry into force: 2003).

following three years of discussion. It was ratified in 1954, amended with a new protocol in 1967 (which expanded its scope to all refugees, not just those fleeing Europe) and today has 145 signatories.

The 1951 Convention allowed for the IRO, set up to deal with refugees of the Second World War, to be replaced by the United Nations High Commissioner for Refugees (UNHCR). It describes the parameters of 'persecution', the rights to which asylum seekers are entitled and the duties which states have in relation to them. As noted in the introduction, a refugee is defined as someone fleeing their country of origin:

> owing to well-founded fear of being persecuted for reasons of race, religion, nationality, membership of a particular social group or political opinion, is outside the country of his nationality and is unable or, owing to such fear, is unwilling to avail himself of the protection of that country; or who, not having a nationality and being outside the country of his former habitual residence as a result of such events, is unable or, owing to such fear, is unwilling to return to it. (United Nations, 28 July 1951)

Since its inception, the 1951 Convention has been celebrated by NGOs advocating for refugee rights, international organisations and academics as a pivotal progressive moment in extending rights to displaced people (Feller 2001; Obokata and O'Connell 2010). In the academic literature there has, of course, been much criticism relating to the parameters of the refugee definition (Foster 2007; Kalin 1991; Keely 2001). Nevertheless, there is a tendency to focus on recent deviations from convention obligations by wealthy nations as lying at the core of 'Western' asylum problems, as opposed to longer term exclusions of particular people from full *de facto* humanity and the rights associated with it. Related to this focus on recent policy change is the fact that asylum seekers in the middle of the twentieth century are often represented as European, while contemporary asylum seekers are non-European. In short, the policy has changed because the asylum seekers have changed. These issues were discussed in chapter 2.

The next section entails an institutional orders analysis of the negotiations surrounding the Geneva Convention on the Status of Refugees and the human rights framework of which it was a part.

Britain and the 1951 Convention: An Institutional Orders Analysis

In this critical juncture two key institutional orders are identified: the colonial order and the transformative order. Though operating in different contexts to the orders identified in previous chapters, continuities can nevertheless be observed. For example, the language of colonialism and anti-colonialism present here was also found at the 1919 Paris Peace Conference. Furthermore, invocations of the ties of blood and a belief in the immutability of racial difference is again seen here. The data used comes from the British National Archives and the United Nations Archives, as well as secondary sources, with the analysis focusing on those seeking to influence the outcome of the human, and specifically asylum, rights agenda. My interest is particularly in efforts by the British government to restrict access to rights on the basis of colonial status and resistance to this from others.

The Colonial Order and Human Rights

Table 6.1 identifies individuals and organisations categorised for the purposes of this analysis as the 'colonial institutional order'. In the mid-twentieth century Britain was led by a Labour government (1945–51) and a Conservative government (1951–55). Though these two political parties had very different national agendas, the majority of cabinet ministers of both governments were deeply embedded in the activities of the Empire both politically and economically, and they were also wedded to ideologies which justified such

Table 6.1. The Colonial Order

Level	Who?	How?
Official delegation	Government: Cabinet UK Representatives at the United Nations (UN) Civil Service Foreign Office Colonial Office Commonwealth Relations Office Home Office	Deliberation in Cabinet meetings, ultimate decision making on behalf of the British state. Representing the position of the government in UN negotiations. Research, report writing, briefings to the Cabinet. Cross-departmental working group on human rights.
Colonial actors a.	Political figures of the Empire (e.g. Jan Smuts) Other colonial powers	Speeches to the UN, involvement in negotiations and convention drafting. Allies in UN discussions, mutually supporting the position of those countries who held dominion over colonised territories.
Colonial actors b.	Colonial administrators	Feeding opinions back to the metropole through letters and reports.

activities (Saville 1993; Toye 2010). The colonial order was made up of the powerful and, as such, had a decisive role to play in determining the official British response to calls for a legal framework for human rights. Members of this order were against the institutionalisation of human rights, particularly if it affected activities in the Empire. They were also against immigration of 'coloured' populations from the colonies, while in favour of supporting 'deserving' refugees from Europe.

Jan Smuts, noted at level 2 in table 6.1, is an individual worthy of discussion. This is in part because he had a high-profile role in both the British Empire and the League of Nations, which provides a useful introductory illustration of the entanglement of human rights with the Empire, and in part because his views on 'race' are indicative of establishment thinking at the time. South African Prime Minister (1919–1924 and 1939–1948), architect of white settler nationalism and advocate of racial segregation, Jan Smuts was deeply embedded in the milieu of British institutional politics (see Smuts 1944). Churchill described him as 'a warrior-statesman and philosopher who was more fitted to guide struggling humanity through its sufferings and perils towards a better day than anyone' (cited in Gilbert 1988: 434). He was a member of the British Imperial War Cabinet during the First World War, the creator of the British Royal Air Force and the first Dominion Prime Minister to be allowed to speak to the two Houses of the British Parliament. Mazower (2009: 30) describes him as 'above all a figure of Empire – of the British Empire at the very height of its global power'. He goes on: 'Smuts was a leading member of the generation that followed [nineteenth-century colonialism], who sought to prolong the life of an Empire of white rule through international cooperation' (Mazower 2009: 30).

Delivering the Rhodes Memorial Lectures at Oxford University in 1929, Smuts said of 'the black African':

> It has largely remained a child type, with a child psychology and outlook. A child-like human cannot be a bad human ... the African easily forgets past troubles and does not anticipate future troubles. This happy-go-lucky disposition is a great asset, but it also has its drawbacks. There is no inward incentive to improvement. (Smuts 1944: 39)

For Smuts, evidence could be found for these assertions in the fact that black Africans (according to him) had no religion, no art and no architecture. Note the use of the pronoun 'it'. Smuts' ideas were founded upon ideas of racial hierarchy, and white supremacy particularly.

Despite being remembered (at least by some) as a racist, in his lifetime Smuts 'enjoyed a positive world reputation as a liberal visionary and fair minded statesman' (Scheub 1996: 12). He conceived the idea of the League of

Nations, putting it first to the British Cabinet before convincing US President Woodrow Wilson to champion the project. In 1945 he wrote the Preamble for the UN Charter, delivering it to widespread political acclaim at a conference in San Francisco. The preamble has been described as the most influential text in international relations (Marshall 2001). It outlines a commitment to 'reaffirm faith in fundamental human rights, in the dignity and worth of the human person, in the equal rights of men and women and of nations large and small', as well as to promote justice and freedom (United Nations 1985). Yet the author of the charter was not advocating global equality and respect of fundamental rights. The central contradiction within this and the other key documents in the early life of the UN is that neither Jan Smuts nor the key powers in the UN argued that colonialism involved any violation of fundamental rights. Smuts provides an example of the acceptability of colonial thinking on the world stage in the middle of the twentieth century. This frames the discussion below of attitudes among the colonial powers regarding the applicability of human rights to non-self-governing territories.

Discussions within the British state on human rights in the late 1940s primarily took place within the Foreign Office. A number of young civil servants in the Foreign Office became enthused about the idea of human rights and drove the issue forward in spite of scepticism from their seniors (Simpson 2004). Indeed, Simpson (2004: 544) suggests that the Foreign Office sought to keep the Cabinet away from the issue as much as possible:

> So far as the Cabinet was concerned the last thing Foreign Office officials wanted was for it to become involved in the details of foreign policy, about which most of its members knew virtually nothing. Where other departments were concerned and there was controversy the preference was always for not using the cabinet as arbitrator.

The Foreign Office and Cabinet Office jointly led an interdepartmental working party of officials which included the Home Office and the Colonial Office (Cabinet Office 1947). Set up in 1946, the lead taken by the Foreign Office indicates that human rights was considered an issue of foreign relations, but also that there was an awareness that it could affect a range of departments on the home, colonial and foreign fronts. The main concern of the Colonial Office lay in the danger posed by the UN, and particularly its human rights agenda, for British colonial interests (Colonial Office 1952).

The working party, an offshoot of the Steering Committee on International Organisations, worked diligently in 1946 and 1947, eventually producing a proposed draft Bill of International Human Rights for the assistance of the Drafting Committee at the UN (Cabinet Office 1947). Such preparations allowed the UK representative the upper hand at the UN meeting, as few other delegations had worked so hard on the issue, and requests for assistance had not been issued. However, there were a number of issues which remained unresolved throughout the life of the working party. One which consumed a significant amount of time and cross-departmental consultation was concern about the connection between the International Labour Organisation Convention on Forced Labour and the human rights document, and particularly the applicability of enforced labour provisions in the colonies. For example, in a meeting of the working party on 9 June 1947, Mr. Grossmith stated that 'The convention provided that forced labour be abolished in the shortest possible time, but at the present stage it would be impossible to develop certain of the colonial territories unless some degree of forced labour were imposed' (Colonial Office 1952: np).

The working group appears to have faded in the late 1940s, but there must have been some residue of enthusiasm, particularly in the Foreign Office, as in a 1951 correspondence with the Colonial Office, a Foreign Office civil servant warned of the danger that 'it is becoming difficult to maintain that questions of human rights are purely domestic ... I have the impression from what is said and written in relation to human rights by the representatives of other Departments that some of them do not recognise that' (Colonial Office 1952).

In addition, despite putting off going to the Cabinet with specific advice for as long as possible, the cross-departmental group of civil servants could not ignore the ultimate power of their ministerial overlords. The Cabinet appears to have been the primary context in which ministers discussed the convention. Their discussions imply both much less knowledge of the details of the convention and the drafting process than the working party and much less enthusiasm for it.

Table 6.2 shows the discourses present in the practice of government in relation to the response to the human and refugee rights framework. For the remainder of this section I will elaborate on the discourses identified in the table above, developing three key points:

1. British ministers were initially uninterested, then hostile to any human rights conventions which might place demands on the British state.
2. The British government was especially reluctant to sign the conventions if they applied to people in the colonies.
3. The British state, alongside other European states and the United States, was prepared to aid non-European refugees located in other parts of the world, but not to include them under the rubric of the Refugee Convention.

First, British ministers were initially uninterested, then hostile to any human rights conventions which might place demands on the British state. For imperial institutionalists, the UN 'was to be a device for cushioning the British

Table 6.2. Colonial Order Discourses

Discourse	General Focus/Argument	Use for the Colonial Order	Key Interpretations (by all or some of the alliance)
1. (British tradition of) law and justice – Sovereignty over	Supreme system, must maintain sovereignty over.	Justifies objections to international law.	Undesirable to lose sovereignty to an international body.
2. (British tradition of) rights, liberties and protection of refugees	Rooted in tacit understanding, not necessary to enshrine in international law – must maintain sovereignty over.	Justifies objections to international law, particularly foreign conceptions of rights. Justifies selective refugee assistance.	Undesirable to lose sovereignty to an international body, particularly if undermines colonial activities, rooted in tacit understanding of 'right'.
3. Human hierarchy (white supremacy)	Human beings can be organised into distinct 'races' which are hierarchically organised.	Justifies exceptionalism in rights while supporting commitment to certain categories of refugees and immigrants.	All human beings not equal, therefore all should not have equal access to human rights. Some must be tutored first.
4. Civilisation	Human beings can be organised into distinct 'races', found in various societies, all of whom have varying levels of civilisation. Inequality inherent, duty on the part of the civilised to look after the uncivilised (the white man's burden).	In-here/out-there binary justifies exceptionalism.	As above.

Empire, cementing its ties with the United States, and coming to terms with the unfortunate but tolerable fact that the Soviet Union had become a world power' (Mazower 2009: 104). When proposals came along which placed demands inconsistent with the activities of the Empire, therefore, they were not well received (Colonial Office 1952). The Cabinet Secretary's notebooks from the period show that there were long discussions between senior British ministers regarding their reluctance to be bound by the human rights convention, but equal reluctance to be seen as against it. There was a belief that the British had an innate understanding of rights, liberties and justice, and that this was so intrinsic to the national character that it was not necessary to codify it in law. If there were exceptions to the rule (in the colonies, for example), they were always for the good of people who were not yet able to look after themselves. In the UK submission to the UN yearbook on human rights in 1946, where each member country reported on their perspective on human rights and the situation in their country, Sir Cecil Carr concluded,

> Although human rights in Britain do not rest upon a written constitution, this brief survey will have shown that what Lord Wright described as 'the good sense of the people' and 'the representative and responsible government which has been evolved here' have produced a society in which the fundamental human liberties are respected and protected to the full. (Carr 1946: 321)

There was concern that a legally binding human rights convention would put in place a body of law above the sovereign British legislature and over the judicial review functions of the House of Lords. This provided a legally inflected nationalistic justification for objecting to inconvenient international legal constraints. According to Simpson (2004: 18), another objection 'was a vague notion that bills of rights were evil simply because they were foreign'. These suspicions, however, did not develop into solid opposition for two years, primarily because many senior British ministers did not take human rights particularly seriously.

Indicative of this view are the diaries of Sir Alexander Cadogan, Britain's Permanent Representative to the United Nations. The General Assembly debated the Universal Declaration of Human Rights over a number of months in 1948, and on 10 December a final draft was adopted. Writing on the subject, Simpson (2004: 40) notes, 'in the history of the subject this has come to rank as an event of major significance, commemorated annually throughout the world as Human Rights Day. One might expect to find, in Cadogan's diary, some hint of excitement, or pleasure, or even mild interest. But no'. On 8 December Cadogan wrote,

> I then went on to the Plenary for a bit, and came out, ostentatiously, in the middle of the long harangue by Vyshinsky. Ian went off to the American Hospital to have a boil cut out of his neck. Went with Theodosia to a concert at which Kempff played the piano divinely. He got and gave a number of encores, and we got home rather late. The Plenary was sitting, also the first committee, but I think it was high time to play truant, and I ignored them.

On Friday, 10 December, the date of the final signing of the Declaration, he wrote,

I ignored the Assembly and all its works.

And on 11 December,

> Still no Council, and I have finished with that foul Assembly. (cited in Simpson 2004: 41)

The Universal Declaration is never mentioned. The working party on human rights had briefed Cadogan on human rights extensively (Cabinet Office 1947) and he had apparently taken a lead in the earlier discussions at the UN, as previously noted.

There was pressure on the government from within (primarily the Foreign Office) to support a European Convention on Human Rights within the context of Cold War politics. Thus, in a memorandum to the Cabinet marked 'secret', a civil servant wrote in October 1949 that

> The Council of Europe is an important element in the structure which we have been building in Europe with the object of creating a feeling of confidence and unity amongst the Western nations ... it is one of the major weapons in the cold war. Whatever, therefore, may be our opinions as to the ultimate relationship between this country and the Continent, or between the continental nations, we should do nothing now to undermine the general hopes of solidarity and co-operation which the Council of Europe has aroused. (Bevin, 24 October 1949: 3)

Despite such guidance, the Cabinet remained sceptical. Cleavages between 'administering authorities' (those with colonies) and 'non-administering authorities' (those without) in the UN General Assembly and Trusteeship Council were reported to the Cabinet (Jones 1949). For example, Creech Jones described attacks from non-administering authorities as filled with 'prejudice and ignorance ... superficial, largely platitudinous' on the occasion of the Third General Assembly in 1949 (Jones 1949: 1). A Cabinet Secretary's notebook shows the following exchange in a Cabinet meeting discussion of the European Convention on Human Rights in August 1950:

> **P.M.**[*] All the Greeks etc will vote for it, even tho' they won't carry it out. We shall look v. foolish if we vote against it.
>
> **Att.G.**[†] Policy of workg. for a Convention has gone on too long to reverse it now.

---

[*] Prime Minister Attlee.

[†] Attorney General Hartley William Shawcross. He was the lead British prosecutor at the Nuremberg war crimes tribunal.

J.* No pol. advantage. For Russians and others won't pay the slightest attention to Convention and we shall feel obliged to.

J.G.† Political diffy. is tht. we shall have to oppose it in public in Assembly.
Hope therefore we may take opportunity of seeking amendments in the Council of Ministers, in private. Esp. Art. 23.‡
Parallel Convention under disc'n in U.N. That restricts right of petition to States. If this is carried in C/Europe same principle may be inserted in U.N. draft.
Urge therefore omission of Art. 23 or at least its modification.

K.Y.§ But can we go back on genl. policy of support for a Convention.

H.McN.¶ Only hope is to try to reduce it to a declaration. Or kill it by a 1,000 cuts at particular provisions.

Att.G. There's bn. a declaration already. Too late for that line.
We have agreed to go ahead with Convent'n.
If we oppose it now we shall be alone with the Greeks.
Best line wd. be to stall on this, on drafting grounds.

K.Y. Cab. shd. realise that it will be seen, at Assembly stage, tht. we have made volte face.**

When it came to declaring a public position, the British government determined to be in favour of a European Human Rights Convention since, as the Foreign Office had pointed out, it would bring closer ties to Europe within the context of the Cold War. In this they had supporters. Speaking as Vice President of the Parliamentary Assembly of the Council of Europe, Walter Layton spoke in the House of Lords in 1950 of how

> quick progress needs to be made with the Convention on Human Rights drafted by the Strasbourg Assembly. That draft would establish a joint responsibility for the maintenance of a limited number of rights, but including the cardinal political rights of free Parliaments, with the right to form an Opposition, free speech and freedom from arbitrary arrest ... It is most desirable that they should be established. (House of Lords, 8 March 1950)

For the time being the government remained privately against a UN convention, however, as there were no discernible benefits and many dangers.

---

* Lord Jowitt, Chancellor.
† James Griffiths, Secretary of State for the Colonies.
‡ Article 23 related to forced labour.
§ Kenneth Younger, Acting Foreign Secretary, headed the British delegation to the UN General Assembly.
¶ Hector McNeil, Secretary of State for Scotland.
** This is an edited extract.

This was despite apparent enthusiasm from some in the Foreign Office, who were leading the working party (Cabinet Office 1947). However, one of the central dangers for both the Cabinet and Colonial Offices lay in the colonial question. Simply put (the second key point in this section), those in British government were reluctant to sign the conventions if they applied to people in the colonies. As early as 1947 the problems raised by colonial activities within the context of a proposed International Bill of Human Rights were causing concern. The Cabinet Secretary's notebook entry for 30 October that year records David Rees-Williams, Undersecretary of State for the Colonies, as saying: 'In formula, don't use phrase "Col. Territories". There are 8 areas where comp. Labour in force. Words "exceptional cond'ns ..." will cover our case' (Brook 1947: np).

At this point, government ministers do not, from the records, appear to be *too* concerned about the bill. There was an assumption that they could insert their 'exceptional conditions' clause without too many problems. Such a clause would exclude certain groups from rights claims with the justification that 'exceptional conditions' necessitated such action. Those groups to be excluded were colonial subjects. In a memo to the Cabinet from the Foreign Office in 1949, it was recommended that the Foreign Secretary should accept in principle that a convention should be drawn up but that he 'should, if possible, refrain at the present stage from taking up a position on the application of the convention to colonial territories' (Brook 1949: np). The Foreign Secretary duly refrained in public, but by January 1951 the issue was looking more problematic, as this conversation from the Cabinet Secretary's notebooks (Brook 1951: np) shows:

J.G. Want it clear tht. Protocols may be accepted separately in Col. Territories. Cd. Not apply 7 at once in Colonies.

J. Second Protocol '... so far as resources permit.' Who is to judge? Can Comm'n rule our resources allow of our doing more for education in a Colony?

H.M.[*] I have always bn. against this Convention – all of it. Humbug.

A.[†] Prefer a frontal attack of this nonsense. Don't express any sympathy.

Att.G. Not merely Layton. Some Tories & Labour supporters keenly favour it.

P.M. 3rd Protocol: restrict to home territories.[‡]

---

[*] Herbert Morrison, who succeeded Ernest Bevin as Secretary of State for Foreign Affairs two months later.
[†] Viscount Addison, leader of the House of Lords and Lord Privy Seal.
[‡] This is an edited extract.

In April 1951 the Cabinet discussion continues with increasing anxiety (Brook 1951: np):

H.M. I don't know anything about this – except that we are in a mess. Started as anti-Soviet propaganda. As it goes on, it looks as tho' it will put us on the spot – especially re. Colonies.

J.G. Col. Appl'n clause is out now, by U.N. vote. We couldn't apply this Covenant in the Colonies. Tho' politically dangerous for us to w'draw. If we stay in, we mght. guide disc'n usefully.

J. Stay in and make difficulties. V. difficult for us to walk out.

G.W.[*] As it stands, w'out Col. Appl'n clause, it is unacceptable to us. We should realise that.[†]

This extract clearly shows Cabinet ministers stating that their support for human rights as an instrument of anti-Soviet propaganda has been directly challenged by the realisation that it could curtail British colonial activities. Without the 'colonial application clause' – a clause in the convention which would allow administering authorities to decide in which of their colonies human rights should be applied – the convention would be 'unacceptable'. Such a clause would of course allow Britain to *exclude* many colonised peoples from accessing international human rights, including the right to asylum. Yet this issue presented a dilemma to the British Cabinet: if they withdrew, then they would lose any ability to guide the convention in ways which would be advantageous to their country, at the same time as *looking* bad in relation to the Soviets, whom they had planned to accuse of human rights abuses.

In March the following year, the discussion appears as follows (Brook 1952: np):

S.Ll.[‡] [Human rights] Designed to embarrass Russians, has ended up by embarrassing us and U.S. much more because of coloured popul'ns. One Covenant signed. This one will surely emerge in a form wh. we can't ratify. We must go on with the knowledge that we will never ratify.

O.L.[§] Can't ratify anything wh. involves enforcement.

M-F.[**] We cdn't reverse engines on enforcemt.

O.L. V. well. Let's pursue policy of steady obstruction by legal quibbles.

---

[*] Patrick Gordon-Walker, Secretary of State for Commonwealth Relations.
[†] This is an edited extract.
[‡] John Selwyn-Lloyd, Foreign Secretary.
[§] Oliver Lyttleton, Secretary of State for the Colonies.
[**] David Maxwell-Fyfe, Home Secretary.

This extract conveys a sense of rising concern. The human rights agenda is moving forward and will result in a convention. 'Steady obstruction via legal quibbles' is the only option presented in the meeting, and though John Selwyn-Lloyd suggests that Britain can 'never ratify' a convention of the kind that is emerging from the negotiations, there is a sense here that such a situation is inevitable. The fact that the issue is the colonies, or, in the words of Selwyn-Lloyd, the 'coloured populations', and that this is proving embarrassing, suggests that the administering powers do not feel free to speak in the open forum of the UN in the language of racial hierarchy and civilisation. Yet, at the same time, the behind-the-scenes discussions suggest that such ideas are precisely the rationales upon which colonised peoples were to be excluded from human rights.

The third key point in this section is that that the British state was prepared to aid non-European refugees located in other parts of the world, but not to include them under the rubric of the Refugee Convention. Though the most commonly told story of the history of the right to asylum focuses on the Second World War and its impact in Europe, that does not mean that there were no asylum seekers in other parts of the world in the mid-twentieth century. Refugees (asylum seekers only existed in law post the Geneva Convention) were present outside of Europe in the late 1940s and early 1950s, but the records show that their plight and the burden on their hosts were not recognised as being of immediate concern to the convention.

Arab (Palestinian) and Korean refuges were discussed more in Parliament in 1951 than European refugees (House of Commons, 15 March 1951, 19 March 1951). Yet despite non-European refugee issues being raised on a regular basis in the British Parliament throughout the 1950s, and the country providing significant sums of bilateral aid, my analysis of the Parliamentary debate transcripts found no discussion of extending the UN right to asylum to non-Europeans. In the negotiations on human rights at the UN, the British delegation pushed for a colonial application clause. Such clauses were inserted into treaties so that the British state was under no obligation to apply them in the colonies, as outlined above. Meanwhile, the government publicly argued that non-application was a means of promoting self-determination and democracy in the colonies (Simpson 2004).

The records of the UN Ad Hoc Committee on Refugees and Stateless Persons (17 February 1950) and the UN Conference of Plenipotentiaries on the Status of Refugees and Stateless Persons (27 November 1951, 3 July 1951) show these bodies deferring back to discussions on colonial application covered in the human rights convention discussions. In these discussions, which specifically relate to asylum, Samuel Hoare, the delegate for the United Kingdom emphasized that the question before the Committee was not whether it was right or wrong that a colonial system should still exist in the twentieth Century but merely whether, with such system in existence a colonial clause should be incorporated in the Covenant. The U.K. had never claimed that the peoples of the territories under its administration were sovereign and independent. No one could deny however that those peoples were constantly progressing along the road to self-government and independence ... If the colonial clause were omitted, the participation of colonies in an international convention would become automatic and those territories would thus find themselves deprived of the right to decide for themselves. (UN Conference of Plenipotentiaries on the Status of Refugees and Stateless Persons, 3 July 1951: np)

Those in agreement with the UK delegate were France, Belgium, Greece, Australia, New Zealand and Canada (UN Conference of Plenipotentiaries on the Status of Refugees and Stateless Persons, 3 July 1951: np). These were the major colonial powers and major white settler colonial Dominions. Those against, whose objections are elaborated in the next section, included India, Syria, Ethiopia, Pakistan, Iraq, Saudi Arabia, Indonesia, Lebanon, Mexico, Chile and Afghanistan, amongst others. In other words, disproportionately represented amongst those against a colonial application clause were the delegations representing formerly colonised peoples, despite the British claim that such a clause would facilitate independence (UN Conference of Plenipotentiaries on the Status of Refugees and Stateless Persons, 3 July 1951).

In the Ad Hoc Committee on Refugees and Stateless Persons (17 February 1950: np) the UK delegate again argued strongly for a colonial application clause. The same reasoning was used as in the case of the broader human rights framework, with a nod to the persistent criticism from anti-colonials:

The United Kingdom Government was in much the same position as the French Government and must insist on the inclusion of the clause for constitutional reasons. All its dependent territories were advancing towards a greater degree of self-government, and it was a principle of United Kingdom administration that, whatever the degree of advancement of any territory, it would not be committed to accession to any international instrument without prior consultation to ascertain whether it was ready to accept the obligations entailed and prepared to make any domestic legislative changes required. (UN Conference of Plenipotentiaries on the Status of Refugees and Stateless Persons, 27 November 1951: np)

Here, the public case is being made not in terms of racial inferiority, as was the case thirty years earlier (see chapter 5), but using the rhetoric of respect and independence. The UK representative insisted that 'a colonial clause was not a means of excluding Non-Self-Governing Territories from the application of any international agreement, but the only constitutional method of extending its application to them' (UN Conference of Plenipotentiaries on the Status of Refugees and Stateless Persons, 27 November 1951). To *impose* the right to asylum upon colonised peoples would be disrespectful and colonial, suggesting that a deracialised discourse had now become 'politically correct'. However, this public statement of support for the advancement of non-self-governing territories towards independence is belied by the private discussions outlined earlier in this chapter. This is a rhetorical device designed to secure a colonial application clause in the convention. The representatives of those territories who had recently gained independence were not fooled, as we shall see shortly.

In the human rights negotiations the 'colonial application clause' proposal was defeated by the forceful resistance of anti-colonials. However, the colonial powers were successful in inserting an adequate replacement (from their perspective), a 'territorial application clause' in the Refugee Convention. Here, again, there was much controversy over this clause. However, with threats from the United Kingdom, Belgium and France that they would be very reluctant to sign without such a clause, the article containing the clause was adopted by eighteen votes to one with five abstentions, in the 27th meeting of the Conference of Plenipotentiaries on the Status of Refugees and Stateless Persons (27 November 1951). The record does not show how national delegations voted. However, it may be relevant to note that of the eighteen countries represented that day, ten were colonial powers and two were British Dominions.† Such ratios suggest that the colonial powers were in a strong position to have their proposal adopted.

Article 40, paragraph 1 of the final Refugee Convention document, the territorial application clause, thus stated,

> Any State may, at the time of signature, ratification or accession, declare that this Convention shall extend to all or any of the territories for the international relations of which it is responsible. Such a declaration shall take effect when the Convention enters into force for the State concerned. (UNHCR 1951)

Despite at this time governing significant overseas territories, the United Kingdom chose to extend the convention only to the Channel Islands and the Isle of Man. Later, under pressure from a number of colonies and within the context of growing social movements for decolonisation, the United Kingdom extended the application of the convention. These changes came in 1956, 1957, 1960, 1968 and 1970 (United Nations, 28 July 1951).

---

† Australia, Belgium, Canada, Denmark, Germany, France, Italy, Netherlands, Norway, Sweden and the United Kingdom. Other likely supporters included the United States, Switzerland, Luxembourg and Monaco.

In 1952 China requested at a UN General Assembly meeting that Chinese citizens fleeing communism be considered refugees under the mandate of the UNHCR. Most had sought asylum in British-administered Hong Kong. The British government refused to recognise them lest it encourage further flight from China, a territory which they argued should not be recognised as a state (Davies 2007). In 1957 Jewish people in the colonial territory of Egypt were again not permitted to be considered under the rubric of the 1951 Convention. The extract below (from a letter to the Foreign Office from a Home Office official) demonstrates this:

> We are disposed to agree with the Dutch view that the Convention does not apply in strictness to stateless Jews from Egypt who have been admitted to the United Kingdom ... Our view is that the Convention ought to be interpreted according to the ordinary meaning of words. If we start stretching and straining their meaning so as to take them outside their normal context we shall never be happy about entering in to international agreements of this kind. (Lyon, 24 May 1957)

These examples demonstrate the ways in which British governments were able to follow the logic of colonial exceptionalism, an in-here/out-there distinction based on racial classification and geographies of colonialism. Indeed, that a previous government had been reluctant to *sign* the convention makes this later reluctance to 'start stretching and straining' its meaning within the context of new incidences of persecution and displacement entirely unsurprising.

The Geneva Convention on the Status of Refugees was ratified on 11 March 1954. When in 1956 and 1957 Greece brought proceedings against Britain over Cyprus 'at once there was talk of denouncing it [the Human Rights Convention], or of refusing to co-operate; it was as if ratification and extension to the colonies had all been a horrible mistake, or the consequence of some bizarre fit of absence of mind' (Simpson 2004: 12). Yet the conversations cited above show that this kind of situation had been a consistent concern for the government. A belief in Britain as the birthplace of rights and home of justice may appear incompatible with the imperative to exclude people living under colonial rule from the human rights framework. Yet the in-here/out-there binary justifies such an inconsistency. A distinction must be made: between the rhetorical justification for the Empire from a state keen to promote an image of fairness and justice and the behind-the-scenes acknowledgement of a hierarchical ordering of fundamental rights entitlement, as demonstrated in the extracts above.

The next section is concerned with the transformative order. Those included in this order consistently opposed efforts to exclude colonised peoples from the human rights framework. This contrasting order demonstrates the strength of resistance to exclusionary conceptions of humanity, and in doing so highlights a number of non-European refugee production and reception contexts in the middle of the twentieth century. Thus it will be shown that people became refugees in other parts of the world long before the 1990s.

The Transformative Order and Human Rights

This section details the transformative institutional order involved in the negotiations around human rights in the late 1940s and early 1950s. Before outlining those included in this order, however, a note on the context of the time is necessary. Indeed, the immediate context to the 1951 Convention was not only the situation resulting from Adolf Hitler's leadership of Germany. A further contextual factor was the global explosion of struggles for decolonisation. At the end of the Second World War, running through the convention discussions, the majority of the world's population lived under colonial rule and some were actively contesting the legitimacy of the colonial state. The colonised of the British Empire (as well as those of other empires) fought sometimes violent, sometimes protracted struggles for their right to be viewed as capable of running their own countries (Thomas 2008). The people of some of the first independent states, India and Pakistan, for example, had long been seen by the British as incapable of self-government on the basis of racial inferiority. In 1947, two years after Jan Smuts gave his rousing speech on human rights to the UN, and a century after beginning the struggle, they successfully broke the colonial yoke (Chandra 1989).

Though achieving self-determination would appear to be a significant triumph for the idea of human rights, decolonisation is rarely (if ever) included in narratives of the history of human rights or the context surrounding the emergence of asylum and refugee rights. The displacements resulting from the process of decolonisation are especially notable within the context of this study. As Pierson et al. (1998: 270) point out, 'in this century of the displaced person [the twentieth century], India's partition of 1947 still remains one of the greatest social upheavals' with an estimated ten million people uprooted from their homes. Indeed, there were people making this very point during the UN discussions on the Refugee Convention. Yet these refugees, and those defending them, are rarely characters in academic accounts of the history of refugees and asylum seekers.

This section makes a contribution to the foregrounding of such histories. The focus is the transformative order in 1951 and its response to human and refugee rights. Much like the institutional orders identified in previous chapters, the order challenging the powerful (colonial) order was more dispersed, less centrally organised and less coherent in many ways. Nevertheless, such an order can be identified for the purposes of analysis in that there were individuals and institutions at this time fighting against colonial political, social and economic domination who were highly critical of the human rights framework. Table 6.3 identifies those individuals and institutions included within this order for the purposes of my analysis.

Many people sought to influence the direction of the human rights agenda (including that on refugee rights) in the 1940s. Table 6.3 identifies first those attempting to influence the agenda at the level of the UN. Representatives of the countries listed took an anti-colonial position in the negotiations, but from differing standpoints. India and Pakistan had been British colonies, were now independent and were experiencing population displacements. The Soviet Union consistently attacked the Western European colonial powers, opposing anything that the old powers of Europe proposed or favoured. At the next level are those individuals and organisations that sought to influence the UN talks via their national delegations. Following this are the individual activists and anti-colonial organisations who produced journals, newsletters, letters to the government and more mainstream journalistic output where possible.

Table 6.4 addresses the discourses drawn on by these various members of the anti-colonial order. Discussions regarding the territorial applicability of the Refugee Convention were very much framed within discussions of a colonial application clause in the Human Rights Convention. As previously stated, the old colonial powers, Britain included, were very much in favour of such a clause. In response, many of the objections to the clause came from delegations with experience, currently or in the recent past, of living under colonial rule. These objections were often articulated in terms of anti-colonialism. For example, the representative of Indonesia 'pointed out that if the clause were included the General Assembly would in effect be giving a privileged class of human beings the right to decide arbitrarily how far the rights enjoyed unreservedly by themselves could be granted to less favoured classes' (United Nations, 17 February 1950).

This quote foregrounds the idea of humanity – unequal access to the idea of humanity as articulated in the human rights discourse – using the concept of 'class' and thus echoing the discourse of the racial sciences discussed in chapter 4. The representative of Saudi Arabia

> explained the effects of the colonial situation upon the problem under discussion, so long as the colonies remained indispensable to the economic survival of the metropolitan powers, those powers could not afford to allow the dependent peoples to enjoy the advantages of instruments like the Covenant which would make them conscious of their rights. (United Nations, 17 February 1950: np)

This draws attention to the issue of power, subverting the power relation by pointing out that the economic fortunes of metropolitan powers depended on maintaining colonial subjects in a position of ignorance regarding their potential claim to human rights.

Table 6.3. The Anti-Colonial Order

Level	Who?	How?
1. Within the UN	Within the United Nations (UN), often formerly colonised countries. Notable examples: India Lebanon Mexico Pakistan Soviet Union	Questioning/discussing/challenging the wording of draft conventions during UN General Assembly discussions. Economic and Social Affairs Committee at UN. UN Conference of Plenipotentiaries on Refugees and Stateless Persons.
2. Attempting to influence the UN	British-based individuals and organisations seeking to influence the British position at the UN *From within Parliament:* Nye Bevan Fenner Brockway (Labour Member of Parliament [MP]) Lesley Hale (Labour MP) William Gallacher and Phil Piratin (Communist Party of Great Britain MPs) *From outside of Parliament:* George Padmore The League of Coloured Peoples Ethiopian World Federation Movement for colonial freedom Congress of Peoples Against Imperialism (COPAI) Union of Democratic Control Socialist Fellowship (pressure group) *Other:* US delegation influence: NAACP, notably W.E.B. Du Bois	Anti-colonial speeches in Parliament. Proposing a Human Rights Bill. Arguing for the expansion of the application of human rights. Producing newsletters. Organising international anti-colonial conferences and meetings. Lobbying British Empire politicians and statesmen, including those at the UN negotiations. Letter writing exchanges and information sharing. Direct lobbying of US delegation through status as representatives at the talks. Producing newsletters. Organising meetings, conferences and information exchanges with other anti-colonial, anti-racist groups.
3. Indirect participants – supporters not engaging in direct lobbying	Anti-colonial journalists, writers, critics and organisations	Writing newspaper and newsletter articles.

Chapter Six

Table 6.4. Transformative Order Discourses

Discourse	General Focus/Argument	Use for the Transformative Order	Key Interpretations (by all or some of the alliance)
1. (British tradition of) rights, liberties and protection of refugees	Innate respect for human rights, moral authority.	Justifies signing up to international law which seeks to protect British subjects around the world. Justifies universal refugee assistance.	Undesirable to lose sovereignty to an international body, particularly if it undermines colonial activities, rooted in tacit understanding of 'right'.
2. Anti-racist	Human beings are often wrongly organised into distinct 'races' which are hierarchically organised.	Justifies signing up to human rights conventions in most expansive sense possible.	Human hierarchy leads to the unfair exploitation of some to the advantage of others. All human beings are equal; therefore all should have equal access to human rights. Human rights as 'universal' in principle facilitate an anti-racist argument.
3. Anti-colonial	The colonial system must end.	Justifies universal application of human rights as stepping stone to freedom.	The resistance of the colonial powers to universal application of human rights exposes their ulterior motives of domination and subjugation. Exposing them aids the anti-colonial cause. All human beings are equal; therefore all should have equal access to human rights.
3. Civilisation	Human beings can be organised into distinct 'races', found in various societies, all of whom have varying levels of civilisation. Inequality inherent, duty on the part of the civilised to look after the uncivilised (the white man's burden).	Justifies human rights for the colonies.	Civilising mission demands human rights for the colonies as education. Part of path to self-determination.

Echoing this, the representative of Afghanistan stated that 'those who claimed they were trying to civilize the peoples whom they were colonizing should at least give them the right to learn how to become conscious of their human dignity' (United Nations, 17 February 1950: np). Here we can see the articulation of what Spivak (1988) would later characterise as the inability of the subaltern to speak in the terms that are demanded of her. The representative of Afghanistan is arguing that curtailing the possibility of colonised peoples demanding 'human' dignity while at the same time arguing that they are being 'civilised' reveals the fallacy of benevolence within the discourse of colonial rule. In becoming conscious of its rights, the subaltern might (would, inevitably) speak, and what was spoken would not enable the continuation of the colonial project.

The delegation from India was 'convinced that the colonial clause gave the metropolitan powers the right to impose their will upon the peoples of the Non-Self-Governing Territories'. He pointed out that 'it was precisely in the Non-Self-Governing Territories and in the colonies that the Covenant should be especially applied, since it was there that violations of human rights were unfortunately most frequent' (United Nations, 17 February 1950: np). Here the Indian representative is taking the argument further, making a direct connection between colonial rule and what would soon be defined as 'human rights violations'. Not only should rights be extended to colonial territories, then, but the idea that metropolitan powers are human rights violators is presented to the conference. This is a bold and explicitly anti-colonial accusation to make in the UN forum, and its gravity should be borne in mind when the statements of the colonial order (discussed above) are considered.

Alongside these concerns regarding the colonial application clause, the records of the discussions at the UN on the Convention for Refugees and Displaced Persons show clear and consistent resistance from some states (all former colonies) regarding the refugee definition. This resistance resulted from a proposal to limit the label 'refugee' to European displaced people. For example, in November 1949 the Pakistani representative called for a revision of the refugee definition. He pointed out that

> As defined in the Constitution of the IRO, that term only applied to victims of events which had occurred during the Second World War in Europe. After the end of hostilities, however, other events had taken place in other parts of the world. If the United Nations was to be entrusted with that problem, it should consider it on a world-wide basis. For example, a year and a half earlier, Pakistan had been compelled to receive from 6 to 7 million refugees coming from various parts of India. More recently it had had to give asylum to 500,000 or 600,000 fugitives from Kashmir. (UN General Assembly, 10 November 1949)

In the following meeting, the representative of India noted that although India was not a member of the IRO, 'it had done its utmost to aid both UNRRA and the IRO and had helped six thousand European refugees to settle in its territory after the war' while also coping with its own refugee problem, namely six million Indian refugees who had to be looked after and resettled. He 'hoped the United Nations would acknowledge that India was performing an international as well as a national duty by helping those people, and that it would not be asked to shoulder any further responsibility regarding European refugees'. This was followed by support for the Pakistani representative's suggestion that the IRO be maintained and that it address itself to the drafting of a convention on the legal protection of refugees *everywhere* (UN General Assembly, 10 November 1949).

These extracts show that not only were there significant numbers of refugees outside of Europe at the time of the drafting of the Geneva Convention, but the drafting delegations were made fully aware of the extent of these displaced populations. They were further made aware of the fact that both the Indian and Pakistani states, amongst others, had hosted European refugees uprooted as a result of the Nazi regime and the Second World War. And yet Eleanor Roosevelt (United Nations, 17 February 1950: np), representing the United States, replied that 'the matter required very careful consideration', and she wondered 'whether the General Assembly would be prepared at the present juncture to assume responsibility for other groups of refugees than those defined in the IRO Constitution'. She dismissed the query, as the Economic and Social Council had set up an ad hoc committee to review existing conventions providing protection for refugees and she assumed therefore that this matter would be discussed there.

The Pakistani representative welcomed the formation of this committee but reiterated the fact that 'if the proposal before the Committee were adopted, Pakistan would have to share in financing the legal protection of an undefined number of refugees in Europe, while obtaining no benefits for the excess of refugees in its own country'. Indeed, 'there was no mention in any formal proposal of extending the protection of the new organization to all categories of refugees and he hoped that some concrete amendments would be submitted in order to allay his anxiety'. Karim Azkoul of Lebanon concurred that the draft resolution left out new categories of refugees who did not come under the protection of the IRO, specifying Greece, Pakistan, India and China as examples. He said, 'it should be possible for the United Nations to extend his services to cover all refugees' (UN General Assembly, 11 November 1949).

These are clear and precise expressions of concern and demands for simple rewording within the final convention. Furthermore, that universal human rights might fulfil the rhetoric surrounding their inscription – that they would be applied to all human beings – seems like a reasonable demand. Its simplicity, in fact, further foregrounds inequalities in the idea of the 'human' amongst some of the delegations in attendance and begs the question of whether all human lives were considered of equal value. At the next meeting the Pakistani representative again raised the issue of the refugee definition, stating that

> he had gathered the unfortunate impression that some delegations entertained serious doubts as to the purely humanitarian aspect of the problem of refugees and also that politics had perhaps made an unwelcome intrusion into the question. Furthermore, he deplored a situation in which refugees might find themselves mere pawns on the international chessboard.

He suggested that 'the only firm stands had been made by the Indian delegation, which had opposed the draft resolution, and the Mexican and Brazilian delegations, which had expressed grave misgivings about its ultimate implications'. The transcript of the meeting suggests that the Pakistani representative was exasperated, condemning the vagueness of the proposed text and its implications. The implication that 'other categories might be added at some later stage' begged the question of 'what other categories, or when and how they might so be added [it has] never been made clear'.

Regarding the definition of the term 'refugee', he had significant objections to the direction of the talks:

> it was proposed that the matter should be left to the discretion of the General Assembly, which might make appropriate decisions from time to time. It was difficult to vote for hypothetical possibilities. It was true that the General Assembly might one day decide to include the seven million refugees in Pakistan within the High Commissioner's terms of reference. But Mr. Bokhari could not, on that mere assumption, ask the refugees in his own country, who sadly lacked food and shelter and not merely legal protection, to forgo part of the already inadequate help they received for unspecified categories of refugees, over an unspecified period, to be administered by a High Commissioner whose relationship with them also remained unspecified.

The representative for Iraq expressed 'full support for the views outlined by the representative of Pakistan', as did the Lebanese representative. In response the representative of France suggested that the Pakistani representative was merely confused and 'regretted that [such] a confusion between refugees and stateless persons continued'. This did not placate the objectors, and the Iraqi, Indian, Brazilian and Ethiopian representatives all expressed similar concerns (UN General Assembly, 16 November 1949).

Though the UN was not a European institution, the final definition of legitimate grounds for claiming asylum left little chance that non-Europeans fleeing events after 1 January 1951 would be granted refugee status. This was due first to the nature of the refugee definition, which remained narrow, and second to the fact that it was left to the discretion of the General Assembly whether 'other' categories of refugees not originally envisaged as recipients of UNHCR Convention support would be included within it. Of the forty-three countries that could vote, twenty-six voted 'for', twelve abstained and five voted 'against'. Here, silence speaks volumes.

It is important to note here that Pakistan, India and some other former colonies were represented at the UN and were therefore able to voice their concerns because they had gained independence. Yet in the early stages of the talks on human rights in 1945 there were accusations that the Indian delegation had been hand-picked by the British. Mahatma Gandhi commented in the *Hindustan Times* in March 1945 that 'the camouflage of Indian representation through Indians nominated by British imperialism will be worse than no representation. Either India at San Francisco is represented by an elected representative, or represented not at all' (cited in Anand 2010: 18). Other voices could not be heard in any capacity, though rarely for want of trying. For example, in 1945 the African members of Nigeria's Legislative Council passed a resolution unanimously asking the British government to approve a delegation of two unofficial (i.e. African) members to attend the San Francisco conference on human rights (Sherwood 1996). The British Colonial Office replied that 'no such observers were to be allowed' (Sherwood 1996: 81). This was despite the United States allowing a number of NGOs, including the delegation of African-Americans, of whom W.E.B. Du Bois was one, to attend. It should be noted, however, that the British government was extremely perturbed by this action on the part of the United States.

At level 2 in table 6.3 are those actors who sought to influence the UN talks from the outside. The independence of the colonies was a peripheral project for the Labour government and the Cabinet contained a number of committed enthusiasts for the Empire (Saville 1993). There was, however, one committed anti-colonial in the Cabinet: Aneurin Bevan, Minister of Health. Bevan had been outspoken in Parliament against colonialism in the past – for example, saying 'our boast about this country being a good coloniser is baseless' during a rousing anti-colonial speech in 1938 (House of Commons, 28 February 1938). But as an anti-colonial he had been kept away from involvement in the government of the British Empire. He showed an interest in the post of Colonial Secretary in 1950 but was, according to Hugh Dalton, not to be trusted '(a) not to waste money (b) not to be carried away by his colour prejudice, pro-black and anti-white' (cited in Gupta 2002). Busy with the task of setting up the National Health Service, there is therefore no evidence that I have found of him intervening on the question of human rights for the colonies.

There was an anti-colonial presence in the wider Labour party, though not great in number. Archibald Fenner Brockway, Member of Parliament (MP), was the leader of this grouping. He worked closely with George Padmore and other black pan-Africanists in pamphleting, lecturing and the setting up of various organisations and conferences (Padmore 1953; Adi, Sherwood and Padmore 1995). In Parliament, he used his first speech as MP for Eton and Slough to call for a 'full-scale Debate on the Colonial Empire' and later that year made a speech on South Africa in which he stated

> I suggest to the Minister that if any Government takes that course, as the South African Government is now doing, it is not merely excluding another race from the all-embracing human family but is excluding itself from the mind and morality of the world. The Declaration on Human Rights of the United Nations says that we are all born equal, equal in human dignities and in human rights. It is on that principle that this Government ought to stand. (House of Commons, 5 December 1951)

Here he is invoking the same ideas as the anti-colonial delegations at the UN quoted above. Indeed, those in the transformative order made direct links between the hierarchical ordering of humanity inaugurated by racial scientists, and promoted through colonial activities, and unequal international power relations, which were illustrated by unequal access to human rights.

While human rights law was used in an exclusionary way by the colonial powers, it also offered a discourse through which anti-colonials could articulate their legitimate claims of human equality. Following this logic, in December 1951 Brockway proposed a Human Rights Bill in the House of Commons. The bill was

> to establish throughout the United Kingdom *and the non-self-governing Colonies* and Protectorates a standard of Human Rights and Freedoms applicable to all His Majesty's subjects without distinction of race, colour, sex, language, religion, birth or other status. (House of Commons, 5 December 1951, emphasis added)

The main focus was abolishing all forms of racial discrimination throughout the Empire. The Colonial Office had 'grave apprehensions' about this, describing it as 'completely unrealistic' and 'impracticable', and committed to prevent its success (Colonial Office 1951–1952). The plan was to either vote down or talk out the bill in Parliament. Telegrams were sent to officers administering colonies all over the world, briefings for ministers and the Attorney General were produced, colonial legislation in a number of specific areas was surveyed, detailed responses to every article were formulated and the Colonial Office, Home Office and Commonwealth Office all produced separate briefs.

The extent of these preparations indicate that the government was strongly against extending human rights to colonised peoples, and that some in the government and civil service believed Brockway had a chance of success. However, when the bill was debated the following May it was not well received, and it appears all this effort planning a counter-attack was wasted. The discussion quickly descended into a debate on colonial policy with lengthy reminders from the (Conservative) opposition of all that the British had done for the Africans, notably freeing them from slavery and aiding their development. Equal treatment of the 'races' would mean that Africans would be free to buy 'intoxicating liquor', and much was said about whether removing this law, which was said to be for the Africans' protection, would be beneficial or (more likely) not. Such elaborate distractions from the real issue of the day were resisted by some. For example, Cuthbert Alport, MP for Colchester, endorsed the principle of the bill, if not the entire substance:

> What we must not do is to give the impression that we do not realise and understand the grave difficulties which exist in Africa and make it appear that we are prepared simply to make a carte blanche declaration of this sort. We should, rather, encourage all developments which are going on here and overseas which aim at improving the partnership and co-operation between the two races. (House of Commons, 23 May 1952)

Ultimately, after lengthy discussion (mostly off-topic), the bill was not adopted and this ambitious idea appears to have been abandoned by Brockway.

Though there is little evidence that the wider party was privy to the details of the negotiations going on at the UN (relating to the colonial application clause etc.), Brockway did press for the human rights declaration to be applied in the colonies following 1951 – for example, urging Henry Hopkinson (then Minister for Colonial Affairs) to include human rights in the Rhodesia and Nyasaland Federation Bill in 1953 (House of Commons, 24 June 1953). So great, however, was the association of refugees with Europe that the issue of application outside of Europe was not taken up in Parliament. Indeed, the Refugee Convention was in fact discussed very little in Parliament.

The most documented efforts to influence a delegation from outside the Parliamentary sphere are those efforts made by African-Americans (Sherwood 1996; Anderson 2003), but the pan-Africanism which fuelled activities in the United States was international in scope. For those living under British rule, the task was made somewhat difficult by the censoring of British and colonial press during the Second World War. Designated 'radicals' were easily imprisoned. Sherwood (1996) identifies the Indian National

Congress leaders, Jamaican activists Richard Hart and W.A. Domingo and trade unionists I.T.A. Wallace Johnson of Sierra Leone and Michael Imoudou of Nigeria as just some of those jailed. This made efforts to be heard significantly more difficult for the transformative order outside of the UN.

Anti-colonials were, when in a position to do so, outspoken in the mainstream media. Nnamdi Azikiwe, the owner and editor of the *West African Pilot*, based in Nigeria (then a British colony), was consistently critical of the human rights talks taking place. He wrote in a 1945 editorial about the exclusion of the colonies from the San Francisco conference:

> We are pessimistic because there is no new deal for the blackman at San Francisco. We are worried about San Francisco because colonialism and economic enslavement of the Negro are to be maintained ... We shall not be happy until the world is rescued from its half slavery and half freedom. God grant that this miracle happens at Frisco. (cited in Sherwood 1996: 82)

Meanwhile, Kumar Goshal predicted in the *Pittsburgh Courier* that the British would present at the UN the '"white man's burden" theory in its post-World War second clothes' and would legitimate it through colonial '"representatives" furnished in the shape of three Indian stooges' (cited in Von Eschen 1997: 81).

A key node in the anti-colonial network was W.E.B. Du Bois, an African-American academic activist and pan-Africanist. Joseph M. Proskauer, president of the American Jewish Committee, wrote to Du Bois in 1944 and included a declaration of human rights which his organisation had drafted. It was specifically targeted at stateless and displaced people in the mould of the German Jew. Du Bois did not respond enthusiastically; he wrote, 'this is very easily understood as a declaration of Jewish rights but it has apparently no thought to the rights of Negroes, Indians and South Sea Islanders. Why then call it a Declaration of Human Rights?' (Du Bois 1978: 25). The following year, Du Bois wrote to the leaders of the US delegation to the UN talks that their proposed declaration

> leaves out the mass of people living in the colonies, against whom discrimination is customary and unjustifiable. We believe that a declaration should lay down the principle and implement it so as to provide for the transition of all colonial peoples from colonial status to such autonomy as they desire. The eventual disappearance of the colonial system is the best insurance of peace. This domestic principle, the international organization has not recognised. (Du Bois 1978)

For Du Bois, human rights offered the possibility of progress towards emancipation for African-Americans and people living under European colonial rule. But human rights as a legal framework could only work if universally applied and not augmented to suit the prejudices and financial interests of the United States and the old colonial powers.

Du Bois was a prolific letter writer and sought to build networks with like-minded people across the globe. In 1945 anti-colonial activist George Padmore, who had been Kwame Nkrumah's personal representative in London during the struggle for Ghanaian independence, wrote to Du Bois on the nature of anti-colonial activism in Britain:

> The British Negro lives away from the British Isles, and those individuals who are here constitute an alien minority, although they are subjects of the same crown. As a result, when the negro comes to this country ... he tends to get together with other Colonial organisations to advocate and propagate his own political aspirations which ... concentrate on the question of self-determination from the country whence he comes. (Du Bois 1978: 77)

Yet there were nevertheless anti-colonial and black activist networks in Britain who disseminated their views through newsletters. One such organisation was the League of Coloured Peoples, whose publication *The News Letter* covered the emerging human rights agenda in the UN:

> The Union of South Africa, although it is represented abroad as a democracy with a system of Parliamentary government, manifests essentially the same characteristics as [Nazi Germany] ... While they [South African Labour Party and Trade Unions] may SPEAK abroad of equality for all and opportunity for all, they do not for a single moment include the non-Europeans. (The League of Coloured Peoples 1946: 72)

This is a clear articulation of the core message of this chapter. Universal humanity was not intended, at the founding of the right to asylum in international law, as including all human beings. Colonially informed ideas of a racially stratified human hierarchy underpinned the distinction between inclusion and exclusion. The authors of the *News Letter* described such ideas as 'racial indoctrination' and suggested that 'Smuts' claim in the house of assembly on 14th March 1945, that ALL in South Africa are agreed on the mission of the Europeans to rule over the non-Europeans in perpetuity, ALL – except those who are "mad, quite mad" was the perfect illustration' (The League of Coloured Peoples 1946: 72).

Later in the same newsletter extracts are provided from the 'Declaration to Imperialist Powers of the World', a document which emerged from the Manchester Pan-African Congress in 1945. The opening paragraph appears as follows:

> We demand for Black Africa autonomy and independence, so far and no further than it is possible, in this 'ONE WORLD' for groups and peoples to rule

themselves subject to inevitable world unity and federation. We are not ashamed to have been an age long patient people. We are willing even now to sacrifice and strive to correct all our too human faults. But we are unwilling to starve any longer while doing the world's drudgery, in order to support by our poverty and ignorance, a false aristocracy and a discredited imperialism. (The League of Coloured Peoples 1946: 77)

The declaration later lays out the basis for action:

> The object of the imperial powers is to exploit. By granting emancipation and self-government, they would defeat this objective and they are therefore unlikely to pursue such a policy. The only option is to fight and struggle for decolonisation from below. (The League of Coloured Peoples 1946: 78)

These extracts illustrate the way in which many people observing and attempting to influence the UN negotiations from the outside understood human rights as emerging from a context in which colonial rationales dominated the priorities of powerful states. Colonial norms were not therefore accepted by all, or by any means uncontested. Rationales of differential humanity were recognised and consciously, articulately challenged. In the closing section the issues arising from the interaction of these orders and the implications for our understanding of asylum policy in the present time are addressed.

Human Rights, Refugee Rights and the Legacy of Differential Humanity

In this chapter I have identified two institutional orders which influenced the UN negotiations on both the broader Convention on Human Rights, and the more specific Convention on the Status of Refugees. These two institutional orders were, as in the previous two chapters, the 'colonial' and the 'transformative'. The colonial order, made up of powerful colonial state actors, was ultimately successful in making human rights exclusive to certain territories and consequently excluding large numbers of the world's population. This situation did not occur without resistance, however. A coalition of actors and institutions in the transformative order, most influentially led by newly independent states, articulated their resistance clearly and consistently. That such challenges were necessary reflects the enduring relevance of ideas of differential humanity amongst politicians in the middle of the twentieth century. The British government documents cited in this chapter suggest a genuine belief that colonised and previously colonised peoples were like children, completely unequipped for self-determination and insufficiently developed to deserve human rights on a par with colonis*ing* (white) peoples. These ideas are very close to those expressed by both abolitionists and slavers in chapter 4, suggesting that ideas of human hierarchy (civilisational and racial) have had an enduring appeal over long periods of time.

There are two vital contextual factors to the discussions elaborated in this chapter. Both relate to the themes of differential humanity, racial classification and colonialism addressed in the previous two chapters. The first is the colonised struggling for decolonisation and the second is the response of the British government to colonial immigration. Decolonisation came as a direct result of the struggles of the colonised to be considered capable of self-government within the context of exclusionary ideas of human hierarchy (Fanon 1967; McIntyre 1998). These struggles dominated the 1950s and 1960s and reconfigured the political geography of the world (Thomas 2008). Decolonisation in many cases led to massive population displacements (Pierson, Chaudhuri and McAuley 1998; Marfleet 2006). However, the 'myth of difference' at the time of drafting the convention presented non-European refugees as radically different from European and therefore requiring solutions outside of the convention (Chimni 1998). The British government, along with other European powers and the United States, was therefore aware of other refugee-producing situations in 1951, and was willing to provide significant financial aid to alleviate these situations but nevertheless saw them as external to the Refugee Conventions. As custodians of the world, it was in some sense their responsibility to protect the 'children of the Earth', especially if this could be done in situ.

This 'myth of difference' directly challenges the universality of the Convention – how can it be universal if most of the world's refugees cannot be provided for within its framework? And yet the exclusivity of rights inscribed in the convention is not problematised by the British government today. It is the failure of asylum applicants to fit into what has been decreed as just grounds for claiming asylum in a foreign land. This is a false logic which makes sense only within the context of the kinds of connected histories which have been identified in this chapter. It is the logic of coloniality/modernity. When colonial histories, including ideas of racial classification informed by racial science, are brought together with histories of refugee and asylum law, contemporary exclusions can be better understood. European powers had long classified their imperial subjects as less human, less civilised, than themselves; why would this logic cease to be operational in 1951 just because a handful had gained independence? Vitally, what evidence do we have to suggest that this has ceased to be operational today?

The second contextual factor is colonial immigration to the United Kingdom. At the same time as signing the Geneva Convention, the Attlee government was working out ways to restrict immigration from the former Empire. These activities have been well documented elsewhere (Rex and Thomlinson 1979; Joshi and Carter 1984; Gilroy 2004), but it may nevertheless be useful to note that the same Cabinet Secretaries' notebooks which contain the discussions over human rights cited in this chapter also contain lengthy discussions which explicitly identify 'coloured' immigration from the colonies as a problem in itself, the danger of being seen as racist if the issue is raised in public (which is of more concern than actually being racist) and the desirability of a *de facto* colour bar in employment, particularly the post office (see Brook 1952). This issue, of course, became more pressing as decolonisation continued. The distinction between the need to protect desirable and deserving refugees and the need to keep 'coloured' people out of the country followed the in-here/out-there distinction of the old Empire. All subjects of the Empire were legally equal, but when non-white subjects sought a home in Great Britain, great effort was made to limit their number.

As Rex and Tomlinson (1979: 288) pointed out in their *Colonial Immigrants in a British City*, the end of the Empire did not herald a new dawn of equality but 'hostile beliefs and attitudes ... came to be sanctioned by the highest moral authority', leading to a 'vicious cumulative spiral of escalating racism' (Rex and Tomlinson 1979: 291). These events, then, integral to understanding conceptions of 'insiders' and 'outsiders', and occurring concurrently with the development of the asylum regime, are highly pertinent to the history of refugee and asylum policy and to understanding the response of governments like the British to asylum seekers today.

King and Smith (2005) suggest that their racial institutional orders framework is particularly useful in that it can help explain many features of politics that may appear unrelated to 'race'. They include contemporary immigration policies in their list of examples suggesting that racial ideas have been 'constitutively interwoven with many other highly significant institutional orders, including gender and class hierarchies' (King and Smith 2005: 78). In the case of asylum policy, the underlying legal framework of human rights posits a universal human being who is putatively *protected* from discrimination on the grounds of 'race'. However, as the institutional orders analysis in this chapter has shown, though this is a policy area which may appear unrelated to 'race', or more specifically to colonially derived ideas of racial hierarchy, this has not historically been the case. It is by looking at history that we can begin to understand these connections, and specifically the framework of colonaility/modernity, which enables us to see that while hostility to asylum seekers is often deracialised in official discourse, the restrictive impulse is deeply embedded in the same histories and logics as those of colonial racism.

As I discussed in chapter 2, the British state has sought to limit the reach of the Geneva Convention in recent decades. This is often seen as a U-turn on commitments made in 1951 which have become the totemic markers of high moral aspirations. This interpretation is problematic because it renders the negation of duties to asylum seekers on behalf of states such as Britain in the late twentieth century as explicable only on the basis of the sudden arrival in the world of non-European refugees. Connected colonial histories are obscured, as are historical attempts to systematically exclude large portions of the world's population from rights and justice. Indeed, within the context of the response to colonial immigrants, current policies appear to be 'business as usual'.

This chapter has demonstrated that not only were refugees not exclusively European in the middle of the twentieth century, but that there were extensive discussions at the UN about the injustice of having a narrow geographical conception of the right to asylum. Furthermore, the empirical evidence has shown that the British government was reluctant to extend both human rights and refugee rights to non-European refugees, particularly colonial subjects, in the post-war period. The evidence suggests that contemporary British asylum and refugee policy must be understood within the context of colonialism and decolonisation as these rationales linger on. Countries which had experienced colonialism were well aware of perceived racial hierarchies which rationalised their exclusion from human rights instruments and fought against them at every opportunity. This history must be incorporated into not only our analyses of the past but also of the present.

Chapter Seven

Dehumanisation

Asylum Seeker Support in the Twenty-First Century

In previous chapters a thread had been traced through disparate historical moments which are linked through the contestation of ideas of differential, hierarchically organised human worth. With each leap forward in time we have seen both transformative change, visible in increased equality, and also the stubborn persistence of unequal access to rights which are meant to be available to all human beings. In chapter 3 I argued that the exclusionary nature of the supposedly universal category of 'man' and the colonial origins of this exclusion are central to understanding unequal access to human rights in the present. Having charted this history through the methodological device of three critical junctures, in this chapter we arrive in the contemporary period. The focus of the analysis are the policies and contestations over welfare support provision for asylum seekers and non-returnable failed asylum seekers. Here, we find again (as in the previous chapter) that powerful actors are unwilling to outwardly *articulate* the exclusion of some human beings from access to equal humanity in explicitly racial or colonial terms, and yet that those very exclusions continue to occur. Key legislative changes in the United Kingdom, particularly the Human Rights Act, mean increased legal means for accessing human rights. Yet the priority of decreasing the number of asylum applications and limiting the rights of those who do manage to make a claim, regardless of the wider contexts of violence and persecution from whence such migrants came, are the overriding objectives of policy-making. The point of this book is to answer the question 'how can this be so?' through deep engagement with histories of differential humanity.

What has changed between the time period of the last chapter and this one? The vast majority of colonised countries have gained independence, apartheid in South Africa, segregation in the United States and the Cold War have all ended and racism has been made a criminal offense in Britain. Since the immediate aftermath of the Second World War the right to asylum has been expanded with a new protocol in 1967, making it applicable to everybody in the world, not just those displaced in Europe. We might think of 1967 as a moment of 'peak rights' for asylum seekers – when expansion was the order of the day and increased protection was viewed as an international political imperative which was, at a minimum, tolerated by Western states as those who were newly independent demanded inclusion in these legal measures of common humanity.

Unfortunately, this toleration did not last long. The end of the Cold War (and therefore the end of politically and ideologically convenient Cold War refugees) coincided with an increase in violent conflict and displacement outside of Europe – in the formerly colonised world. Forced migrants seeking asylum began to arrive in Europe in increased numbers. It was at this point, in the 1990s, that European states, as well as the former white settler colonies, started to seek ways of limiting their obligations under the Geneva Convention. Asylum seekers were prevented from arriving in destination countries, where they would have the right under international law to have their application for asylum assessed. The legal definition of a refugee was restricted, and a wide range of punitive policies rolled out across Europe which were meant to act as deterrence measures for would-be asylum seekers. This phenomenon has been dubbed the rise of 'Fortress Europe' (Crawley 2005). While some scholars would have us think that this response was a rational reaction to the high numbers of applicants, I am arguing here that it was not their number but their countries of origin and position in an imagined racial hierarchy, the rise of which I discussed in earlier chapters, that triggered the response. These populations were never the targeted recipients of the right to asylum, as we saw in the previous chapter; they were actively excluded at the moment of inception.

It is hard to examine the roster of policy changes introduced in Britain since the early 1990s and not conclude that the asylum regime is dehumanising. Indeed, many migrants and asylum advocacy organisations make that very accusation on a regular basis. If the effect is dehumanisation, the underlying rationale of the policies is that the humanity of asylum applicants is something to be respected to the bare minimum of legal obligation, and only where that legal obligation is enforced in the courts. Efforts at repealing the Human Rights Act, which enshrines the European Convention on Human Rights (ECHR) in UK domestic law, reveal the threadbare extent to which this obligation is respected. Through policy measures the government treats asylum seekers as less than human in ways that are clearly informed by a long tradition of differential rights. This is, however, resisted, as with every other exclusionary effort discussed in this book. Today, the call is still for equal humanity by a coalition of citizens and non-citizens who are self-consciously aware of the differential rights afforded to different groups of people.

This chapter focuses on the discussions surrounding a particular legal contestation in order to explore two things: first, the bureaucratic, institutional and legal practices and processes through which the dehumanisation of asylum seekers is possible in contemporary Britain, and second, how this dehumanisation is contested in the public sphere. The legal and policy contestation that the analysis focuses on is the rates of support paid to asylum applicants building up to a judicial review case brought against the government by a British NGO – Refugee Action – in 2013, which concluded in April 2014. Since there was no legal route to challenge the actual levels of asylum support, Refugee Action was challenging the fact that support rates had not increased since 2011, and the process by which this decision was made. This was a complex legal intervention which was really an attempt at intervening in what, by this time, had become an almost impenetrable regime, always moving towards greater closure and exclusion within the parameters of what was legally permitted. Even this led only to legal costs, and not to policy change, and is an example both of how narrow the parameters of possible resistance have become, and how unlikely even marginal gains on legal technicalities are to be successful.

But who are we talking about when we speak of the legal category of 'asylum seekers', a group who many argue are dehumanised? We are speaking of non-Europeans, often people of colour, often coming from formerly colonised countries. It is important to point this out because the neutralised legal language of asylum hides a lot in terms of histories of differential humanity and in turn closes down avenues for more radical critique. The chapter begins with a discussion of the policy area of concern in this chapter. It proceeds through an institutional orders analysis of, firstly, the transformative order which seeks change and regularly draws attention to the inhumane treatment of asylum seekers in Britain. Next comes a discussion of the arguments made by what I call here the 'anti-asylum institutional order', an order infused with the coloniality of power. The final section brings these analyses together with some concluding thoughts which then lead through to the next chapter where the prospects for asylum after empire are addressed.

ASYLUM SUPPORT IN CONTEMPORARY BRITAIN

It is not normally permissible for asylum seekers in the United Kingdom to enter the labour market (Mayblin 2016a, 2016b). In the absence of the right to work and support themselves, asylum seekers are supported by the UK government in a welfare system separate to that which supports unemployed citizens. Such support ensures that the UK government is not violating asylum seeker's human rights by forcing them to live in destitution. However, the support received by asylum seekers is not any more than the absolute minimum required by human rights law, and even then there is considerable debate as to whether the levels of poverty experienced by asylum seekers in the United Kingdom constitute a human rights violation (discussed further below). Understanding this situation requires some knowledge of the highly technical bureaucratic context of asylum support, which I have attempted to explain simply as far as possible below.

Asylum seekers have two support options: financial assistance only (where they have friends or family to stay with) or financial assistance plus housing. The 1993 Asylum and Immigration Appeals Act gave in-port asylum applicants (those who made their application for asylum as soon as they arrived in the United Kingdom) 90 percent of the welfare support provided to citizens, and the 1996 Asylum and Immigration Act reduced this to 70 percent of the income support payments made to unemployed British citizens (Kissoon 2010). The European Council's 2003 Reception Conditions Directive determines that the Home Secretary has a duty to provide support in respect of essential living needs, though what might count as 'essential' is at the discretion of the Minister. Until 2008, increases to the rates of asylum support were made on an annual basis and broadly in line with increases to income support. In 2008 the link to income support was broken and for 2009 the separate rate for single adults aged twenty-five and over was removed. The amounts were increased annually in line with inflation until 2012, when such increases stopped.

Current levels are at around 50 percent of income support. Under Section 55 of the Nationality, Immigration and Asylum Act 2002, asylum seekers are not entitled to support whilst their asylum application is under consideration if they are found not to have applied for asylum 'as soon as reasonably practicable', which can be difficult in situations where, for example, a war breaks out in the country of origin while an individual is studying in the United Kingdom. There are exceptions for families, people with special needs and cases where a refusal of support would be a breach of the individual's human rights. The rate of support has been £36.95 per person per week since August 2015. This is a substantial reduction in support for single parents and families with children who previously received a larger sum. Extra one-off payments are provided to pregnant women, women with new babies and those with children under three. The changes are shown in table 7.1 and are discussed further below. Before this reduction, support rates had not increased since 2011, While the year 2012–13 saw a 5.2 percent rise in income support payments.

If an asylum seeker has their application for asylum refused, support is withdrawn and the UK government asks them to leave the United Kingdom.

Table 7.1. Asylum Support Rates Before and After 2015 Change

	Single Parent + 1 Child	Single Parent + 2 Children	Couple + 1 Child	Couple + 2 Children
Payment per week before change	£96.90	£149.86	£125.48	£178.44
New payment (from 2015)	£73.90	£110.85	£110.85	£147.80

Source: Home Office

There is a voluntary returns policy which includes free travel and a lump sum payment upon arrival. Nevertheless, numbers of returns are low. This is for a variety of reasons, including the presence of war in countries of origin making return impossible, individuals having a lack of valid travel documents and home countries refusing or being unable to issue new ones. This may be because the individual in question is of an ethnic group which their government rejects. Many refused asylum seekers therefore choose to stay in the United Kingdom and live in a situation of poverty or destitution with no clear future (Crawley, Hemmings and Price 2011). If refused asylum seekers are unable to return, have a judicial review pending or are complying with processes aimed at returning them in the future (such as applying for travel documents), then a 'Section 4' support of £35.39 per person per week is loaded on a payment card, valid in select shops, plus accommodation can be applied for.

Poverty and even destitution are very common amongst asylum seekers in the United Kingdom (Allsopp, Sigona and Phillimore 2014). This is not an accident; such experiences are policy tools to discourage asylum seekers from choosing the United Kingdom and encourage those who are here to leave, particularly if their application for asylum has been refused (British Red Cross and Boaz Trust 2013). The impacts on asylum seekers include mental health problems (Refugee Action 2006; Lindsay et al. 2010; Lewis 2007; Phillimore et al. 2007; Cohen 2008; Pettitt 2013; Pinter 2012), high levels of hunger (Taylor 2009; Children's Society 2013; Reacroft 2008), high levels of maternal and infant mortality (Maternity Action and Refugee Council 2013; Cheung and Phillimore 2013) and difficulty navigating the legal process (Refugee Action 2006; British Red Cross and Boaz Trust 2013). In their review of research into poverty amongst asylum seekers and refugees Allsopp et al. (2014: 20) found poverty 'to be present among some of the most vulnerable parts of the asylum seeker population, including pregnant women and newborn babies ... children ... LGBTI individuals ... and torture survivors'. This is a finding which is supported by a wide range of different stakeholders, as we shall see in the next section. But it is also something which is denied by the UK government, which, I will argue here, remains steadfastly committed to the institutionalised dehumanisation of asylum seekers.

Reasserting a Common Humanity: The Battleground of Asylum Support

In this contemporary juncture two key institutional orders are identified: a broad-based transformative order and an institution, perhaps too narrow to be conceptualised as an order, in the form of the UK government and Home Office ministry. Though operating in different contexts to the orders identified in previous chapters, continuities can nevertheless be observed. For example, in the sense that those hailing from outside Europe and the white settler colonies do not require quite such thorough access to human rights, or dignity, as might be afforded to British citizens. What is different here is that it is not yet possible (since the events are so recent) to access private records such as Cabinet Secretaries' diaries or internal Home Office briefing documents. This means that the materials that are available for research are public, not private; are bureaucratic rather than political; are carefully deracialised; and use technical and legalistic language and methods. They are much like the public pronouncements in the last chapter. This is why chapters 4, 5 and 6 were necessary for this book to make sense. When one can observe dehumanisation in a policy regime, and yet find no trace of the age-old language of dehumanisation – human hierarchy often articulated in racial, religious or cultural terms – one must reach back into the long history of dehumanisation in order to contextualise what is being done in the present and name it as not the outcome of rational and fair deliberation on the parameters of human rights law, but as purposefully exclusionary and degrading to particular human beings.

The data used here comes from a range of primary and secondary sources, particularly the Hansard records of parliamentary activity, parliamentary publications, legal reports also accessed via Hansard, the websites of refugee and children's NGOs and community organisations and the official reports of various inquiries. The analysis focuses on those seeking to influence asylum policy in relation to the support given to otherwise destitute asylum seekers by the British state. My interest is particularly in efforts by the British government to restrict access to rights on the basis of immigration status, and resistance to this from others.

The Transformative Order

The range of actors that make up the transformative order are shown in table 7.2. There have been, in recent years, two key groups undertaking

Table 7.2. Transformative Order

Level	Who?	How?
1. Extra-parliamentary leaders	NGOs: Refugee Action, The Refugee Council, Children's Society, Still Human Still Here (coalition of sixty non-governmental and community organisations)	Legal action. Cross-party inquiry (calling/contributing to). Responding to government consultations on asylum support rates.
2. Parliamentary champions	Individual Members of Parliament (MPs), particularly Labour and Liberal Democrat	Private Member's Bills. Willing to sign Early Day Motions (EDMs) and vote in favour of legislative amendments to increase asylum support or extend the right to work.
	Peers in the House of Lords	Proposing amendments to legislation. Resisting changes to the support regime through oral and written questions, & votes on legislation.
3. Parliamentary sympathisers	Parliamentary groups: Home Affairs Committee, All-Party Parliamentary Group Refugees	Parliamentary committee inquiries and reports. Organising support for other parliamentary activity (e.g. EDMs) and liaising with NGOs on grassroots issues.
4. Key stakeholders	Asylum seekers and refugees	Local actions aimed at lobbying MPs. Giving testimony to NGOs and researchers.
5. Other interested parties	International bodies and organisations: United Nations Special Rapporteur on Torture and other Cruel, Inhuman or Degrading Treatment or Punishment, European Union	Minimal interventions critiquing British government policy.

particular types of activities, which resisted the impoverishment of asylum seekers: NGOs and Members of Parliament (MPs), particularly Labour and Liberal Democrat MPs but occasionally a Conservative. The most coordinated NGO activity is a coalition united under the banner 'Still Human Still Here' which has been in existence since 2007. This coalition of over sixty organisations includes local and national refugee charities, local authorities and NGOs such as Amnesty International, The British Red Cross and Oxfam.

Still Human Still Here works primarily to end destitution amongst refused asylum seekers in the United Kingdom but also campaigns for the right to work and against poverty and destitution amongst asylum seekers at all stages in their asylum claim. The leader of Still Human Still Here, Mike Kaye, gave evidence to all of the parliamentary inquiries described below, coordinated a national campaign around the right to work from 2008 to 2010 and produced a significant body of work published on the coalition's website.

This work was primarily focused on policy change around the technical details of support provision rather than influencing public opinion, which is broadly hostile to immigrants in general and unlikely to change dramatically (Blinder 2015). There have, however, been a number of NGO campaigns which have sought to influence public opinion. Following the 2015 cuts to support rates, Refugee Action started a campaign titled 'Bring Back Dignity' (to the asylum support system) which asked members of the public to sign a petition for fair asylum support, donate to their destitution fund and make others aware of the cuts by sharing their campaign statement on social media. The petition garnered 4,368 signatures and was presented to the Home Office a week before the decision to cut rates even further was announced.

MPs have sought parliamentary means of influence such as inquiries, Early Day Motions (EDMs), Private Member's Bills, written and oral questions to the House and select committee reports – all efforts which are time-consuming but are not central to the activities of legislative development in Parliament. These activities have also consistently gone against the grain of dominant opinion on asylum amongst MPs and Home Secretaries, which may explain their lack of success in changing policy.

Table 7.3 shows the key discourses employed by the transformative order. The entry points for challenging current policy by this time are technocratic and legalistic over and above any other feature. Human rights and children's rights have wider moral concerns than the narrow interpretation of the law. Yet by this point the conventions on these topics have become a baseline protection over and above a generous aspiration and are therefore used in order to argue that the government has a legal obligation to increase rates of asylum support. In parliamentary debates and other textual sources moral claims are made in relation to the dehumanisation of asylum seekers and the shame of treating children particularly in this way, but the perceived routes to possible policy change are nevertheless primarily in arguing against the lawfulness of support rates or the process employed in setting them. If the aim is therefore to argue for a common humanity, the openings for realising this in policy terms are much less expansive. These arguments are relatively coherent with one another; there are few 'strange bedfellows' here, as the focused nature of the challenge in one policy area brings together actors with closely aligned agendas.

Dehumanisation 155

Table 7.3. Transformative Order Discourses

Discourse	General Focus/ Argument	Use for the Transformative Order	Key Interpretations (by all or some of the alliance)
Human rights	All human beings should have access to certain rights simply on the basis that they are members of humanity.	Delegitimises maintaining low support rates.	Asylum seekers not treated as equal human beings, they are maintained in situations of poverty which are seen as unacceptable for citizens.
Children's rights	Children are a special group at particular risk and require extra protection.	Delegitimises maintaining low support rates.	Current levels of asylum support contravene the UN Convention on the Rights of the Child. Highly vulnerable children are living in situations of poverty which is detrimental to their physical and mental well-being.
Rationality and due process	Public policy must be the outcome of rational decision making through logical and thorough processes.	Delegitimises maintaining low support rates.	Asylum support levels decided on the basis of irrational decision making – focus on punitive measures rather than due process.
Anti-poverty	Poverty is bad not only for individuals but also for wider society and should therefore be reduced if not eradicated.	Delegitimises maintaining low support rates.	Asylum support levels, in combination with the limit on working, are such that asylum seekers are forced to live in poverty. This is bad for the mental and physical health of asylum seekers, who are highly vulnerable, but it also has wider negative implications (and costs) for society.

In 2012 a national charity, the Children's Society, began an inquiry into asylum support for children and young people. There was hope that this inquiry would shock policymakers and MPs into pushing for change since children are widely seen in the United Kingdom to have a special status as particularly vulnerable and inherently innocent. They are also additionally protected in human rights law by the 1989 Convention on the Rights of the Child. The inquiry was led by Liberal Democrat MP Sarah Teather, who was at that time the Chair of the All Party Parliamentary Group for Refugees. All involved with the inquiry, apart from the government, were highly critical of the provision of asylum support. Sarah Teather was joined by two Conservative MPs, two Labour MPs, a Liberal Democrat Peer, a Labour Peer, a Bishop in the Lords, a children's rights barrister and the chief executive of the Children's Society. The panel heard oral evidence from 21 expert witnesses, received 40 written submissions of evidence relating to asylum support and got 150 responses to a request for information from local authorities, safeguarding boards, child protection committees and a government department.

An important element of the case made in the report for increasing support levels was the Joseph Rowntree Foundation (JRF) Minimum Income Standard for the United Kingdom, which the organisation has been producing annually since 2008. This is a figure based on what members of the British public think people need for an acceptable minimum standard of living. The figure given by JRF for 2015 was £175.81, excluding rent, council tax, childcare and water rates. Mainstream welfare benefits claimants received just 40 percent of this figure in 2015, and JRF used their work in anti-poverty campaigns. Asylum support rates were, however, even lower, set at just 20 percent of the Minimum Income Standard amount. This became important later as the Home Office used a very different measure – the expenditure of the poorest 10 percent of citizens – to argue that asylum support rates were appropriate, if not generous (Hirsch 2015).

Participants in the inquiry started to draw attention to the issue of support levels even before the report was published. For example, in May 2012 Baroness Lister of Burtersett (Labour), who was on the inquiry panel, posed a question to the government in the House of Lords: 'what action [do] they propose, as part of their review of the level of asylum support, to tackle severe poverty experienced by children in asylum-seeking families[?]' She went on:

> the Children's Society and refugee organisations have reported alarming evidence of growing destitution among asylum-seeking children, young people and families, due in part to levels of financial assistance well below those of income support. Can the Minister explain how this state of affairs is compatible with the Government's obligations under Article 27 of the UN Convention on the Rights of the Child and Article 11 of the International Covenant on Economic, Social and Cultural Rights, both of which uphold the right to an adequate standard of living? (House of Lords, 23 May 2012)

The inquiry report was published in January 2013. The panel noted that while income support (which is paid to unemployed citizens) increased 5.2 percent in 2012–13, no increment was added to asylum support, which at that point was 70 percent of income support, 'making it even more difficult for families to survive'. It concluded that 'the current levels of support provided to families are too low to meet children's essential living needs' (The Children's Society 2013: 2). Low levels of asylum support were, expert witnesses (academic researchers, social workers, local authorities and health professionals) suggested, producing malnutrition, high infant and maternal mortality rates, disrupted education for children, mental health problems, health problems related to living in dirty damp conditions and having inadequate clothing, risk of exploitation and domestic violence. In short, the impacts identified were all symptoms of living in poverty with factors such as forced dispersal and histories of persecution compounding the impacts of poverty.

The inquiry report suggested that poverty and even destitution (in the case of refused asylum seekers) are used as policy tools to deter people from making applications for asylum in the United Kingdom, and then to encourage them to leave the country if their application is rejected. The authors refuted the basis of such actions, suggesting that there is no correlation between support levels and the numbers of asylum seekers in the United Kingdom and that enforced destitution does little to increase the numbers of removals. Maggie Atkinson, Children's Commissioner for England (a government-appointed office given statutory authority to promote and protect the rights of all children in England in accordance with the United Nations Convention on the Rights of the Child) responded publicly by saying that

> It is clear from the shocking evidence gathered by the inquiry that the current support arrangements for children in asylum seeking families fall short of the Government's obligations under the Convention. I urge the Government to seriously and urgently consider the measured and sensible recommendations that have arisen from the inquiry which will go a long way to redressing the current unacceptable situation. (Atkinson 2013)

Four months later, in April 2013, the Home Affairs Committee of the UK Parliament published the findings of their own inquiry on asylum, which included an investigation of support levels. In their evidence to the inquiry the Scottish Refugee Council stated,

> The level of income most widely used as a signifier of living in poverty is below 60% of male median income. Asylum support stands at less than 31% of that level. The UKBA arguments about costs such as utility bills and housing being met and that these make up the shortfall is a disingenuous one. A 35%-49% shortfall is not made up by asylum seekers not having to meet these costs. (House of Commons Home Affairs Committee 2013: 34)

In April 2012 a government representative had told the Home Affairs Select Committee that the Home Office was reviewing aspects of support policy, which they took to mean that support levels were likely to increase (Home Affair Select Committee 2013, Ev 48, para 33). However, by June 2012, the Minister for Immigration had announced his decision not to increase support levels. The committee noted that in surveys of asylum seekers receiving support, 50 percent of respondents had reported experiencing hunger, 70 percent were unable to buy essential toiletries and 94 percent were unable to buy clothing. They also suggested that this 'relative poverty' was compounded by the restrictions on working, which was a policy they urged the government to consider changing. The inquiry report concluded that there was a 'culture of disbelief' at the UK Border Agency, as well as other efforts to limit the chances of a claim being successful (such as poor legal advice and having inadequate access to interpreters), and this meant that asylum seekers were waiting too long for a decision on their application and were not then receiving fair judgements. In the meantime, they live in poverty and are liable to become destitute at all stages in the process of making an asylum claim, including once they have been recognised as a refugee.

Also in April of 2013 Sarah Teather, who had chaired the Children's Society inquiry put forward a Private Member's Bill in Parliament, with the support of two Liberal Democrat MP, four Labour MPs, one Social Democratic and Labour Party MP, one Conservative MP and one Green MP. The bill aimed at amending the Immigration and Asylum Act 1999 in order that asylum support rates must be reviewed annually, that they must be increased in line with increases in mainstream benefits when goods prices have increased and that Section 4 support should cease to be delivered via vouchers. The bill was scheduled for a second reading in the House of Commons, but since it was a Private Member's Bill, that meant that it would only be debated if there was time on the day of the scheduled debate. As the tenth bill on the list to be discussed on 3 May 2013, it had little hope of being debated and went no further.

In July 2013 the charity Freedom from Torture, which supports torture survivors, published a research report on poverty amongst asylum seekers, refused asylum seekers and refugees (Pettitt 2013). In his foreword Juan E. Méndez, United Nations Special Rapporteur on Torture and Other Cruel, Inhuman or Degrading Treatment or Punishment, wrote,

> The research [documented in this report] demonstrates that torture survivors living in exile in the UK are pushed into poverty by government systems that are meant to support them as they pass through the asylum determination system and beyond. I know through the work of my mandate internationally that many torture survivors who manage to reach and claim protection in States such as the UK may not have directly experienced these levels of absolute or relative poverty before. (Pettitt 2013: 2)

The sample size in the Freedom from Torture research was small: just eighty-five participants covering all categories of legal status from refused asylum seeker to recognised refugee, a fact which diminished the impact of the report when presented as evidence in the courts later. Nineteen people surveyed were asylum seekers on Section 95 support. Eight of these were '*never* or *not often* able to buy enough food of sufficient quality and variety to meet their needs for a nutritionally balanced diet' and '*never* or *not often* able to buy enough food of any quality to prevent them from being hungry'. Fourteen were '*never* or *not often* able to buy appropriate clothing which is adequate to keep them warm, clean and dry'. Specific items that people said they were unable to afford included non-prescription medicines, sanitary products, nappies for babies and personal or household cleaning products and toiletries. The authors of the report wrote,

> apart from the potential health impacts, people also reported a loss of dignity and self-respect when they were unable to take care of themselves in the way that they would normally expect - and humiliation when they were forced to ask others for personal items such as sanitary towels. (Pettitt 2013: 29)

Many said that they 'do not have enough money to pay for essential travel expenses connected with their asylum claim, such as attending appointments with their legal representative and including attending required "reporting" appointments with the UK Border Agency'. Many others said that they 'can only sometimes afford to pay for transport to get to these appointments, depending on what their other essential expenses have been that day/week' (Pettitt 2013: 30). The authors called upon the government to raise asylum support rates, to provide for a standard of living equivalent to mainstream welfare support provision, to at least 70 percent of income support rates and to increase rates in line with annual cost of living increments for mainstream support.

The charity Refugee Action then sought a judicial review of the decision not to increase support levels in 2013–14. The court could not advise on what the appropriate level of support to meet the essential living needs of asylum seekers might be (that judgment is vested by Parliament in the elected government of the day) but could determine whether the decision not to increase support levels was made on the basis of sound evidence, systematic methods and rational decision making and in compliance with legal obligations such as the ECHR. It was noted by the Judge, Hon. Mr. Justice Popplewell, that making an assessment of 'essential living needs' is a subjective exercise and though the scope of these needs was viewed by the Home Secretary in a more restrictive manner than Refugee Action might like, it was within her power to do so: 'what is "essential" is a criterion on which views may differ widely' (Regina (Refugee Action) vs. Secretary of State for the Home Department, para 182).

Mr. Justice Popplewell nevertheless determined that the Secretary of State had failed to take into account a number of items in her assessment of asylum support levels, including essential household goods such as washing powder, special requirements of new mothers such as nappies, non-prescription medication and the opportunity to maintain interpersonal relationships and participate in social, cultural and religious life. He also determined that she had failed to consider whether travel by public transport to attend appointments with legal advisors when not covered by legal aid, telephone calls to maintain contact with families and legal representatives and writing materials where necessary for communication and for the education of children were essential living needs. He did not, however, find that the decision to freeze support rates was completely irrational ('Wednesbury unreasonable' in legal terms) since much of the evidence presented to the court by Refugee Action – from the two inquiries mentioned above, their own research with their clients, witness statements and the Freedom from Torture report – were 'laden with value judgements' and could not be judged as conclusive (Regina (Refugee Action) vs. Secretary of State for the Home Department, para 269). The judge did note that 'although this support for asylum seekers is temporary, it is often required for a substantial period ... The most recent statistics I was given were that, of the 13,412 asylum applicants who came off s. 95 support in 2013 ... 27.5% were on it for over 2 years' (case report, para 20).

The day after the judgement was delivered MP Sarah Teather put an urgent question on asylum support to the immigration minister in Parliament (House of Commons 10 April 2014). She asked whether the Home Secretary 'will make a statement on support provided to meet the essential living needs of asylum seekers under sections 95 and 98 of the Immigration and Asylum Act 1999'. Teather called for a full independent review of support levels with a transparent decision-making process and the right to work for asylum seekers. She said,

> Is not the problem that this decision is a personal fiefdom of the Home Secretary, driven entirely by base political motives? She can and does ignore detailed representations by other Ministers across the Government. She can and does ignore parliamentarians, including the findings of a cross-party inquiry that I chaired last year. She can and does ignore the pleas of those who work with victims of torture, who say that she is exacerbating their trauma and forcing them into severe poverty. It is an indictment of the current process that Refugee Action and the Migrants Law Project had to take the Home Secretary to court to get any kind of oversight of the process. (House of Commons, 10 April 2014)

Labour MP Jeremy Corbyn, then a backbencher, asked, 'will the Minister look at the misery, destitution and waste of human resources that comes from keeping asylum seekers in desperate poverty, and not allowing them to work and contribute to our society and economy?' (House of Commons 10 April 2014), to which the minister's answer was that support levels were appropriate. Labour/Co-operative MP Mark Lazarowicz said that if the level of support was right in 2011 'it is hard to believe that, given the increase in basic living standard costs over the past three years, it is still right in 2014' and asked, 'would it not be sensible to agree an interim increase at this stage, pending the review that, as the Minister said, will take at least some months?' The minister answered that support levels would not be changed as he would not want to pre-empt the outcome of the review. As is often the case with parliamentary debates, the focus of the House then began to scatter, with questions and statements arising variously about Syrian quota refugees, numbers of asylum applications to the United Kingdom generally, the closure of face to face asylum advice services, recognition rates and the right to work. On support rates, however, the minister continued to repeat that support rates would not necessarily be increased following the High Court ruling but were subject to ongoing review.

In June 2014, three months after the High Court ruling, a group of six MPs led by Teresa Pearce (Labour) put forward an EDM in Parliament in response to the High Court judgment on asylum support (EDM 99 of 2014–15). Grass roots organisations all over the country, including the City of Sanctuary movement, the Regional Refugee Forum North East and the Regional Asylum Activism Project mobilised people of various immigration statuses, including citizens, to lobby their local MP to sign the EDM. The text of the EDM stated that the sponsors plus ninety-eight signatories of the motion believed support rates to be 'detrimental to the well-being of refugees including children' and called on the government to raise asylum support rates to at least 70 percent of income support and to increase this in line with inflation annually. Only one Conservative MP signed the EDM and it had no discernible impact on government policy.

On 21 July 2014, MP David Hanson (Labour), Shadow Immigration Minister, formally opposed the cuts to asylum support and tabled an EDM (EDM 340 of 2015–16) which was signed by twenty-two Scottish National Party, Liberal Democrat and Green MPs. On the same day Labour MP John McDonnell tabled another EDM (EDM 344 of 2015–16) opposing the cuts, garnering twenty-seven signatures. In it he noted that the change went against the April High Court judgement. Again, these efforts had no impact on the actual policies, though EDMs are thought important in that they express the concerns of backbench MPs to the government.

In August 2014 the Home Office confirmed that it had conducted a review but remained satisfied that the levels of asylum support should remain unchanged. This meant that despite all their efforts, the judicial review case had no impact on support rates. The following year rates were in fact further reduced (see table 7.1) following a Home Office internal review of asylum support which found that rates were too high, as they did not take into account the economies of scale that are possible within families. The changes introduced a single weekly rate of asylum support (£36.95 per adult or child), which is the same as the amount previously paid to single adult asylum seekers. The change meant a substantial reduction in support for single parents and families with children. Stephen Hale, Chief Executive of Refugee Action, commented in response to this change:

> These cruel cuts will plunge families into further poverty. They will make it agonisingly tough for parents to feed their children, and practically impossible to buy clothes and other essential items. It is deeply concerning that some of the most vulnerable children in our society are being targeted by the Home Office in this way. (Refugee Action 2016)

Judith Dennis, Refugee Council Policy Manager, said,

> These shameful cuts will plunge children further into poverty and could cause even more unnecessary hunger, ill health and anxiety for some of the most vulnerable families in Britain. It's utterly appalling that the Government has chosen to exacerbate the suffering of people who are already living in desperate situations. (The Refugee Council 2016)

Sarah Wollerston, Conservative MP for Totnes, submitted a written request to the Home Secretary, read out in Parliament, to commission an independent review of asylum support rates. This was quickly dismissed by Immigration Minister James Brokenshire (House of Commons, 8 July 2015). Anger amongst the transformative order was in part because these changes were laid before Parliament without consulting with the Liberal Democrat side of the coalition, who often resisted such proposals, or with key third-sector actors outside of Parliament. No one outside of the Home Office had been informed that they were coming and asylum seekers who were about to see a significant reduction in their support were not notified. A number of (particularly Liberal Democrat) parliamentarians and activists, notably MP Sarah Teather, raised concerns about this, and Nick Clegg (Liberal Democrat), in one of his last actions as Deputy Prime Minister, vetoed the regulations.

The new support rates were due to come into force on 6 April 2015, but as a result of Clegg's intervention on 27 March the government reversed its decision to reduce the rate of Section 95 support for children by £16.00 per week.[1] The explanatory note for the second set of regulations simply states: 'On reflection, the Government has decided that not all of these changes should be implemented from 6 April 2015' (2015). Following the 2015 general election, the end of the coalition, and the arrival of a full Conservative government, the original regulations were then re-tabled in the form of the Asylum Support (Amendment No. 3) Regulations 2015. These revoked the Amendment No. 2 Regulations and introduced the flat rate of support that came into effect in August 2015. In short, Clegg's actions had only delayed the reduction in support rates by a matter of months.

There was great anger about this. Baroness Lister of Burtersett stated in the House of Lords,

> As I understand it, the stakeholder forum of voluntary organisations working with asylum seekers was informed on 23 March, just two weeks before the regulations were due to come into force. I learned of the regulations the following day by pure chance. No other parliamentarian whom I contacted, Front Bench or Back Bench, knew anything about them. It is thanks only to the behind-the-scenes intervention of the former MP Sarah Teather, who was a great parliamentary champion of asylum seekers, that they were withdrawn as they had not been agreed by the coalition partners. It was shoddy behaviour on the part of the Home Office to sneak out controversial regulations in this way at a time when Parliament could do nothing about them. (House of Lords, 27 October 2015)

The resistance did not end there, however. The Sanctuary movement mobilised their supporters against the change with local actions. For example, in Huddersfield asylum seeking families produced cards drawn by their children, which they sent to their local MP, asking for Section 95 support to remain the same. The Refugee Council called on the government to commission an independent review of asylum support rates, but the government confirmed that it had no plans to do so. A motion to annul the new regulations was tabled in the House of Lords. That debate saw some passionate speeches based upon a deep knowledge of the issue. Baroness Hamwee said in her opening speech,

> I tabled this Motion after thinking about the impact of arriving in the UK with nothing but the clothes you stand up in, which are probably inadequate for our climate, probably in a fragile state of health, mentally and physically, not being allowed to work and living on sums which I am told are 60% below the poverty line ... The support is designed to avoid destitution. Does it do so? These regulations clearly do not avoid misery ... I am very concerned. (House of Lords, 27 October 2015)

Lord Rosser, Shadow Spokesperson for Home Affairs, described how the Secondary Legislation Scrutiny Committee had decided to draw this issue to the attention of the House because the change being brought in 'had been poorly managed, particularly given the sudden change to claimants' income as there were no transitional provisions'. In fact, none of the concerns raised by the Secondary Legislation Scrutiny Committee in the first iteration of this policy change had been addressed, including the absence of a cost–benefit analysis assessment, the lack of an estimation of the number of households that would be affected, the absence of a definition of 'essential needs' and a policy impact assessment. Lord Rosser characterised the response of the immigration minister to these concerns as 'We have decided, and we do not accept that we must give a reason or explanation for our decision to anyone – certainly not, apparently, to either Parliament or the House of Lords Secondary Legislation Scrutiny Committee'.

Lord Rosser and other contributors to the debate described how asylum seekers were living in poverty, how this particularly endangered children and was likely to be in contravention of the UN Convention on the Rights of the Child and how mental and physical illness were being compounded by insufficient support rates. For example, Lord Alton of Liverpool said that

> It is usually a pretty good test of the decency of any society to examine how it treats its most vulnerable. By anybody's reckoning, you do not come much more vulnerable than children who are members of families seeking safety from persecution or war ... In the 21st century, in the fourth-richest country on earth, people are being reduced to absolute destitution, not by accident or personal tragedy but by deliberate act of policy—and we should therefore certainly reconsider these regulations today by supporting the Motion in the name of the noble Baroness, Lady Hamwee. (House of Lords, 27 October 2015)

Baroness Janke drew attention to the fact that asylum-seeking children are not treated as equal to British children in their need for nutrition and a nurturing environment. She observed that 'on the one hand, public agencies tell us we should have a healthy diet, and how we should bring up our children and avoid disease. Yet there is one rule for our children and another rule for other people's children'. It did not seem too great a challenge, she suggested, to 'allow our children, and the children of other people, to have the same protection, the same rights, the same democracy and the same civilised country that I believe we have'. Here, the discourse of civilisation is, as in previous chapters, associated with helping unfortunate others in the Victorian tradition of Christian charity. By this point this is also bound up with a secular humanitarianism. Lord Berkeley of Knighton Crossbench commented that 'we have heard some very disturbing facts, and I want to be reassured that this Government are a humanitarian Government ... and do care about these issues and about people who are clearly suffering'. Lord Rosser stated that

> The case for the Government changing their approach towards a group of highly vulnerable people is very strong. Whether they will do so is of course a totally different matter, but not doing so will certainly say a great deal about the attitude of this Government to a group of people in our midst currently in real need and

whose position over the past two and a half months has become significantly worse. (House of Lords, 27 October 2015)

At the end of a long debate with unanimous anger from the speakers about the changes and the treatment of asylum seekers in the United Kingdom in general, the House nevertheless rejected the motion to reject the regulation 194 votes to 68.

The Coloniality of Power: The Anti-Asylum Institutional Order

As with all of the previous cases discussed in this volume, the key distinctions to be made between the transformative order and the colonial order (here the anti-asylum institutional order) are in size and power. The order discussed in this section is small, it is not made up of diverse interests or 'strange bedfellows', it is essentially the state – government and civil service – and it is therefore much more powerful than those seeking transformative change.

The discourses employed by these powerful actors within government are close to those used by the transformative order – they speak largely in the same terms. Where they differ is in the conclusions made. So, for example, the Home Office focuses on their fulfilment of statutory duties and human rights commitments as evidence of their fair treatment of fellow humans. However, limitations are placed on the extent of the generosity of the state's payments to working citizens by the requirement to offer value for money to taxpayers. If this is the limit test and justifies the fulfilment of minimum obligations only, then the broad consensus that poverty is bad and should be eliminated from society troubles the argument that asylum support rates should be kept very low. In response, the discursive manoeuvre used by the

Table 7.4. The Anti-Asylum Institutional Order

Level	Who?	How?
1. Government	Home Secretary: Theresa May Immigration Minister: James Brokenshire	Policy making and retaining. Answering written and oral questions in Parliament. Giving evidence in select committees.
2. Civil Service	Home Office officials	Policy making and retaining. Writing policy briefing documents. Undertaking reviews of asylum support. Drafting responses to questions made in Parliament.
	Home Office lawyers	Representing the Home Office at judicial review.

Table 7.5. Discourses Used by Anti-Asylum Actors

Discourse	General Focus/Argument	Use for the Anti-Asylum Order	Key Interpretations (by all or some of the alliance)
Statutory duty (national law)	The state must deliver at least minimum standards of living to asylum seekers and vulnerable groups in general.	Justifies adhering to minimum standards.	Policy meets minimum obligations.
Human rights (international law)	States must deliver at least minimum standards of living to asylum seekers awaiting a decision on their application, to all children, and to non-returnable refused asylum seekers.	Justifies adhering to minimum standards.	Policy meets minimum obligations.
Sovereign duty to taxpaying citizens	The state has a duty to deliver 'value for money' in public spending.	Support levels must not be too generous otherwise will not be fair on taxpayers.	Support rates must be low to deliver value for money for the taxpayer.
Anti-poverty	Poverty is bad for individuals and societies.	Support levels are not as low as they could be and do not result in poverty.	Support rates are in fact generous.

Home Office is that asylum support rates are not as low as they might be and are in fact generous.

The review which led to the freezing of asylum support rates in 2013–14 was conducted by the Home Office from late 2012 to April 2013. In a letter dated 5 June 2013 the Home Secretary informed the deputy prime minister, Nick Clegg, of her decision not to increase levels of support for both asylum seekers and refused asylum seekers (on Section 4 support): 'I have concluded that the packages of support provided under section 95 and section 4 of the Immigration and Asylum Act 1999 are sufficient, and meet the statutory requirement to provide for recipients' essential living needs'. She explained that both groups are provided with 'fully furnished and equipped housing provided free of charge with no bills to pay, and modest rates of financial support are paid to meet recipients' other essential living needs'. She went on:

> I have carefully considered whether those rates of financial support are adequate, whether they meet the requirement set by Parliament that they provide the essential living needs of recipients and their dependants if they would otherwise be destitute, and whether they are coherent when compared to changes in the mainstream benefit system. ... I have concluded that the system of support is reasonable and consistent with our statutory obligations, as are the rates of financial support paid. (see case report)

The Home Secretary emphasised that there were two key concerns in setting asylum support levels. The first was whether the rate meets the minimum standards of the statutory test set by Parliament and the obligations under European Union (EU) law (to ensure a standard of living adequate for the health of applicants and capable of ensuring their subsistence). The second was to 'demonstrate fairness to the taxpayer'. On the first point she hit back at NGOs:

> Critics have asserted that the rates of support are insufficient, especially for children, and leave families unable to afford sufficient food. I do not accept that. Under current rates a family of four awaiting the outcome of their asylum application would receive more than £175 per week to pay for their food, toiletries and clothing. Additional funds are paid to pregnant women, and to young children and assistance with the costs of transport and telephone calls are provided where needed. We pay higher rates of asylum support to children than many of our EU contemporaries; and data from the Office for National Statistics shows that support rates are on a par with families' spending on essential items for those households with basic but regular income from employment. Whilst modest, the rates are not ungenerous or insufficient. (see case report)

Note the difference in language style here, when compared to the transformative order. Where the transformative order use passionate, emotive language and appeal to people's moral concerns around child protection and common humanity, the Home Secretary uses a detached, formal tone. She lays out the rational basis for the decision rather than engaging with the more emotive moral claims made by those arguing for increased support rates.

The evidence given to the judicial review by the Home Office is informative in understanding the process by which the decision to freeze rates was made. The process involved the following:

- Visits to twelve asylum accommodation properties in Greater Manchester and London. Observations were made about the quantity of food in the cupboards, types of packaging in the bin and cleanliness of the property.
- Price inflation data for essential goods.
- Comparison with Office for National Statistics (ONS) survey data about average household spending for lowest income groups.

- Comparison with income support (deemed incomparable as it is not temporary, does not allow for economies of scale and provides for a higher standard of living than is necessary to meet the statutory requirements of asylum support).
- Comparison with countries within Europe (deemed incomparable because asylum systems support are so different).

The expenditure of the poorest 10 percent of the UK population – £134.80 per household (1.3 people) per week – was found to be around three times more than the support provided to asylum seekers, but the Home Office noted that a greater proportion of this income would be spent on more discretionary items and not essential living needs. Spending on recreation added up to £18 per week for the poorest 10 percent; spending on hotels and restaurants was £9.80. The ONS data showed that

> the poorest 10% of the UK spend only around £37 per week per household (of 1.3 persons) on essential items (i.e. food and non-alcoholic drink, clothing). Therefore the value of other costs met by those households, and not essential for those receiving asylum support, are significant in determining how much support a person actually requires. (legal report, emphasis in original)

The official giving evidence to the judicial review also commented, without elaboration, that 'it was also noted [in the Home Office review of support rates] that the Red Cross provides food and toiletries parcels to destitute persons (valued at around £10 per week)', as though this might be evidence of the needs of asylum seekers, rather than the capabilities of a charity with limited resources.

Regarding inflationary considerations, the Home Office concluded that 'the basket of goods used to calculate food inflation (2% in September 2012 and 4.2% in January 2013) ... includes most commonly purchased items, some of which will not be essential, and will not be the cheapest choice'. Those items which cannot be considered essential were not identified. It was also noted that prices of clothing and footwear went down by 0.5 percent in September 2012, and were up by 0.2 percent in January 2013, making the need to increase support rates for these items null. Consideration was given to the position of sixteen-/seventeen-year-olds – whether the rates for this group should be increased to the rate paid to children under sixteen. In his oral evidence to the judicial review a Home Office official commented that 'whilst they may have some higher costs (than an adult) if attending college (e.g. transport. stationery and possibly uniform) ... post-16 education is not compulsory for recipients of asylum support)', though this is the case for British young people. There was also mention of preparing sixteen-year-olds for the transition to adulthood (and the lower adult rate), though of course it would be the intention that no asylum seekers were ever on asylum support for years on end.

All of this reasoning points to the fact that the Home Office understood that levels of asylum support would mean that recipients were living quite unpleasant lives in poverty, but the most important considerations were not these but rather whether such measures were legal and cost as little as possible for the public purse. All of the justificatory documents reviewed here repeat in several places that the Home Office has taken into account the requirement under EU law to ensure that asylum seekers have a standard of living adequate for their health and to enable their subsistence and the domestic law requirement to provide support to enable asylum seekers to meet their essential living needs. Account was also taken of Article 3 of the ECHR (prohibition against torture/inhumane treatment) and for children, the duty under Section 55 of the Borders and Citizenship Act 2000. In the judicial review evidence a Home Office spokesman described how, with reference to these legal instruments and the evidence described above, some minimum, or 'floor', requirements could be identified. Those which should be covered under the £36.95 weekly payment are

- sufficient food to keep those on support in health and to avoid illness or malnourishment;
- essential toiletries (or means to pay for them);
- the means to travel to appointments where they are out of reach;
- a contribution to wider socialisation costs to promote children's development; and
- for those in receipt of asylum support for any length of time, the provision of suitable clothing to avoid any danger of illness.

As discussed in the previous section, the judicial review concluded with the Home Office being asked to review its method for determining asylum support levels since some important items were not included. Once this review was completed, the Home Office determined that the levels of support provided were in fact correct and the rates of support should not be increased. Immigration Minister James Brokenshire wrote to the National Asylum Stakeholder Forum, a group whose purpose was to bring together external stakeholders with the Home Office in order to promote dialogue and transparency, with this news. He explained that the ONS data of the expenditure of the poorer 10 percent of UK citizens had been used as the sole basis for the decision. This meant some adjustments, as the poorest of UK citizens were assumed to buy more clothes than was strictly essential and only one bus journey per week (costing £3.00 per return journey, though in many cities the cost of a return journey exceeds this) was deemed necessary for asylum seekers. It was stated that some families were receiving as much as 80 percent of income support payments, and the figure for such units was therefore clearly too high. While those in the transformative order challenging the adequacy of the support rates had compiled a body of evidence from a range of sources which contested the assessment that support levels were adequate, Queen's Counsel (QC) Mr. Sheldon, representing the Home Secretary, dismissed this evidence as 'anecdotal and/or flawed and/or irrelevant' (legal report).

At the Conservative party conference on 7 October 2015 the prime minister promised to tackle 'the scourge of poverty. The brick wall of blocked opportunity' (Cameron 2015). He declared an 'all-out assault on poverty', suggesting that it creates problems for everyone in society and demanding equality of opportunity for all. By 'all' he referred to all *citizens*. During the House of Lords debate on 27 October, which discussed a motion to annul the change which would introduce flat rates for all asylum seekers, the contradiction between this anti-poverty pronouncement and the treatment of asylum seekers was raised. In response, Lord Bates (Home Office Minister in the House of Lords) explained,

> I know that we are talking about vulnerable people. I know that we are talking about people who are hovering precariously above the line of destitution, with all sorts of pressures on their mind. However, those of us who have had families would all recognise that, if you are cooking a meal for four, it is less expensive per unit than if you are providing food for one. (House of Lords, 27 October 2015)

Before reiterating that the UK government is meeting all of its international obligations to meet the essential living needs of asylum seekers, he explained that asylum support is in fact quite generous:

> I have tried to set out that there is a substantial basis of support for asylum seekers. We recognise that they are vulnerable. These cash payments need to be seen in the context of that wider support. When people question whether the cash sums are below the poverty line – we were talking about what poverty was in terms of 60% of median earnings – we need to remember that that is in cash terms. But we are talking here not about that but about all the other things: the homes fully furnished; the repairs already paid for; all the utilities bills paid; all the council tax paid; and all the healthcare paid. All of that is there. (House of Lords, 27 October 2015)

The discursive framing of this issue by the government suggests that support levels meet all aspirations: they fulfil international and national legal duties, are generous to asylum seekers and deliver value for money for taxpayers.

And yet, the only element of this narrative that does not appear to be true is that support levels are generous – the Home Secretary tacitly admitted this when she suggested that support rates should not exceed the spending money of the poorest 10 percent of the British population. Indeed, the expert evidence presented by the transformative order, who have no clear interest in expending excessive amounts of time and energy on a senseless battle with the government, suggests that support levels are in fact inadequate. Indeed, upon closer inspection, there is an inherent contradiction between the various discursive framings of the issue by the government. Support levels must only meet the absolute minimum standard set by the government; this should be lower than the money available to the poorest 10 percent of citizens, and yet levels are also *generous*. Levels of support are lower than the poorest 10 percent of citizens (and poverty amongst this group must be tackled), but they do not place people below the poverty line. Support levels are adequate to respect the needs of children and young people, but asylum-seeking young people are not expected to be in education after the age of sixteen. Furthermore, claims by a leading children's charity and by the Children's Commissioner that asylum-seeking children are living in poverty are implied to be incorrect.

Human Rights, Asylum Seekers' Rights and the Continued Legacies of Differential Humanity

What can we conclude from this brief snapshot in the history of asylum support? Well, we know that a large coalition of MPs, Lords, healthcare professionals, social workers, academic researchers, activists, asylum seekers and refugees, community organisations and large third sector organisations, including very large and well-respected NGOs such as the Red Cross, have all argued ceaselessly and without caveat or caution that the levels of support provided to asylum seekers in the United Kingdom at the present time are inadequate. And they are not just inadequate; they are so low as to have detrimental impacts on the physical and mental health of asylum seekers: baby, child and adult alike. Furthermore, the implications are so grave for children that numerous individuals have questioned whether support levels are in contravention of the UN Convention on the Rights of the Child. This is not surprising since, as discussed above, research has found that anything less than 70 percent of the jobseeker's allowance puts people well below the poverty line.

The response of those with policy-making power to the efforts of these actors and organisations working for change has been variously to ignore them, resist their efforts when forced to respond and to deny that there is any credible evidence to support their claims. Yet what the records of Home

Office responses to the judicial review case brought by Refugee Action in 2013 amount to is an underlying assumption of inequality. While the judge in the judicial review case found that there were certain provisions which had not been factored into the analysis, such as nappies and formula milk, the QC defending the Home Secretary at the judicial review was correct in observing that what was at stake was a value judgement: What are essential living needs? The Home Office determined 'essential' to be commensurate with a 'subsistence' level which is wholly unequal and indeed at odds with anti-poverty ambitions set by the government with respect to citizens. The transformative order meanwhile took 'essential' to mean an adequate standard of living at least in line with that experienced by the poorest 10 percent of UK households. According to the ONS the expenditure of the poorest 10 percent of the United Kingdom is £134.80 per household (1.3 people) per week. Asylum seekers receive £43.10 per household per week. This in itself says a lot about how these different institutional orders view asylum seekers.

Asylum seekers are not equal to citizens and can be expected to live within economic, and indeed educational, constraints, which are deemed unacceptable for citizens. Such constraints are thought unacceptable for citizens in part because they have negative consequences for the individual, and in part because of the impact on the whole of society – in terms of increased use of healthcare for mental and physical health problems, increased criminality, increased infant mortality, etc. The fact that the judge in the judicial review case specifically highlighted the absence of vital and basic provisions for babies such as nappies and formula milk in asylum support calculations and still the Home Office decreased the payments further should give us real pause for thought. Does this amount to dehumanisation? Does it reveal a human hierarchy in which some are more easily, and readily, kept in poverty than others? Or is it simply an issue of citizenship? The state has a sovereign responsibility to protect, look after, foster the flourishing of citizens. Others are outside of that remit. There are two linked responses to these questions.

First, the transformative order is not here seeking equality between citizens and asylum seekers in relation to their access to economic, political and social rights. Rather, they are seeking equality of humanity in relation to access to basic living conditions and freedom from state-enforced poverty. Second, and leading on from this, the British state has signed conventions stating that people should have access to certain rights when their own state has let them down. The assumption within the human rights conventions is that all are equal as human beings. And yet, as we saw in the previous chapter, those conventions were never intended for all human beings; they were differentiated with a higher level of protection being reserved for the non-colonised peoples of the world. With the expansion of those rights in 1967 such inequality was meant to be erased, but we can see such a rationale active in Britain today, in the maintaining of asylum seekers in a situation of poverty. The only thing standing between this situation and destitution is the minimum standard set in the human rights convention, a convention that Britain explicitly did not wish to be extended to the non-colonised.

However, by this time there is little in the way of bold moves to transform, and rehumanise, the whole asylum regime on the part of the transformative order. Activities pursued are focused on trying to curb the worst excesses of the regime. There is little public interest in rehumanising the system, making this a marginal activity where NGOs and refugee community organisations work together to try to get slightly less worse outcomes for asylum seekers. The issue is not grand, then; it is bureaucratic and technocratic, and yet what is at stake is something much greater. This case study suggests that since there is such a weak commitment to human rights when they affect the least desirable people, it is their legal authority that is vital, over and above any pretence at a moral commitment. Interventions are therefore made on a highly technical and legalistic basis, attempting to put a dent in the regime but with no ambition of seeing its downfall. The human rights framework is a minimum, a barrier preventing descent into the worst excesses of dehumanisation, and in this sense it works. But it does not guarantee human equality; it does not wholly protect people from less powerful states, especially when they are most vulnerable. The sovereign power to determine the parameters of acceptable treatment, in this case 'essential living needs', remains with the state, and the state enacts that power through a regime of differential humanity so old it can no longer be named. The legalistic language therefore masks ill treatment and transforms disempowerment into legitimate action.

The letter of the human rights conventions, but not the spirit, is therefore met. The aspiration of hospitality has been replaced by the fulfilling of minimum standards in order to avoid international embarrassment or sanctions. By contrast, the UK government over the past decade has declared a war on poverty, particularly amongst children. It is clear, then, that there is a practical regime of differential humanity operating here, that conditions of impoverishment and endangerment are simply more tolerable for some human beings than for others in Britain today. How do we make sense of this regime of differential humanity, where even children, who are widely seen to be inherently innocent and in need of special protection and care, are not deemed worthy of the same levels of care if they are seeking asylum? The preceding three chapters give the answer to this question. Through them I have panned through time, zooming in at particular historical moments, in order to chart the coloniality of power. Indeed, let us remind ourselves of who are the targets of these policies. The main countries of origin of asylum seekers change every year with the ebb and flow of displacement-inducing events, but consistently these are people coming from outside of Europe, often former colonies, always from those countries that Britain so determinedly sought to exclude from the right to asylum in 1951. The coloniality of power is not an empty academic phrase; it refers to those very empirically identifiable practices of human classification and differentiation which set some apart from others and give rise to unequal treatment. If coloniality is a way of looking at the world in civilisational terms, it is this concept which names the practices of dehumanisation described in this chapter.

NOTE

1. Asylum Support (Amendment) Regulations 2015, SI 2015/645, revoked and replaced by Asylum Support (Amendment No.2) Regulations 2015, SI 2015/944.

Chapter Eight

Asylum after Empire

Through empirical cases spanning more than two hundred years, this book has charted the development, evolution and mutation of ideas of human hierarchy. A whole host of complexly entangled histories have been brought together to argue that the logics of excludability not only *result in* dehumanisation, but also *emerge from* long-standing modes of thinking about the world, and the various people in it, in colonial/modern hierarchical terms. The introduction began with the observation that many forced and undocumented migrants make connections between their present situation and histories of colonial domination and its attendant racism. That this is not the starting point of many scholars working on the British context is perhaps part of a wider colonial amnesia in which events taking place within the geographical space of Europe, such as the Cold War and the two world wars of the twentieth century, are more readily brought to mind as contextually significant to contemporary politics and policy than five hundred years of European colonialism.

The book began with a discussion of the rise of asylum as an issue of significant political concern since the 1980s, a concern which was mirrored by the development of refugee studies as an academic field. While asylum seekers have come to be understood as a problem to be solved, largely through exclusionary means, academics responding to this policy agenda have sought a variety of critical inroads in analysing the politics and public policy of asylum. Though much of this work makes important contributions to our understanding of the policy regime and its impacts on the lives of asylum seekers, the almost exclusive focus on the present means that history is neglected. This and the lack of serious theoretical engagement are well-established criticisms of the field (see Elie 2014). A 'standard narrative' on the history which is relevant to the current moment was therefore identified in chapter 2. This narrative focuses on a select European history which inevitably leads to contemporary asylum seekers being conceptualised as 'new' and 'different', rather than historically consistent. I critiqued this standard narrative by focusing on the 'sociology of absences' – what is missing from the dominant account.

Chapter 3 offered an alternative standpoint from which to approach the politics of asylum. The standard narrative was problematised, drawing on the work of B.S. Chimni, as a 'myth of difference' and the inadequacy of theories of 'racism' or 'racialisation' to account for the hostile policy regime explained. This chapter offered an alternative theoretical starting point drawing on the postcolonial and decolonial critique of modernity as deeply interwoven with histories of colonialism. Following Michel-Rolph Trouillot, Walter Mignolo and Sylvia Wynter, the entanglement of exclusionary and hierarchical ideas of 'man' and the 'human' with ideas of modernity was discussed and developed as a means of making sense of the contemporary non-entrée regime for asylum seekers. Central to this is the concept of coloniality/modernity – coloniality and modernity as two sides of the same coin which have informed hegemonic Western modes of understanding the world over time and into the present.

Chapters 4, 5 and 6 traced three critical junctures which together provided the empirical evidence required for wider claims to be made about the connections between colonialism and contemporary asylum policy. Chapter 4 was concerned with the role that slavery played in influencing early conceptions of humanity and differential rights, and how this ideology was augmented by the campaign for abolition. While this is a history which is not usually associated with the idea of the refugee, and may not be what Marfleet (2007) had in mind when he called upon refugee studies scholars to undertake historical work, starting here was, for me, absolutely necessary in moving away from 'the European refugee' as the central figure in the story of the development of the non-entrée regime. The case focuses on one of the earliest legal expansions of the category of 'man' which would later be used as a basis for human rights. It offered an exploration of the debates around the humanity of black bodies and the possibility of extending rights to them in the past. This legislation represents the first critical juncture in a long series of connected histories which have contributed to the framing and understanding of the deserving and the undeserving, the familiar and the 'other' in Britain. In this book a pragmatic decision was made to undertake four 'snapshots' in the form of the diachronic analysis, but these snapshots are part of a much larger set of globally interconnected histories.

Chapter 5 was then concerned with the rise of conceptions of racial hierarchy in the nineteenth century and the ways in which these taxonomies influenced international relations in the twentieth century. If refugee studies scholars address the Paris Peace Conference, it is most likely to be because the

League of Nations which was founded at the conference oversaw early international responses to refugee displacement in Europe. Here, I was interested not in specific mechanisms for dealing with European refugees but in tracing historical continuities in modes of viewing non-Europeans in the colonial world before such peoples had access to the right to asylum. This, for me, is the relevant context to the current moment. Without this context the expansion of the right to asylum to non-Europeans in 1967 and beyond is simply a depoliticised expansion, a logical outcome of progress, demonstrating the liberal and progressive principles that now underpin national and international politics. This is not the view of history advanced in this book. Rather, chapter 6 shows that powerful ideas of human hierarchy had an enduring impact in world politics into the twentieth century.

Chapter 6 was concerned with the institutionalisation of human rights, and by extension the right to asylum, in the mid-twentieth century. The focus here was on the 1951 United Nations (UN) Geneva Convention on the Status of Refugees, one part of the international legal framework for human rights which emerged in this period. The Geneva Convention is central to scholarship on refugee and asylum issues and has come to be associated with the very idea of a universalised rights-bearing human being. Yet the focus on European asylum seekers is only one part of the story. The period in question was also one of the dismantling of colonialism and a profound reshaping of the world order which involved massive displacements outside of Europe. Drawing out the relevance of these histories to the founding of human rights in international law is the task of this case study. The themes addressed in chapters 5 and 6 are of course of vital relevance here. By selecting this founding moment of contemporary asylum rights as a critical juncture, I was able to exposit the entanglement of colonialism and decolonisation with the institutionalisation of asylum policy, and thus call for a reconsideration of the bases for critical analysis in which we engage. While this example *is* about the history of the refugee, my aim was to demonstrate how this history is linked not just to the history of refugee reception internationally, but also, vitally, to colonial histories and worldviews.

Chapter 7 detailed the complex case of contestations around asylum support in Britain in recent years. This case study demonstrates the institutional, legal and procedural means through which asylum seekers are effectively dehumanised, and yet also how this dehumanising process is undertaken in very carefully deracialised and depoliticised terms. Without the previous three chapters, the administrative means through which asylum seekers and failed asylum seekers are purposefully, and legally, impoverished in the United Kingdom today would be difficult to label in terms of the history of racism, of human hierarchy and of the exclusionary framework of modernity. With them, this case is a clear example of the coloniality of power, historically emergent and ever evolving. The chapter therefore explored the ways in which long-standing (modern) notions of human hierarchy continue to be quietly active in the contemporary asylum regime.

BEYOND AHISTORICITY

When asylum seekers make an application for asylum in Britain today, they are seeking asylum after Empire. The fact that non-Europeans can apply for asylum is a result of successful struggles for decolonisation, and then the subsequent struggle of non-Europeans to be included within the remit of the Refugee Convention. The original human rights conventions, including the Geneva Convention on the Status of Refugees, was written at a time when much of the world's population lived under colonial rule, and the assumptions of differential humanity underpinning the projects of the European empires also underpinned the 1951 negotiations. These histories, at and preceding 1951, are integral to making sense of the non-entrée regime that has attracted so much scholarly attention in recent years. But the coloniality of power which cuts through this policy area now and in the past is rarely acknowledged.

Such an analysis is only possible when the relevance of history is taken seriously. As the situation of asylum seekers, both within Britain and beyond, is so urgent, and appears to be subject to ever more authoritarian, rights-diminishing policies and practices, looking to history is for many an indulgent academic exercise. Should we not be critiquing the immediate impacts of policies and proposing alternative, more sympathetic and indeed *human* modes of responding to the existence of forced migrants in the world? Indeed we should, but incorporating history into our critiques can also aid the project of making sense of the non-entrée regime and of hostility to asylum seekers in broader society, as I hope this study has shown. Developments today can, therefore, be understood as part of historic developments, not just in relation to *refugee* histories as some (Marfleet 2007) have argued, but more fundamentally in relation to global histories of inclusion and exclusion. Acknowledging these histories is part of the process of making sense of the realities facing asylum seekers today and uncovering the power dynamics that make these realities possible.

This book is a historical sociology but it is not a history of the refugee. The aim of the project was to historicise Britain's contemporary response to asylum seekers, not to tell the story of different groups of displaced people over time. Though much empirical material has been shared, this has been done in order to trace the rise of ideas of human hierarchy over time in order to make sense of the present, rather than primarily to say, 'look, there were refugees in the past and they were treated better/worse/just as badly'. This historical work has been necessary because in order to theorise the British state's hostility to asylum seekers, it was also necessary to engage with those histories which also help us to theorise racism today. Hostility to asylum seekers is not straightforwardly racism, but it does have its origins in the same regimes of differential humanity which have marked anti-black racism, Islamophobia and other such phenomena. These things are colonial; they must be understood as a feature of the coloniality of power.

This book is by no means the final word on this topic; rather, it offers up a set of propositions and provocations to be explored further. It is a starting point at thinking beyond ahistoricity *with* postcoloniality and decoloniality. I have built upon Chimni's (1998) challenge to the 'myth of difference' and suggested some first steps towards thinking through hostility to asylum seekers within the context of colonial histories, but there is so much more to do to identify the coloniality of power in the present and through time.

Racism, Man and Human, Coloniality/Modernity

Many people in different contexts suggest that asylum policy in Britain today is dehumanising. Many have also observed that the dehumanising policy regime is coupled with a wider social context of hostility to asylum seekers which has many of the features of racism (in that it is directed at people from countries, cultures and religions which have not traditionally been categorised as 'British' – despite the global nature of the British Empire, and indeed that many asylum seekers are not white). And yet no systematic effort has been made to analyse the policy regime as explicitly dehumanising through a serious theoretical engagement with what that might mean conceptually. Equally, those studies that have named hostility to asylum seekers as racism are let down by a whole set of issues including the carefully deracialised language of policy makers and the empirical diversity of the legal category 'asylum seekers'.

The charge of racism has no analytical purchase if we focus only on acts of apparent racism in the present. There is not enough solid evidence for the charge because of the deracialisation of policy and political discourse and because asylum seekers are a legal category. But if we elaborate racism as emergent of colonialism and trace the history of coloniality/modernity, we then get a route map through which to explain how this hostility is linked to racism and how dehumanisation is possible by the state even in the post-racial policy language of the contemporary moment. In contrast to this presentist mode of analysis, I started in this study from the idea of modernity, of modern countries and modern people. Such ideas are rooted in the philosophical traditions of the Age of Enlightenment, and in colonial encounters. When Sylvia Wynter (2003) writes that '"man" is not the human, although it represents itself as if it were', she is explaining that the supposedly universal category of human, which has its origins in the idea of 'man', has been historically racialised, and yet at the same time it is today represented as unproblematically applicable to all human beings as though the old power relations are no longer relevant. Fanon too observed in the year that the Geneva Convention was expanded beyond Europe, 'your humanism claims we are at one with the rest of humanity but your racist methods set us apart' (Fanon 1967: 8). That this statement resonates so acutely in the present moment suggests that we have not come quite as far since 1967 as many imagine. Indeed, the history of the 'human' in human rights is also far more troubled than many would have us believe.

Bhabha (2005 [1994]) has observed that it is through the spatial metaphor that the social relations of modernity are conceived. And where is that spatial metaphor more visible than in the unsanctioned movement of people across borders? He further points out that 'the "value" of modernity is not located, a priori, in the passive fact of an ephochal event or idea – of progress, civility, the law – but has to be negotiated *within* the "enunciative" present of the discourse' (Bhabha 2005: 241). In other words, the idea of the modern, a concept which only has meaning in relation to *other* times and/or *other* places, is given meaning, negotiated and renegotiated in the present – over and over again. The process whereby asylum seekers came to be marked as different in line with a narrative of unwanted, alien 'others' from the 'underdeveloped', 'non-modern world' is one which is very specifically informed by histories of 'race' science but endures today because of the continued logics of coloniality – the legacies of the justificatory discourses of colonialism. In short, human rights must also be understood as fundamentally rooted in histories of colonial exclusion and discrimination. And yet shifts in vocabulary – from racialised to deracialised, from colonial to humanitarian – conceal the fact that those same hegemonic power structures are maintained in the present.

My analysis therefore links these histories to the present and provides a means of understanding hostility to asylum seekers today. While the analysis presented focuses on the British case, the study has broader ramifications for all who study borders and refugee movements in the contemporary world. Indeed, it is highly significant for scholars of international relations who look at migration, mobilities and border making more generally. Through the concept of coloniality we find that certain human bodies are often seen to exist in the past, while others (most often in the 'West') inhabit a modern present and embody the future. Some categories of migrant, including asylum seekers, are assigned non-modern status, thus making them undesirable to modern states. This standpoint exposes the limits of current approaches to the politics of asylum and suggests avenues for further work from this perspective in the field.

References

2014. Regina (Refugee Action) *v* Secretary of State for the Home Department. In *Hon. Mr Justice Popplewell*: Royal Courts of Justice Administrative Court. *The Asylum Support (Amendment No.2) Regulations 2015*.

Adi, H., M. Sherwood and G. Padmore. 1995. *The 1945 Manchester Pan-African Congress Revisited*. 3rd ed. London: New Beacon Books.

Allsopp, J., N. Sigona and J. Phillimore. 2014. 'Poverty among Refugees and Asylum Seekers in the UK: An Evidence and Policy Review.' *IRIS WORKING PAPER SERIES* NO.1/2014.

Amenta, E. 2009. 'Making the Most of an Historical Case Study: Configuration, Sequence, Casing, and the US Old Age Pension Movement.' In *The Sage Handbook of Case-Based Methods*, edited by D. Byrne and C.C. Ragin. London: Sage.

Amin, A. 2003. 'Unruly Strangers? The 2001 Urban Riots in Britain.' *International Journal of Urban and Regional Research* 27 (2): 460–463.

Anand, R.P. 2010. 'The Formation of International Organizations and India: A Historical Study.' *Leiden Journal of International Law* 23 (1): 5–21.

Anderson, C.E. 2003. *Eyes off the Prize: The United Nations and the African American Struggle for Human Rights, 1944–1955*. Cambridge: Cambridge University Press.

Anghie, A. 2008. *Imperialism, Sovereignty, and the Making of International Law, Cambridge Studies in International and Comparative Law*. Cambridge: Cambridge University Press.

Appleyard, R. 2001. 'International Migration Policies: 1950–2000.' *International Migration* 39 (6): 7–20.

Atkinson, M. 2013. 'Statement on the Report of the Parliamentary Inquiry into Asylum Support for Children and Young People.' http://www.childrenscommissioner.gov.uk/news/statement-report-parliamentary-inquiry-asylum-support-children9, Accessed on 1 June 2016.

Banton, M. 1997. *Ethnic and Racial Consciousness*. 2nd ed. London: Longman.

Banton, M. 1998. *Racial Theories*. 2nd ed. Cambridge: Cambridge University Press.

Banton, M. 2009. 'The Idiom of Race: A Critique of Presentism.' In *Theories of Race and Racism: A Reader*, edited by L. Back and J. Solomos, 55–67. London: Routledge.

Barber, M. and S. Ripley. 1988. 'Refugee Rights.' In *Human Rights in the United Kingdom*, edited by P. Sieghart. London: Human Rights Network.

Barclay, A. 1827. *A Practical View of the Present State of Slavery in the West Indies, or, An Examination of Mr. Stephen's Slavery of the British West India Colonies*. London: Smith, Elder & Co.

Barker, A.J. 1978. *The African Link: British Attitudes to the Negro in the Era of the Atlantic Slave Trade*. London: Frank Cass.

Barot, R. and J. Bird. 2001. 'Racialization: The Genealogy and Critique of a Concept.' *Ethnic and Racial Studies* 24 (4): 601–618.

Bennett, N. 2001. 'White Discrimination against Japan: Britain, the Dominions and the United States, 1908–1928.' *New Zealand Journal of Asian Studies* 2 (2): 91–105.

Bernasconi, R. 2001. 'Who Invented the Concept of Race?' In *Race*, 11–56. Oxford: Wiley-Blackwell.

Bernasconi, R. 2002. 'Kant as an Unfamiliar Source of Racism.' In *Philosophers on Race: Critical Essays*, edited by J.K. Ward and T.L. Lott. Oxford: Wiley-Blackwell.

Bernasconi, Robert. 2010. 'Defining Race Scientifically: A response to Michael Banton.' *Ethnicities* 10 (1): 141–148.

Berthoud, R. 1999. *Young Caribbean Men and the Labour Market: A Comparison with Other Ethnic Groups*. York: Joseph Rowntree Foundation.

Bevin, E. 24 October 1949. *Cabinet: Memoranda. Council of Europe*. CO 936/108: National Archives.

Bhabha, H.K. 2005 [1994]. *The Location of Culture*. London: Routledge.

Bhambra, G.K. 2007. *Rethinking Modernity: Postcolonialism and the Sociological Imagination*. Basingstoke: Palgrave Macmillan.

Bhatnagar, J. 1981. *Educating Immigrants*. London: Palgrave Macmillan.

Blackburn, R. 1988. *The Overthrow of Colonial Slavery 1776–1848*. London: Verso.

Bleich, E. 2005. 'The Legacies of History? Colonization and Immigrant Integration in Britain and France.' *Theory and Society* 34 (2): 171–195.

Blinder, S. 2015. *Public Opinion: Overall Attitudes and Level of Concern*. Oxford: The Migration Observatory at the University of Oxford.

Bloch, A. 1999. 'Introduction.' In *Refugees, Citizenship and Social Policy in Europe*, edited by A. Bloch and C. Levy, 1–11. Bascingstoke: Macmillan Press.

Bloch, A. and L. Schuster. 2002. 'Asylum and Welfare: Contemporary Debates.' *Critical Social Policy* 22 (3): 393–414.

Bloch, A. and L. Schuster. 2005. 'At the Extremes of Exclusion: Deportation, Detention and Dispersal.' *Ethnic and Racial Studies* 28 (3): 491–512.

Blumenbach, J.F. 1969 [1779]. *On the Natural Varieties of Mankind*. Translated by T. Bendyshe. New York: Bergman.

Boccardi, I. 2002. *Europe and Refugees: Towards an EU Asylum Policy*. London: Kluwer Law International.

Bogues, A. 2003. *Black Heretics, Black Prophets: Radical Political Intellectuals*. London: Routledge.

Bohmer, C. and A. Shuman. 2008. *Rejecting Refugees: Political Asylum in the 21st Century*. London: Routledge.
Bonnett, A. 1998. 'How the British Working Class Became White: The Symbolic (Re)formation of Racialized Capitalism.' *Journal of Historical Sociology* 11 (3): 316–340.
Bressey, C. 2007. 'The Black Presence in England and Wales after the Abolition Act, 1807–1930.' *Parliamentary History* 26 (1): 224–237.
British Red Cross and Boaz Trust. 2013. *A Decade of Destitution: Time to Make Change*. Manchester: British Red Cross.
Brook, N. 1947. *Notebook: Cabinet Minutes*. CAB 195/5: National Archives.
Brook, N. 1949. *Notebook: Cabinet Minutes*. CAB 195/7: National Archives.
Brook, N. 1951. *Notebook: Cabinet Minutes*. CAB 195/8: National Archives.
Brook, N. 1952. *Notebook: Cabinet Minutes*. CAB 195/10: National Archives.
Brooks, D. and K. Singh. 1978. 'Ethnic Commitment versus Structural Reality: South Asian Immigrant Workers in Britain.' *Journal of Ethnic and Migration Studies* 7 (1): 19–30.
Brown, W. 2010. *Walled States, Waning Sovereignty*. New York: Zone.
Buchanan, S., B. Grillo-Simpson and T. Threadgold. 2003. *What's the Story? Results from Research into Media Coverage of Refugees and Asylum Seekers in the UK*. London: Article 19.
Buck-Morss, S. 2009. *Hegel, Haiti and Universal History*. Pittsburgh, PA: University of Pittsburgh Press.
Buffon, G.L.L. 1776. *The Natural History of Animals, Vegetables, and Minerals; With the Theory of the Earth in General*. Translated by W. Kenrick, L.L.D. and Others. London: T. Bell.
Burkman, T.W. 2008. *Japan and the League of Nations: Empire and World Order, 1914–1938*. USA: University of Hawaii Press.
Cabinet Office, 1912–1923. *Committee of Imperial Defence and Standing Defence Sub-committee: Minutes. 'Most Secret' Minutes of Meeting of Committee of Imperial Defence, June 20th 1921*. CAB 2/3: National Archives.
Cabinet Office, 1917. *Imperial War Cabinet Meetings of Minutes*. CAB 23/43: National Archives.
Cabinet Office, 1918a. *War Cabinet and Cabinet: Memoranda. Papers nos. 5701-5800*. CAB 24/64: National Archives.
Cabinet Office, 1918b. *War Cabinet and Cabinet: Minutes*. CAB 23/42: National Archives.
Cabinet Office, 1919. *Draft resolutions and miscellaneous papers submitted to the Peace Conference 'P.B.' series 1-28*. CAB 29/36: National Archives.
Cabinet Office, 1947. *Working Party on Human Rights April 26th-Dec 31st*. CAB 134/422: National Archives.
Cameron, D. 2015. Speech to Conservative Party Conference. Available at: http://www.independent.co.uk/news/uk/politics/tory-party-conference-2015-david-camerons-speech-in-full-a6684656.html. The Conservative Party.
Carey, B. 2005. *British Abolitionism and the Rhetoric of Sensibility: Writing, Sentiment and Slavery, 1760–1807, Palgrave Studies in the Enlightenment, Romanticism and the Cultures of Print*. Basingstoke: Palgrave Macmillan.

Carr, Cecil. 1946. 'Human Rights and Fundamental Freedoms in the United Kingdom.' In *Yearbook on Human Rights*. New York: United Nations.

Carter, R. 2000. *Realism and Racism: Concepts of Race in Sociological Research*. London: Routledge.

Carter, R. 2007. 'Genes, Genomes and Genealogy: The Return of Scientific Racism?' *Ethnic and Racial Studies* 30 (4): 546–556.

Chandra, B. 1989. *India's Struggle for Independence: 1857–1947*. London: Penguin.

Cheung, S.Y. and J. Phillimore. 2013. *Social Networks, Social Capital and Refugee Integration*. London: Nuffield Foundation.

Chi-Kwan, M. 2007. 'The 'Problem of People': British Colonials, Cold War Powers, and the Chinese Refugees in Hong Kong, 1949–62.' *Modern Asian Studies* 41 (6): 1145–1181.

Children's Society. 2013. *Report of the Parliamentary Inquiry into Asylum Support for Children and Young People 2013*. London: The Children's Society.

Chimni, B.S. 1998. 'The Geopolitics of Refugee Studies: A View from the South.' *Journal of Refugee Studies* 11 (4): 350–374.

Chimni, B.S. 2009. 'The Birth of a "Discipline": From Refugee to Forced Migration Studies.' *Journal of Refugee Studies* 22 (1): 11–29.

Cissé, M. 1997. *The Sans-Papiers—A Woman Draws the First Lessons: The New Movement of Asylum Seekers and Immigrants Without Papers in France*. London: Crossroads Books.

Clarkson, T. 2006 [1808]. *The History of the Rise, Progress, and Accomplishment of the Abolition of the Slave-Trade by the British Parliament*. Teddington: Echo Library.

Cohen, J. 2008. 'Safe in Our Hands? A Study of Suicide and Self-Harm in Asylum Seekers.' *Journal of Forensic and Legal Medicine* 15 (4): 235–244.

Cole, M. 2009. 'A Plethora of 'suitable enemies': British racism at the dawn of the twenty-first century.' *Ethnic and Racial Studies* 32 (9): 1671–1685.

Colonial Office, 1919. *Dominions Original Correspondence*. CO 532/139: National Archives.

Colonial Office, 1951–1952. *Racial discrimination: Declaration of Human Rights Bill*. CO 859/249: National Archives.

Colonial Office, 1952. *Domestic Jurisdiction and Human Rights [in particular minute of 16 July 1952]*. CO 936/108: National Archives.

Cook, M. 1936. 'Jean-Jacques Rousseau and the Negro.' *The Journal of Negro History* 21 (3): 294–303.

Crawley, H., J Hemmings and N. Price. 2011. *Coping with Destitution: Survival and Livelihood Strategies of Refused Asylum Seekers Living in the UK*. Oxford: Oxfam.

Crawley, H. 2005. 'Europe: Fortress or Refuge?' *Forced Migration Review* 23: 14–16.

Crisp, J. 2003. 'The Refugee and the Global Politics of Asylum.' *Political Quarterly* 74 (1): 75–87.

Cugoano, O. 1825. *Narrative of the Enslavement of Ottobah Cugoano*. London: Hatchard, and J. and A. Arch.

Curtin, P. 1969. *The Atlantic Slave Trade: A Census*. Madison: University of Wisconsin Press.

Darwin, C. 1859. *On the Origin of the Species by Means of Natural Selection*. London: John Murray.

Davies, S.E. 2007. 'Redundant or Essential? How Politics Shaped the Outcome of the 1967 Protocol.' *International Journal of Refugee Law* 19 (4): 703–728.

Davis, D.B. 1966. *The Problem of Slavery in Western Culture*. Ithaca, NY: Cornell University Press.

Davis, D.B. 1975. *The Problem of Slavery in the Age of Revolution, 1770–1823*. London: Cornell University Press.

Dean, D.W. 1987. 'Coping with Colonial Immigration, the Cold War and Colonial Policy: The Labour Government and Black Communities in Great Britain 1945–51.' *Immigrants and Minorities* 6 (3): 305–334.

Drescher, S. 1990a. 'People and Parliament: The Rhetoric of the British Slave Trade.' *Journal of Interdisciplinary History* 20 (4): 561–580.

Drescher, S. 1990b. 'The Ending of the Slave Trade and the Evolution of European Scientific Racism.' *Social Science History* 14 (3): 415–450.

Drescher, S. 1994. 'Whose Abolition? Popular Pressure and the Ending of the British Slave Trade.' *Past and Present* 143: 136–166.

Du Bois, W.E.B. 1997. *The Correspondence of W.E.B. Du Bois, Volume 3*. US: University of Massachusetts Press.

Dummett, A. and A.G.L. Nicol. 1990. *Subjects, Citizens, Aliens and Others: Nationality and Immigration Law*. London: Weidenfeld and Nicolson.

Elie, J. 2014. 'Histories of Refugee and Forced Migration Studies.' In *The Oxford Handbook of Refugee and Forced Migration Studies*, edited by E. Fiddian-Qasmiyeh, G. Loescher, K. Long and N. Sigona. Oxford: Oxford University Press.

Fanon, F. 1967. *The Wretched of the Earth*. Harmondsworth: Penguin.

Fekete, L. 2001. 'The Emergence of Xeno-Racism.' *Race and Class* 43 (2): 23–40.

Fekete, L. 2009. *A Suitable Enemy: Racism, Migration and Islamophobia in Europe*. London: Pluto Press.

Feller, E. 2001. 'The Convention at 50: The Way Ahead for Refugee Protection.' *Forced Migration Review* 10 (April): 6–10.

Fischer, S. 2004. *Modernity Disavowed: Haiti and the Cultures of Slavery in the Age of Revolution*. United States: Duke University Press.

Flynn, D. 2005. 'New borders, New Management: The Dilemmas of Modern Immigration Policies.' *Ethnic and Racial Studies* 28 (3): 463–490.

Foreign Office, 1918–1919. *Paris Peace Conference*. FO 1011/118: National Archives.

Foreign Office, 1919a. *Foreign Office: Peace Conference of 1919 to 1920: Handbooks*. FO 373/4/15: National Archives.

Foreign Office, 1919b. *Japanese Claims in Connection with the League of Nations*. FO 608/240: National Archives.

Foreign Office, 1919c. *Races: Racial Equality Under the League of Nations*. FO 608/243/12: National Archives.

Foreign Office, 1921. *General Correspondence: Far-Eastern: Japan* FO 371/6684: National Archives.

Foster, M. 2007. *International Refugee Law and Socio-Economic Rights: Refuge from Deprivation*. Cambridge: Cambridge University Press.

Friedman, E. and R. Kelin. 2008. *Reluctant Refuge: The Story of Asylum in Britain*. London: The British Library.

Fryer, P. 1984. *Staying Power: Black People in Britain since 1504*. Atlantic Highlands, NJ: Humanities Press.

Gabrielatos, C. and P. Baker. 2008. 'Fleeing, Sneaking, Flooding: A Corpus Analysis of Discursive Constructions of Refugees and Asylum Seekers in the UK Press, 1996–2005.' *Journal of English Linguistics* 36 (1): 5–38.

Gallicchio, M.S. 2000. *The African American Encounter with Japan and China*. USA: The University of North Carolina Press.

Garner, S. 2013. 'The Racialisation of Asylum in Provincial England: Class, Place and Whiteness.' *Identities: Global Studies in Culture and Power* 20 (5): 503–521.

Gates Jr, H.L. 1988. *The Signifying Monkey: A Theory of African-American Literary Criticism*. Oxford: Oxford University Press.

George, A. and A. Bennett. 2005. 'Process Tracing and Historical Explanation.' In *Case Studies and Theory Development in the Social Sciences*, edited by A. George and A. Bennett. MIT Press.

Gibney, M. 2003. 'The State of Asylum: Democratisation, Judicialisation and Evolution of Refugee Policy.' In *The Refugees Convention 50 Years On*, edited by S. Kneebone. Aldershot: Ashgate.

Gibney, M. 2004. *The Ethics and Politics of Asylum: Liberal Democracy and the Response to Refugees*. Cambridge: Cambridge University Press.

Gibney, M. 2006. '"A Thousand Little Guantanamos": Western States and Measures to Prevent the Arrival of Refugees.' In *Displacement, Asylum, Migration*, edited by K.E. Tunstall. Oxford: Oxford University Press.

Gibson W.E. 1996. *Thomas Clarkson: A Biography*. 2nd ed. York: William Sessions.

Giddens, A. 1990. *The Consequences of Modernity*. Cambridge: Polity Press.

Gilbert, M. 1988. *Never Despair: Winston S. Churchill, 1945–1965*. Portsmouth, New Hampshire: Heinemann.

Gillborn, D. 1990. *'Race,' Ethnicity and Education*. London: Routledge.

Gilroy, P. 2002. *There Ain't No Black in the Union Jack: The Cultural Politics of Race and Nation*. London: Routledge.

Gilroy, P. 2003. '"Where Ignorant Armies Clash by Night": Homogeneous Community and the Planetary Aspect.' *International Journal of Cultural Studies* 6 (3): 261–276.

Gilroy, P. 2004. *After Empire: Melancholia or Convivial Culture?* Abingdon: Routledge.

Goldstein, E. 1991. *Winning the Peace: British Diplomatic Strategy, Peace Planning, and the Paris Peace Conference 1916–1920*. Oxford: Clarendon Press.

Goldstein, E. 2002. *The First World War Peace Settlements, 1919–1925*. Harlow, Essex: Pearson Education.

Goodwin-Gill, G.S. 2001. 'After the Cold War: Asylum and the Refugee Concept Move On.' *Forced Migration Review* 10: 14–16.

Gupta, P.S. 2002. *Imperialism and the British Labour Movement, 1914–1964*. New Delhi: Sage.

Haddad, E. 2008. *The Refugee in International Society: Between Sovereigns*. Cambridge: Cambridge University Press.

Hall, A. 2012. *Border Watch: Cultures of Immigration, Detention and Control.* London: Pluto Press.

Hall, C., K. McClelland, N. Draper, K. Donington and R. Lang. 2014. *Legacies of British Slave-Ownership: Colonial Slavery and the Formation of Victorian Britain.* Cambridge: Cambridge University Press.

Hall, S. 1996. 'The West and the Rest: Discourse and Power.' In *Modernity: Introduction to the Modern Societies*, edited by S. Hall, D. Held, D. Hubert and K. Thompson. Oxford: Blackwell.

Hampshire, J. 2005. *Citizenship and Belonging: Immigration and the Politics of Demographic Governance in Postwar Britain.* Basingstoke: Palgrave Macmillan.

Hansen, R. 2000. *Citizenship and Immigration in Post-War Britain: The Institutional Origins of a Multicultural Nation.* Oxford: Oxford University Press.

Hansen, R. 2003. 'Migration to Europe since 1945: Its History and Its Lessons.' *Political Quarterly* 74 (1): 25–38.

Hassan, L. 2000. 'Deterrence Measures and the Preservation of Asylum in the United Kingdom and United States.' *Journal of Refugee Studies* 13 (2): 184–204.

Hathaway, J.C. 1990. 'A Reconsideration of the Underlying Premise of Refugee Law.' *Harvard International Law Journal* 31 (1): 129–182.

Hay, C. 2002. *Political Analysis: A Critical Introduction.* Basingstoke: Palgrave.

Headley, C. 2005. 'Otherness and the Impossible in the Wake of Sylvia Wynter's Notion of the "After Man."' In *After Man, Towards the Human: Critical Essays on Sylvia Wynter*, edited by A. Bogues, 57–75. Kingston, Jamaica: Ian Randle.

Helmke, G. and S. Levitsky. 2004. 'Informal Institutions and Comparative Politics: A Research Agenda.' *Perspectives on Politics* 2 (4): 725–740.

Hirsch, D. 2015. *A Minimum Income Standard for the UK in 2015.* York: Joseph Rowntree Foundation.

Home Office. 2005. Controlling our Borders: Making Migration Work for Britain. Five Year Strategy for Asylum and Immigration. London: HM Government.

Home Office. 2015. National Statistics: Asylum. https://www.gov.uk/government/publications/immigration-statistics-april-to-june-2015/asylum, Accessed on 21 August 2016.

Horne, G. 2004. *Race War: White Supremacy and the Japanese Attack On the British Empire.* London: New York University Press.

Horvath, R.J. 1972. 'A Definition of Colonialism.' *Current Anthropology* 13 (1): 45–57.

House of Commons. 10 February 1807. Slave Trade Abolition Bill. Hansard 1803–2005: UK Parliament.

House of Commons. 16 March 1807. Minutes. Hansard 1803–2005: UK Parliament.

House of Commons. 31 July 1833. Debate: Ministerial Plan for the Abolition of Slavery. Hansard 1803–2005: UK Parliament.

House of Commons. 1 May 1848. Removal of Aliens Bill. Hansard 1803–2005: UK Parliament.

House of Commons. 24 April 1850. Juvenile Offenders' Bill. Hansard 1803–2005: UK Parliament.

House of Commons. 7 May 1861. The Ionian Islands, Papers Moved for. Hansard 1803–2005: UK Parliament.
House of Commons. 25 March 1867. Representation of the People Bill (2nd reading). Hansard 1803–2005: UK Parliament.
House of Commons. 10 May 1870. East India (Opium Revenue) Resolution.
House of Commons. 28 February 1938. *Civil Estimates and Estimates For Revenue Departments, 1938 (Vote on Account), Vol. 332, cc 763–860*. online: Hansard.
House of Commons. 15 March 1951. *Arab Refugees, Vol. 485, cc 1868–1885*. online: Hansard.
House of Commons. 19 March 1951. *Korea (Relief Programme), Vol. 485, cc 2102–2103*. online: Hansard.
House of Commons. 5 December 1951. *Declaration of Human Rights Bill, Vol. 494, cc 2392–2393*. online: Hansard.
House of Commons. 23 May 1952. *Declaration of Human Rights Bill, Vol. 501, cc 889–908*. online: Hansard.
House of Commons. 24 June 1953. *Rhodesia and Nyasaland Federation Bill Clause 1. -(Power by Order in Council to Establish Federation, Etc.), Vol. 516, cc 1911–2033*. online: Hansard.
House of Commons. 10 April 2014. Asylum Seekers (Support). Hansard.
House of Commons. 8 July 2015. Asylum: Finance: Written question – 6175. Hansard.
House of Commons and Home Affairs Committee. 2013. Asylum: Seventh Report of Session 2013–14 HC 71: The Stationary Office.
House of Lords. 16 May 1806. Slave Importation Restriction Bill. Hansard 1803–2005: UK Parliament.
House of Lords. 5 February 1807. Slave Trade Abolition Bill. Cart Whip and Billy Roller: Antislavery and Reform Symbolism in Industrializing Britain. Hansard 1803–2005: UK Parliament.
House of Lords. 23 May 1898. Aliens Bill. Hansard 1803–2005: UK Parliament.
House of Lords. 8 March 1950. *The King's Speech: Address in Reply, Vol. 166, cc 117–151*. online: Hansard.
House of Lords. 23 May 2012. Asylum Seekers: Children. Hansard.
House of Lords. 27 October 2015. Asylum Support (Amendment No. 3) Regulations 2015 Motion to Annul. Hansard.
Hubbard, P. 2005. 'Accommodating Otherness: Anti-Asylum Centre Protest and the Maintenance of White Privilege.' *Transactions of the Institute of British Geographers* 30 (1): 52–65.
Hudson, N. 2001. '"Britons Will Never Be Slaves": National Myth, Conservatism, and the Beginnings of British Anti-Slavery.' *Eighteenth Century Studies* 34 (4): 559–576.
Hughes, W.M. 1929. *The Splendid Adventure: A Review of Empire Relations Within and Without the Commonwealth of Britannic Nations*. London: Ernest Benn.
Hunt, J. 1863. *On The Negro's Place in Nature*. London: Published for the Anthropological Society by Trubner.
Jamaica Assembly. 1805. The Report from a committee of the House of Assembly of Jamaica, appointed in a session, which began on the 23d of October, 1804, to

inquire into the proceedings of the imperial parliament of Great Britain and Ireland relative to the slave trade, &c. &c [microform]. London: The House of Assembly.

Joly, D. 1996. *Haven or Hell? Asylum Policies and Refugees in Europe*. Basingstoke: Palgrave Macmillan.

Joly, D. 2002. 'Introduction.' In *Global Changes in Asylum Regimes*, edited by D. Joly. Basingstoke: Palgrave.

Jones, A.C. 1949. *Memorandum 7th February, 1949. United Nations: Non-Self-Governing Territories and Trusteeship*. 24 / 0024 vols. Vol. CAB 129/32, *Cabinet Papers*. CAB 129/32: The National Archives, Kew.

Joshi, S. and B. Carter. 1984. 'The Role of Labour in the Creation of a Racist Britain.' *Race and Class* 3.

Jowell, R. and P. Prescott-Clarke. 1970. 'Racial Discrimination and White-collar Workers in Britain.' *Race & Class* 11 (4): 397–417.

Kalin, W. 1991. 'Refugees and Civil Wars: Only a Matter of Interpretation?' *International Journal of Refugee Law* 3 (3): 435–451.

Keck, M.E. 1998. *Activists Beyond Borders: Advocacy Networks in International Politics*. New York: Cornell University Press.

Keely, C.B. 2001. 'The International Refugee Regime(s): The End of the Cold War Matters.' *International Migration Review* 35 (1): 303–314.

Keith, M. 1993. *Race, Riots and Policing: Lore and Disorder in a Multi-Racist Society*. London: UCL Press.

King, D.S. and R. Smith. 2005. 'Racial Orders in American Political Development.' *American Political Science Review* 99 (1): 75–92.

Kissoon, P. 2010. 'From Persecution to Destitution: A Snapshot of Asylum Seekers' Housing and Settlement Experiences in Canada and the United Kingdom.' *Journal of Immigrant and Refugee Studies* 8 (1): 4–31.

Koser, K. 2001. 'New Approaches to Asylum?' *International Migration* 39 (6): 85–101.

Kotef, H. 2015. *Movement and the Ordering of Freedom: On Liberal Governances of Mobility*. London: Duke University Press.

Kriegel, A.D. 1987. 'A Convergence of Ethics: Saints and Whigs in British Antislavery.' *Journal of British Studies* 26 (4): 423–450.

Kushner, T. 2006. *Remembering Refugees: Then and Now*. Manchester: Manchester University Press.

Lake, M. and H. Reynolds. 2008. *Drawing the Global Colour Line: White Men's Countries and the International Challenge of Racial Equality*. Cambridge: Cambridge University Press.

Lambert, D. 2005. 'The Counter-Revolutionary Atlantic: White West Indian Petitions and Proslavery Networks.' *Social and Cultural Geography* 6 (3): 405–420.

Langa, N. 2015. 'About the Refugee Movement in Kreuzberg/Berlin.' *Movements journal für kritische migrations-und grenzregimeforschung*. http://movements-journal.org/issues/02.kaempfe/08.langa--refugee-movement-kreuzberg-berlin.html, Accessed on 23 May 2016.

Lawrence, C.R. 1970. 'Foreword.' In *The Africa That Never Was: Four Centuries of British Writing about Africa*, edited by D. Hammon and A. Jablow. New York: Twayne.

Lawrence, W. 1822. *Lectures on Physiology, Zoology, and the Natural History of Man*. London: Benbow.
Lentin, A. 2008. *Racism*. Oxford: Oneworld.
Lewis, H. 2007. *Destitution in Leeds: The Experiences of People Seeking Asylum and Supporting Agencies*. Yorkshire: Joseph Rowntree Charitable Trust.
Lindsay, K., et al. 2010. *Refugees' Experiences and Views of Poverty in Scotland*. Glasgow: Scottish Poverty Information Unit.
Loescher, G. 1993. *Beyond Charity: International Cooperation and the Global Refugee Crisis*. Oxford: Oxford University Press.
Long, E. 1772. *Candid Reflections upon the Judgement Lately Awarded by the Court of King's Bench, in Westminster-Hall, on What is Commonly Called the Negroe-Cause, by a Planter*. London: Printed for T. Lowndes.
Long, E. 1774. *The History of Jamaica, or, General Survey of the Antient and Modern State of that Island with Reflections on its Situation, Settlements, Inhabitants, Climate, Products, Commerce, Laws, and Government*. London: Printed for T. Lowndes.
Long, K. 2013. 'When Refugees Stopped Being Migrants: Movement, Labour and Humanitarian Protection.' *Migration Studies* 1 (1): 4–26.
Lyon, W.B. 24 May 1957. *Letter to P.S.Falla*. HO 352/158: The National Archives.
Malkki, L.H. 1995. 'Refugees and Exile: From "Refugee Studies" to the National Order of Things.' *Annual Review of Anthropology* 24: 495–523.
Marshall, P. 2001. 'Smuts and the Preamble to the UN Charter.' *The Round Table: The Commonwealth Journal of International Affairs* 90 (358): 55–65.
Marfleet, P. 2006. *Refugees in a Global Era*. Basingstoke: Palgrave Macmillan.
Marfleet, P. 2007. 'Refugees and History: Why We Must Address the Past.' *Refugee Survey Quarterly* 26 (3): 136–148.
Maternity Action and Refugee Council. 2013. *When Maternity Doesn't Matter: Dispersing Pregnant Women Seeking Asylum*. London: Maternity Action.
Mayblin, L. 2016a. 'Troubling the Exclusive Privileges of Citizenship: Mobile Solidarities, Asylum Seekers, and the Right to Work.' *Citizenship Studies* 20 (2): 192–207.
Mayblin, L. 2016b. 'Complexity reduction and policy consensus: Asylum seekers, the right to work, and the "pull factor" thesis in the UK context.' *British Journal of Politics and International Relations* Online first (DOI: 10.1177/1369148116656986).
Mayblin, L. 2013. 'Never Look Back: Political Thought and the Abolition of Slavery.' *Cambridge Review of International Affairs*, 26(1): 93–110.
Mayblin, L. 2014. 'Colonialism, Decolonisation, and the Right to be Human: Britain and the 1951 Geneva Convention on the Status of Refugees.' *Journal of Historical Sociology* 27 (3): 423–441.
Mazower, M. 2009. *No Enchanted Palace: The End of Empire and the Ideological Origins of the United Nations*. Woodstock: Princeton University Press.
McIntyre, W.D. 1998. *British Decolonisation, 1946–1997: 'When, Why and How did the British Empire Fall?'*. Basingstoke: Palgrave Macmillan.

Midgley, C. 1992. *Women Against Slavery: the British Campaigns, 1780–1870.* London; New York: Routledge.

Mignolo, W. 2009. 'Who Speaks for the "Human" in Human Rights?' *Hispanic Issues On Line* 5 (1): 7–24.

Mignolo, W. 2011. *The Darker Side of Western Modernity: Global Futures, Decolonial Options.* Durham: Duke University Press.

Mignolo, W. 2000. *Local Histories/Global Designs.* Chichester: Princeton University Press.

Mignolo, W. 2007. 'DELINKING: The Rhetoric of Modernity, the Logic of Coloniality and the Grammar of De-coloniality.' *Cultural Studies* 21 (2): 449–514.

Morris, B. 2003. *The Birth of the Palestinian Refugee Problem Revisited.* Cambridge: Cambridge University Press.

Morris, L. 2002. 'Britain's asylum, and immigration regime: the shifting contours of rights.' *Journal of Ethnic and Migration Studies* 28 (3): 409–425.

Morton, E. 2002. 'Race and Racism in the Works of David Hume.' *Journal on African Philosophy* 1 (1): online: http://www.africanphilosophy.com/vol1.1/morton.html.

Murji, K and J. Solomos. 2005. *Racialization: Studies in Theory and Practice.* Oxford: Oxford University Press.

Neumayer, E. 2005. 'Bogus Refugees? The Determinants of Asylum Migration to Western Europe.' *International Studies Quarterly* 49 (3): 389–410. DOI: 10.1111/j.1468-2478.2005.00370.x.

Nickolls, R.B. 1788. *Letter to the treasurer of the Society Instituted for the Purpose of Effecting the Abolition of the Slave Trade.* 4th ed. London: James Phillips.

Noll, G. 2003. 'Visions of the Exceptional: Legal and Theoretical Issues Raised by Transit Processing Centres and Protection Zones.' *European Journal of Migration and Law* 5 (3): 303–341.

Nyers, P. 2003. *Rethinking Refugees.* London: Routledge.

Obokata, T. and R. O'Connell. 2010. 'Ambition, Achievement and Potential: The UK and the Universal Declaration of Human Rights at Sixty.' *The International Journal of Human Rights* 14 (3): 394–406.

Offe, C. 1985. 'New Social Movements: Challenging the Boundaries of Institutional Politics.' *Social Research* 52 (4): 817–868.

Ogborn, M. 2008. *Global Lives: Britain and the World, 1550–1800, Cambridge studies in historical geography.* Cambridge: Cambridge University Press.

Omi, M. and H. Winant. 1994. *Racial Formation in the United States: From the 1960s to the 1990s.* 2nd ed. New York: Routledge.

Onishi, Y. 2007. 'The New Negro of the Pacific: How African Americans Forged Cross-Racial Solidarity with Japan, 1917–1922.' *The Journal of African American History* 92 (2): 191–213.

Orchard, P. 2014. *A Right to Flee: Refugees, States, and the Construction of International Cooperation.*

Orren, K. and S. Skowronek. 2004. *The Search for American Political Development.* Cambridge, UK; New York: Cambridge University Press.

Padmore, G. 1953. 'Behind the Mau Mau.' *Phylon (1940–1956)* 14 (4): 355–372.

Page, M.E. 2003. *Colonialism: An International Social, Cultural, and Political Encyclopedia*. Santa Barbara, CA: ABC-CLIO.

Paine, T. 1775. 'American Slavery in America.' *Pennsylvania Journal* 8th March 1775.

Patterson, S. 1965. *Dark Strangers: A Study of West Indians in London*. Abridged ed. Penguin.

Patterson, S. 2007. 'The Imperial Idea: Ideas of Honor in British India.' *Journal of Colonialism and Colonial History* 8 (1).

Peach, C. 1998. 'South Asian and Caribbean Ethnic Minority Housing Choice in Britain.' *Studies* 35 (10): 1657–1680.

Peach, C. and M. Byron. 1993. 'Caribbean Tenants in Council Housing: "Race", Class and Gender.' *Journal of Ethnic and Migration Studies* 19 (3): 407–423.

Peckard, P. 1788. *Am I Not a Man? And a Brother? With All Humility Addressed to the British Legislature*. Cambridge: J. Archdeacon.

Penson, L.M. 1921. 'The London West India Interest in the Eighteenth Century.' *The English Historical Review* 36 (143): 373–392.

Pettitt, J. 2013. *The Right to Rehabilitation for Survivors of Torture in the UK*. London: Freedom from Torture.

Phillimore, J and L. Goodson. 2006. 'Problem or Opportunity? Asylum Seekers, Refugees, Employment and Social Exclusion in Deprived Urban Areas.' *Urban Studies* 43 (10): 1715–1736.

Phillimore, J., E. Ergun, L. Goodson and D. Hennessy. 2007. *They Do Not Understand the Problem I Have: Refugee Well-Being and Mental Health*. York: Joseph Rowntree Foundation.

Phillips, D. 1998. 'Black Minority Ethnic Concentration, Segregation and Dispersal in Britain.' *Urban Studies* 35 (10): 1681–1702.

Phillips, J.A. and C. Wetherell. 1995. 'The Great Reform Act of 1832 and the Political Modernization of England.' *The American Historical Review* 100 (2): 411–436.

Pierson, R.R., N. Chaudhuri and B. McAuley. 1998. *Nation, Empire, Colony: Historicizing Gender and Race*. Bloomington, Indiana: Indiana University Press.

Pinter, I. 2012. *I Don't Feel Human: Experiences of Destitution among Young Refugees and Migrants*. London: The Children's Society.

Porter, A. 1992. 'Religion and Empire: British Expansion in the Long Nineteenth Century, 1780–1914.' *The Journal of Imperial and Commonwealth History* 20 (3): 370–390.

Prichard, J.C. 1847. *Researches into the Physical History of Mankind*. London: Sherwood, Gilbert and Piper.

Quijano, A. and M. Ennis. 2000. 'Coloniality of Power, Eurocentrism, and Latin America.' *Nepantla: Views from South* 1 (3): 533–580.

Rawley, J.A. and S.D. Behrendt. 2005. *The Transatlantic Slave Trade: A History*. 2nd ed. Lincoln, NE: University of Nebraska Press.

Reacroft, J. 2008. *Like any other child? Children and families in the asylum process*. London: Barnardo's.

Refugee Action. 2006. *The Destitution Trap: Research into Destitution among Refused Asylum Seekers in the UK*. London: Refugee Action.

Refugee Action. 2015. 'Drastic cuts to asylum support will plunge children deeper into poverty.' *Refugee Action*.

Rex, J. and R. Moore. 1967. *Race, Community, and Conflict: A Study of Sparkbrook*. London: Oxford University Press.

Rex, J. 1970. *Race Relations in Sociological Theory*. London: Routledge and Kegan Paul.

Rex, J. and S. Thomlinson. 1979. *Colonial Immigrants in a British City: A Class Analysis*. London: Routledge & Kegan Paul Books.

Rich, P. 1990. *Race and Empire in British Politics*. 2nd ed. Cambridge: Cambridge University Press.

Richmond, AH. 1994. *Global Apartheid: Refugees, Racism, and the New World Order*. Toronto; Oxford: Oxford University Press.

Robinson, V. and J. Sergott. 2002. *Understanding the Decision Making of Asylum Seekers, Home Office Research Study 243*. London: Home Office.

Sales, R. 2002. 'The deserving and the undeserving? Refugees, asylum seekers and welfare in Britain.' *Critical Social Policy* 22 (3): 456–478.

Sandler, S. 1999. *The Korean War: No Victors, No Vanquished*. Kentucky: University Press of Kentucky.

Santos, B.S. 2008. 'The World Social Forum and the Global Left.' *Politics & Society* 36 (2): 247–270.

Saville, J. 1993. *The Politics of Continuity: British Foreign Policy and the Labour Government, 1945–51*. London: Verso.

Scheub, H. 1996. *The Tongue is Fire: South African Storytellers and Apartheid*. Madison: University of Wisconsin Press.

Schulte B.M. 2003. 'British Nationality Policy as a Counter-Revolutionary Strategy During the Napoleonic Wars: The Emergence of Modern Naturalization Regulations.' In *Migration Control in the North Atlantic World: The Evolution of State Practices in Europe and the United States from the French Revolution to the Inter-War Period*, edited by A. Fahrmeir, O. Faron and P. Weil. Oxford: Berghahn Books.

Schuster, L. 2003a. 'Common Sense or Racism? The Treatment of Asylum-Seekers in Europe.' *Patterns of Prejudice* 37 (3): 233–255.

Schuster, L. 2003b. *The Use and Abuse of Political Asylum in Britain and Germany*. London: Frank Cass.

Shamir, R. 2005. 'Without Borders? Notes on Globalization as a Mobility Regime.' *Sociological Theory* 23 (2): 197–217.

Sherwood, M. 1996. '"There Is No New Deal for the Blackman in San Francisco": African Attempts to Influence the Founding Conference of the United Nations, April–July, 1945.' *The International Journal of African Historical Studies* 29 (1): 71–94.

Shimazu, N. 1998. *Japan, Race and Equality: The Racial Equality Proposal of 1919*. London: Routledge.

Shyllon, F.O. 1974. *Black Slaves in Britain*. London: Oxford University Press.

Sigona, N. 2003. 'How can a "Nomad" be a "Refugee"? Kosovo Roma and Labelling Policy in Italy.' *Sociology* 37 (1): 69–79.

Silove, D., I. Sinnerbrink, A. Field, V. Manicavasagar and Z. Steel. 1997. 'Anxiety, Depression and PTSD in Asylum-Seekers: Associations with Pre-migration Trauma and Post-migration Stressors.' *The British Journal of Psychiatry* 202 (2): 351–357.

Simpson, A.W.B. 2004. *Human Rights and the End of Empire: Britain and the Genesis of the European Convention*. Oxford: Oxford University Press.

Sivanandan, A. 2001. 'Poverty is the New Black.' *Race and Class* 43 (2): 1–5.

Smuts, J.C. 1944. *Toward a Better World*. Duell: Sloan and Pearce.

Spencer, I.R.G. 1997. *British Immigration Policy Since 1939: The Making of Multi-Racial Britain*. London: Routledge.

Spencer, M. 1995. *States of Injustice: A Guide to Human Rights and Civil Liberties in the European Union*. London: Pluto Press.

Spencer, S. 2003. 'Introduction.' *Political Quarterly* 74 (1): 1–24.

Spivak, G.C. 1988. 'Can the Subaltern Speak?' In *Marxism and the Interpretation of Culture*, edited by C. Nelson and L. Grossberg. Basingstoke: Macmillan Education.

Squire, V. 2009. *The Exclusionary Politics of Asylum. Edited by Z Layton-Henry and D. Joly, Migration, Minorities and Citizenship*. Basingstoke: Palgrave Macmillan.

Stocking Jr, G.W. 1971. 'What's in a Name? The Origins of the Royal Anthropological Institute (1837-71).' *Man* 6 (3): 369–390.

Strack, T. 1996. 'Philosophical Anthropology on the Eve of Biological Determinism: Immanuel Kant and Georg Forster on the Moral Qualities and Biological Characteristics of the Human Race.' *Central European History* 29 (3): 285–308.

Talbot, I. and G. Singh. 2009. *The Partition of India*. Cambridge: Cambridge University Press.

Tarrow, S. 2001. 'Transnational Politics: Contention and Institutions in International Politics.' *Annual Review of Political Science* 4: 1–20.

Taylor, D. 2009. *Underground Lives: An Investigation into the Living Conditions and Survival Strategies of Destitute Asylum Seekers in the UK*. Leeds: PAFRAS.

The League of Coloured Peoples. 1946. *The News Letter*. Vol. No. 76, Vol. XIII. Westminster: The League of Coloured Peoples.

The Refugee Council. 2015. 'Families' asylum support drastically cut.' *The Refugee Council*.

Thomas, M. 2008. *Crises of Empire: Decolonization and Europe's Imperial States, 1918–1975*. London: Hodder Education.

Tobin, J. 1785. *Cursory Remarks upon the Reverend Mr Ramsay's Essay*. London.

Toye, R. 2010. *Churchill's Empire*. London: Macmillan.

Trouillot, M-R. 1995. *Silencing the Past: Power and the Production of History*. Boston: Beacon Press.

Turnbull, G. 1786. *An Apology for Negro Slavery, or, The West-India Planters Vindicated from the Charge of Inhumanity / by the Author of Letters to a Young Planter*. London: Stuart and Stevenson.

UN Conference of Plenipotentiaries on the Status of Refugees and Stateless Persons. 3 July 1951. *Draft Convention Relating to the Status of Refugees. Memorandum Prepared by the Legal Department*. A/CONF.2/21: UN Archives.

UN Conference of Plenipotentiaries on the Status of Refugees and Stateless Persons. 27 November 1951. Conference of Plenipotentiaries on the Status of Refugees and

Stateless Persons: Summary Record of the Twenty-seventh Meeting. A/CONF.2/SR.27: United Nations Archives.

UN General Assembly. 10 November 1949. *Summary Record of the Two Hundred and Fifty-eighth Meeting Held at Lake Success, New York, on Wednesday, 9 November 1949, at 3 p.m.* A/C.3/SR.258: United Nations Archives.

UN General Assembly. 11 November 1949. *Summary Record of the Two Hundred and Fifty-ninth Meeting Held at lake Success, New York, on Thursday, 10 November 1949, at 10.45 a.m.* Edited by Third Committee. A/C.3/SR.259: United Nations Archives.

UN General Assembly. 16 November 1949. *Provisional Summary Record of the Two Hundred and Sixty-Fourth Meeting Held at Lake Success, New York, on Tuesday, 15 November 1949, at 3 p.m.* A/C.3/SR.264: United Nations Archives.

UNHCR. 1951. Convention relating to the Status of Refugees.

United Nations. 17 February 1950. *Ad Hoc Committee on Statelessness and Related Problems, First Session: Summary Record of the Twenty-Sixth Meeting Held at Lake Success, New York, on Friday, 10 February 1950, at 2.15 p.m.* E/AC.32/SR.25: United Nations Archives.

United Nations. 28 July 1951. 'Convention relating to the Status of Refugees.' United Nations Treaty Series.

United Nations. 1985. *Charter of the United Nations and Statute of the International Court of Justice*. New York: United Nations, Department of Public Information.

van der Veer, P. and H. Lehmann. 1999. *Nation and Religion: Perspectives on Europe and Asia*. Chichester: Princeton University Press.

van Wetten, J.W., C.C.J.H. Bijleveld, F. Heide and N. Dijkhoff. 2001. 'Female Asylum-Seekers in the Netherlands: An Empirical Study.' *International Migration* 39 (3): 85–98.

Verity, R. 1839. *Changes Produced in the Nervous System by Civilization, Considered According to the Evidence of Physiology and the Philosophy of History*. 2nd ed. London: S. Highley.

Vink, M. and Meijerink, F. 2003. 'Asylum Applications and Recognition Rates in EU Member States 1982–2001: A Quantitative Analysis.' *Journal of Refugee Studies* 16 (3): 297–315.

Visram, R. 2002. *Asians in Britain: 400 years of History*. London: Pluto.

Von Eschen, P.M. 1997. *Race Against Empire: Black Americans and Anticolonialism, 1937–57*. Ithaca, NY: Cornell University Press.

Vázquez, R. 2011. 'Translation as Erasure: Thoughts on Modernity's Epistemic Violence.' *Journal of Historical Sociology* 24 (1): 27–44.

Wacquant, L. 2002. 'From Slavery to Mass Incarceration: Rethinking the "Race Question" in the U.S.' *New Left Review* 13: 41–60.

Wagner, P. 2001. *Theorizing Modernity: Inescapability and Attainability in Social Theory*. London: Sage.

Walvin, J. 1986. *England Slaves and Freedom, 1776–1838*. London: Macmillan.

Walvin, J. 2007. 'British Slavery, Abolition of.' In *Encyclopedia of antislavery and abolition*, edited by P.P. Hinks, J.R. McKivigan and R.O. Williams. Westport: Greenwood Press.

Wemyss, G. 2009. *The Invisible Empire: White Discourse, Tolerance and Belonging, Studies in migration and diaspora*. Farnham: Ashgate.
West India Committee. 1785-1792. Standing Committee's Minutes vol. i. In *West India Committee: Acquired Papers*. London: Institute of Commonwealth Studies.
Wynter, S. 2000. 'Africa, the West, and the Analogy of Culture: The Cinematic Text After Man.' In *Symbolic Narratives/African Cinema: Audiences, Theory and the Moving Image*, edited by J. Gianni and I. Baker, 25–75. London: British Film Institute & Palgrave Macmillan.
Wynter, S. 2003. 'Unsettling the Coloniality of Being/Power/Truth/Freedom: Towards the Human, after Man, its Overrepresentation - an Argument.' *The New Centennial Review* 3 (3): 257–37.
Young, L. 1997. 'Rethinking Race for Manchuko: Self and Other in Colonial Contexts.' In *The Construction of Racial Identities in China and Japan*, edited by F. Dikotter. London: Hurst.
Zetter, R. 1991. 'Labelling Refugees: Forming and Transforming a Bureaucratic Identity.' *Journal of Refugee Studies* 4 (1): 39–62.
Zetter, R., D. Griffiths and Sigona N. 2005. 'Social Capital or Social Exclusion? The Impact of Asylum-Seeker Dispersal on UK Refugee Community Organizations.' *Community Development Journal* 40 (2): 169–181.
Zimmern, A.E. 1926. *The Third British Empire*. London: Oxford University Press.
Zolberg, A., A. Suhrke and S. Aguayo. 1989. *Escape from Violence: Conflict and the Refugee Crisis in the Developing World*. Oxford: Oxford University Press.
Zolberg, A.R., A. Suhrke and S. Aguayo (Eds). 1989. *Escape from Violence: Conflict and Refugee Crisis in the Developing World*. Oxford: Oxford University Press.

Index

abolition
  abolitionists (slavery), 56–57, 60–63, 65–67, 70, 71–77, 109, 143
  of racial inequality, 91–98, 105
  of slavery, 6, 11, 45, 48, 51–52, 54–77, 79–80, 88, 108, 110
  of slave trade, 48, 57, 60, 61, 64, 66, 73–75, 88
Anglophone, 100
Africa, African, 19, 42, 52, 53, 57, 59, 61, 63, 67, 70, 72, 74, 75, 78–79, 80, 85, 86, 88, 100, 103, 104, 107, 108, 118, 138, 139, 140, 142, 147
aliens, 10, 13, 14, 15, 37, 142, 180
asylum
  right to, 5, 6–7, 11, 24, 29, 39, 52, 80, 108, 113–116, 126–127, 129, 142, 146, 148, 174, 177
  seekers, 6–7, 15, 17–18, 31–35, 40, 114, 147, 150–151, 159, 171
  support, 17, 48, 149–174
Australia, 93, 97–98, 100, 102, 105–107, 128, 129

blood, 85, 102, 109, 117
Brexit, 19

British Empire, 7–8, 11, 25, 45, 47, 52, 63, 73, 77, 79–80, 83–84, 89, 90, 92–93, 96, 97, 99, 100, 102, 104, 105, 108, 109, 117–118, 120–121, 130, 131, 133, 138, 144–145, 179

Cabinet, Cabinet Office, 48, 65, 90, 98, 100, 102, 107, 117–127, 138, 145, 152
Canada, 93, 100, 107, 128
Caribbean, 53, 56, 59, 63
Chimni, B.S., 5, 20, 22, 29, 30–32, 42, 48, 144, 176, 179
China, Chinese, 22, 90, 95, 107, 111, 130, 136, 184
Christianity, 41, 53, 54, 57, 58, 61–63, 68, 72, 78, 81, 89, 108, 164
civilisation, 2, 37, 39, 41, 68, 77, 81, 83, 87, 88–89, 101, 103, 106, 109, 121, 127, 134, 144, 164, 174
Cold War, 4, 16, 20–21, 30, 123, 124, 147, 148, 175
colonial
  anti-, 92, 94, 99, 117, 128, 132–134, 135, 138–142
  application clause, 126, 127–129, 132, 135

197

coloniality/modernity, 27, 30, 37, 39–40, 42, 43, 44, 46, 81, 83, 114, 179
colonialism, 1–12, 15, 22, 24–27, 30, 36, 37, 39–49, 51–54, 61–81, 87, 94, 95, 98–103, 108, 114, 117–119, 125–132, 139–144, 146, 176, 177, 179–180
Colonial Office, 91, 117, 119, 120, 138–140
colonies, 4, 6, 8, 22, 31, 36, 42, 55–56, 59, 63–64, 69, 73, 76, 84, 88, 102–104, 106, 109, 118, 120, 122–148, 152, 174
Commonwealth, 16, 117, 140
Conservative (party), 16, 19, 117, 140, 153, 156, 158, 161, 162, 163, 170

Darwinism, 36, 85, 86, 87
 social, 33, 36, 87
decolonial, 1, 6, 10, 12, 27, 29, 37, 39, 40, 41, 48, 176, 179
decolonisation, 12, 22, 23, 24, 34, 114, 129, 131, 143, 144, 146, 177, 178
dehumanisation, 1, 12, 147–174, 179
destitution, 150, 151, 156, 157, 160, 163, 164, 170, 173
Du Bois, W.E.B., 92, 99, 133, 138, 141–142
Dominions, 79, 100, 102, 105, 107, 128–129

Early Day Motions, 153, 154, 163, 164
empire(s) 47, 131
Enlightenment, 26, 38, 61, 88, 98, 179
Europe, 3, 7, 8, 10–11, 13–27, 29–42, 46, 52, 53, 56, 58, 61, 68, 70, 71, 72–73, 77, 80, 83, 85–86, 88, 91, 93, 95, 98, 101, 103, 109–110, 113–116, 118, 120, 123, 124, 127, 132, 135, 136–137, 140, 141, 144, 146, 148, 150, 152, 153, 167–168, 173, 175–177, 178, 180

First World War, 15, 31, 90, 93, 115, 118
Foreign Office, 95–99, 100, 102–109, 117, 119–120, 123–125, 130

Geneva Convention (*see* Refugee Convention)
Gilroy, Paul, 25, 26, 34
globalisation, 9, 24–25, 30
Global North, 21, 32
Global South, 21, 30, 31

Habeas Corpus, 59, 63, 69, 74
Haitian Revolution, 43, 56, 80
historical institutionalism, 10, 43–49, 57, 78
historical sociology, 1, 178
Home Office, 18, 117, 119, 130, 140, 152, 154, 156, 157, 161–163, 165–166, 167, 168–170, 172
Home Secretary, 16, 18, 150, 159–160, 162, 165, 166–167, 170, 171, 172
House of Commons, 14–15, 23, 56, 64, 67, 72, 73, 74, 76, 87, 89, 100, 127, 138–140, 157–158, 160–162
House of Lords, 14, 61, 64, 75, 76, 122, 124, 153, 156, 163–165, 170
human rights, 2, 3, 6, 11–12, 17, 23, 26, 29, 40, 42, 48–49, 51–52, 79–80, 84–85, 100, 113–146, 148, 150, 152, 154, 155, 165, 166, 171–174, 176, 177, 178, 180

immigration, immigrants, 4, 7, 14–19, 25, 32–36, 45, 47, 52, 79, 93, 97, 101, 104–107, 118, 121, 144–146, 150, 152, 154, 158, 160–162, 164–166, 169
imperialism, 7–8, 45, 93, 99, 133, 138, 143

India, 23, 89, 95, 100, 107, 109, 128, 131, 132, 133, 135–138, 140–141
International Refugee Organization (IRO), 15, 115, 116, 135–136
institutional orders, 43–49, 51, 54, 56, 78, 84, 90, 108–109, 110, 131, 143, 145, 149, 152, 172
Iraq, 128, 137
Islamophobia, 4, 33, 179

Jamaica, 67, 70, 72–73, 76, 141
Japan, 11, 48, 83–84, 88–110

King, Desmond, 44–45, 46, 49, 51, 78, 145
Korea, 22, 127

Labour party, 17, 18, 117, 120, 133, 138, 139, 153, 156, 158, 160–161
League of Nations, 6, 11, 15, 48, 83, 84, 85, 90, 91, 93–106, 118, 177
Liberal Democrat, 19, 153, 156, 158, 161, 162

man, 1, 5, 10–11, 22, 26, 27, 29, 30, 37, 40–43, 44, 49, 51, 52, 53, 58, 68, 70, 71, 72, 77, 80, 85–88, 147, 176, 179–180
media, 1, 4, 10, 13, 20, 32, 35, 56, 66, 92, 95–96, 98, 106, 133, 141, 154
Mignolo, Walter, 10, 27, 30, 39, 41, 42, 77, 176
mobility, immobility, 16, 24–25, 26, 30
modernity, 1, 3, 10, 26–27, 30, 37–49, 52, 77, 81, 83, 104, 108, 109, 114, 145, 176, 179–180
myth of difference, 5, 23, 27, 30–32, 48, 144, 176, 179

non-governmental organization (NGO), 149, 153–154

Pakistan, 2, 23, 128, 131, 132, 133, 135–138

Paris Peace Conference (1919), 83, 89–108, 117, 176
Parliament (*see also* House of Commons; House of Lords), 14–16, 23, 43, 48, 55, 57, 60, 64, 65, 66, 72–77, 79, 87, 89, 109, 118, 124, 127, 133, 138–142, 152–165, 167
  Members of (MPs), 56, 67, 72, 139, 140, 143, 156, 158, 160–161, 162, 163
postcolonial, 1, 3–6, 10, 12, 25, 27, 29, 37, 41, 43, 48, 176, 179
prejudice, 10, 15, 33, 34, 56, 67, 80, 91, 93, 104, 110, 123, 138, 142
Protocol Relating to the Status of Refugees (1967), 7, 23, 116, 148

Quakers, 54, 57, 62

race
  equality, 6, 8, 11, 48, 83–110
  racialisation, 10, 27, 32–37, 45, 47, 176, 179
  racial science, 45, 85, 144
  racism, 1, 3–4, 6, 9–10, 27, 30, 32–37, 39, 45, 47, 53, 70, 71, 79, 105, 145, 147, 175–177, 179
  relations, 4, 17
refugee, 1–7, 11–12, 14–16, 18–27, 29, 30–31, 39, 42, 47, 79, 84, 113–114, 118, 120, 121, 127–138, 140, 143–149, 151–154, 156–163, 171–173, 175–178, 180
Refugee Convention, 7, 11–12, 15, 18, 20–21, 48, 110, 113, 114–142, 144–45, 177–178, 180
refugee studies, 3, 5, 20, 22, 27, 29, 31, 48, 175, 176
rights, 2, 5, 6, 11–12, 14–19, 22–24, 26, 29, 30, 39–43, 47–49, 51–81, 84, 85, 88, 93, 101, 110, 113–146, 152, 154–157, 164–166, 171–173, 176–178, 180

Second World War, 5, 15, 20, 21, 26, 116, 127, 131, 135, 136, 140, 148
slavery, 6, 11, 41, 45, 48, 51–81, 86, 88, 91, 108–110, 176
slave trade, 14, 48, 51–54, 55, 56, 58–69, 71–75, 77, 78
sociology, 1, 3–4, 10, 13, 21, 22–26, 38, 176, 178
South Africa, 100, 107, 109, 142, 147
Smith, Rogers, 44–45, 46, 49, 51, 78, 145
Smuts, Jan, 100, 117, 118–119, 131, 142

Third World, 5, 10, 27, 29, 31, 36
Third World Approaches to International Law (TWAIL), 10, 27, 29, 30
Trouillot, Michel-Rolph, 10, 27, 30, 41, 42, 43, 53, 63, 71, 176

United Kingdom, 7, 16–21, 46–48, 54, 57, 63, 127–130, 139, 144, 147, 149–151, 154–157, 161, 165, 171–177
United Nations (UN), 3, 11, 24, 47, 48, 90, 110, 113, 115–116, 117, 119–120, 122–124, 127–131, 132, 133, 135–143, 146, 153, 155–158, 164, 171, 177

UNHCR, 7, 116, 129, 130, 138
United States of America (USA), 11, 45, 46, 78, 83–84, 91, 93, 95, 96, 98–99, 102, 105, 106, 107, 109, 120–121, 129, 136, 138, 140, 142, 144, 147

West, Western, 2, 3, 5, 7–9, 13, 16, 20–21, 22, 23, 29, 30–31, 35–36, 38–42, 48, 63, 91, 93, 95, 96, 103–106, 109, 113, 116, 123, 132, 148, 176, 180
West Indies, 56, 61, 65–66, 67, 75, 77
welfare (*see also* asylum), 16, 17, 149–150, 156, 159
white, 4, 6, 8, 31, 33, 35, 36, 41, 44, 46, 57, 58, 61, 63, 65, 70, 76–78, 84–90, 95, 96, 98–102, 104, 106–108, 109, 118, 121, 128, 134, 138, 141, 143, 148, 152, 179
white supremacist, 44, 45, 78, 90, 99, 101
Wynter, Sylvia, 10, 27, 30, 41–42, 176, 179

xeno-racism, 33, 35–36

yellow peril, 84, 93, 96, 101, 104

About the Author

Lucy Mayblin is assistant professor of Sociology at the University of Warwick, UK. She holds degrees in Human Geography (BA, University of Birmingham), European Studies (MA, University of Birmingham), Social Research Methods (MA, University of Warwick) and Sociology (PhD, University of Warwick). She is co-convenor of the British Sociological Association's Study Group on Diaspora, Migration and Transnationalism, has been Visiting Fellow at the European University Institute in Florence and during 2015–2018 holds a prestigious Future Research Leaders fellowship from the UK's Economic and Social Research Council for research into the economic rights of asylum seekers. This book is based on her doctoral research, which was funded by the ESRC.